D0891862

Sane Asylum

Charles Hampden-Turner

Sane Asylum

SAN FRANCISCO BOOK COMPANY, INC.

San Francisco *1976*

Printed in the United States of America

Library of Congress Cataloging in Publication Data

Hampden-Turner, Charles, 1934–
   Sane asylum.

   Bibliography: p.
   1. Delancey Street Foundation. 2. Rehabilitation of criminals—California —San Francisco. 3. Halfway houses—California—San Francisco.
I. Title. [DNLM: 1. Crime. 2. Psychotherapy, Group. 3. Rehabilitation. WM430 H229s]
HV9306.S42D44   365′.9794′61   75-43678
ISBN 0-913374-28-8

Simon and Schuster Order Number 22282

Trade distribution by Simon and Schuster
A Gulf + Western Company

10 9 8 7 6 5 4 3 2 1

Photographs in this book were collected by
SHELLEY LANCASTER HAMPDEN-TURNER.

For Kristin Shannon,
Sandra Hickey,
and Yola,
who made this book possible

Contents

Illustrations follow pages 120 and 248

Prologue

I FIRST CAME TO the Delancey Street Foundation in San Francisco on a spring morning in late February 1974. It was sixty-one degrees. There was not a cloud in the sky, and from the top of the old Mein mansion on the heights of Broadway you could see from the Golden Gate Bridge to Oakland airport clear across the Bay. I had left Boston a few hours earlier in the midst of winter. There had been a temporary thaw, and the snow had melted in places revealing the winter's harvest of cigarette butts and dirty sand. Here the azaleas and the wisteria and exotic blooms I had never seen before tumbled down the steep gardens of some of San Francisco's most beautiful houses. I was being shown around an immaculately kept building by recent criminals and addicts who were exuding more charm, wit, and hospitality than I had known in years.

The pundits had been telling us that the Movement was dead, and indeed the ghetto corporations I'd been working with in the last few years were hanging on by their fingernails in the rubble. I had expected to find the same thing at Delancey Street and was stunned by the contrast. I was in San Francisco to write a report on behalf of a foundation that was considering funding Delancey. I was so amazed that day that I lost all track of time and remembered shortly after 3:00 P.M. that I was supposed to be speaking across the Bay in Berkeley in twenty-five minutes.

Clutching my rolled-up charts on "Interpersonal Process in Schizophrenia," I ran into the road and hailed a taxi. Soon we were making haste down Broadway toward the freeway. I was so excited about Delancey that I had to tell someone. I leaned toward the small hatch that separated me from the driver and shouted my impressions at the back of his neck. It was not an impressive neck. I recall three bulges covered with short grey bristle. They would writhe occasionally as if their owner was yawning, and I thought I detected a grunt or two between gospels. There is a resonance as you cross the Bay Bridge, and I had to raise my voice further so that soon I was quite hoarse.

A sudden annoyance with myself and a revulsion for Three Bulges swept over me. What the hell was I yelling for? Why should *he* care, some yahoo who beats up peace marchers and voted for George Wallace? By the time we reached the University of California, I had settled back into my seat and into my skepticism. Imagine gushing like that! How jejune! . . . Must think of my presentation . . .

The taxi pulled to a halt outside the Wright Institute. I got out and went around to the driver's window. He was an older man with watery eyes, and he seemed to be staring fixedly at his own feet. The meter was blank.

"What do I owe you?"

"Nothing," he said, still looking down. "I know . . . someone . . . got his kid in Delancey. He stole his parents blind for twenty years and now. . . . Anyone who's helping those people is helping me. . . ."

All of a sudden the taxi surges forward, almost decapitating me. I am left on the front steps of the Wright Institute. They are waiting for me. I am late, but my eyes are so full of tears I cannot see. I sit down on the steps, still clutching my charts, and try to compose myself. Someone touches my shoulder.

"Are you all right?" she asks

"I'm fine. . . . Someone was kind to me. . . ."

"Far out," she says.

1

The Curious and the Desperate

TWO KINDS OF PEOPLE come to the Delancey
Street Foundation in San Francisco, the Curious, who have
read about its various dramas in the newspapers or seen
them on television, and the Desperate, who come from jail
or the streets to seek asylum there.

The Curious are welcome on Wednesday and Friday
evenings when there is Open House at the Club, located on
the corner of Fulton and Eighth on the edge of Golden Gate
Park. The old El Portal apartment building has been
remodeled with cedar siding, tiffany shades, gold lettering
on the windows, and touches of art nouveau. If the name
reminds you of New York's Delancey Street, which socialized many thousands of American immigrants in the early
part of this century, that is intentional. The wretched refuse
of this country's teaming prisons wash up at San Francisco's
Delancey Street Foundation regularly to begin a new life.

You will know when you are in the vicinity of the Club by
the long rows of strange vehicles: an open-topped double-
decker bus, replete with brass fittings; a replica of a prison
cell on wheels; an MG sports car; a 1935 Bentley; a motor

home; a three-ton truck; and innumerable vans, jitneys, and small buses.

Assuming you can park and that you get as far as the door, there are certain things you should *not* do. Since I did them, be warned by me. You will see the "manager's desk" and a long bench beyond it, above which hangs a plaque with the words of Anatole France reminding us that "The Law in its majestic equality forbids the rich as well as the poor to sleep under bridges, to beg in the streets, and to steal bread."

If there is a man or a woman sitting on the bench, you should not accost him or her. They are not Curious; they are Desperate—and exceedingly so. I sat down next to a morose young man and engaged him in what I felt was witty and genial conversation. I paused after several seconds, sensing a lack of response, only to hear him tell me, quietly but unmistakably, to engage in coitus with myself at a place as far removed from him as possible.

He had been sitting on the bench for seven hours awaiting the interview that might admit him to Delancey. No one had even acknowledged his existence—by design—until—by accident—an effete Englishman began neighing inanities at him. It was too much. "Madhouse!" he muttered to himself, while I stared. "This is a fuckin' madhouse!"

The other person whom you should not bother, unless absolutely necessary, is the one behind the manager's desk. He is there more for his own sake than for yours. One of the first nonmenial jobs a new resident is given is working at the desk. It teaches him the ropes, and while he certainly manages to learn, only occasionally does he manage to manage. Since he is taught to assert himself before strangers, he will, if you ask him a question, give you the fullest benefit of his inexperience. For example, when a friend inquired for the author, he was told, politely but firmly, that Hampden-Turner had not yet been in residence for sixty days, could not, therefore, see visitors or receive messages, and did my friend realize that he was only feeding my sickness?

The manager is flanked by a large octagonal wheel, which purports to give the current location of every resident, and a large blackboard covered with names. The wheel, the board, and the manager are somewhat akin to the Delphic oracle. They require imaginative interpretation.

It is best to leave both the bench and desk to your left and turn right into a large L-shaped lounge. The architect (or perhaps a mining engineer) appears to have had last minute doubts about the structural soundness of the ceiling, and a number of random pillars and props break up the interior space. These have been put to good use, however, and are festooned with photographs, certificates, honorable citations, and trophies. Delancey's history and its colorful opinions are written on its walls.

A short cut to understanding what all this is about can be found on a pillar immediately facing you as you enter the lounge. There is a framed scroll bearing a resolution adopted by the California Senate's Rules Committee and proposed by Senator George R. Moscone. It reads in part as follows:

Whereas The Delancey Street Foundation, a self-help, residential, and therapeutic community in San Francisco, which was started to help ex-convicts, drug addicts, and anyone else who needs to get their lives back into shape, is deserving of public recognition and the highest commendation for its efforts and successes in returning its residents to the mainstream of society as responsible and productive citizens; and

Whereas established in 1971 by Mr. John Maher the Foundation is currently housing, teaching, training, and employing approximately three hundred people who would otherwise be considered financial and social burdens to the community; and

Whereas The Delancey Street Foundation runs six businesses . . . and each business has formal on-the-job training; and

Whereas the members have the opportunity to attend college and vocational school, an accredited in-house high school, and

may attend private schools in exchange for Delancey Street services; and

Whereas community services, such as escorting senior citizens in
dangerous areas, counseling young children as to the danger of
drugs, and consulting with prisoners and prison administrators in
times of conflict, are performed by members; and

Whereas the spirit and business of the Foundation is self-
reliance and the support of government funds and agencies has not
been sought; and

Whereas . . . the basic belief that people can change their lives
for the better, and that it is possible for them to break the molds
society puts them in . . . is gaining increased support. . . .

Therefore be it resolved. . . .

Some adjacent pictures and blown-up newspaper articles
suggest why the senator, apart from his genuine enthusiasm,
might like to have Delancey on his side. There are pictures
of rallies and parades: Delancey Streeters with Cesar Chavez
and the black eagle of the United Farm Workers, Delancey
Streeters in Ku Klux Klan costume satirizing local Nazis.
There are residents marching with Sinn Feiners, Italian-
Americans, and the Hotel and Restaurant Employees
Union.

The notice board yields evidence of the formidable activity of Delancey's voluntary political clubs, including the
Teapot Dome Republican Club and the Michael James
Curley Democratic Club. Over two hundred canvassers
from Delancey sally into the streets to elect their clubs'
slates of candidates.

If you find the chairwoman of the San Francisco Board of
Supervisors, two members of the school board, a judge, two
candidates for mayor, and a local assemblyman who pumps
your hand with generalized affability while you stand there
bemused, take it in stride. They are friends of Delancey in
more ways than one.

On the opposite wall are pictures of John Maher, Delan-

cey's founder and president, with Jimmy Carter, Governor
of Georgia; with Governor Docking of Kansas; with
Richard Hongisto, Sheriff of San Francisco; with Ron Del-
lums of the Black Congressional Caucus; with Karl Men-
ninger; and with Bayard Rustin. Among dozens of framed
letters of thanks and support are letters from the Prisoners
Union that Delancey helped establish, the Social Services
Union, the Supreme Court of California, and the Massachusetts Department of Corrections.

In a corner by itself, and strangely moving in its simplicity
and directness, is a letter from Randolph Hearst, father of
Patty Hearst, alleged member of the Symbionese Liberation
Army, which kidnapped her in 1974. In the letter Hearst
thanks John and the Foundation "for valuable help and
assistance during the very difficult period in our lives." A
few feet to the left, beneath a huge headline from the *Los
Angeles Times,* one can discover more about Hearst's
attempt to ransom his daughter.

Heroes of Food Give Away Program

The People in Need Program was in near-riot situation,
one reads, until fifty volunteers from Delancey stepped into
the breech to unload trucks and distribute the food in the
ghettos. John is eloquent on the condition he found:

> "Goons," said Maher. "Goons that demanded triple wages
> because they knew Hearst's back was against the wall. Goons that
> sold Hearst $200,000 worth of meat that was all fat and bone
> and nearly started a riot. . . . We accepted no money and no
> food. . . ."
>
> "When a person is under the kind of human pressure Hearst is,
> you don't cheat him," said Maher. "Just like the slumlords in
> Harlem ought to stop cheating the poor people. . . ."

Next to this statement are displays from Delancey's
public service advertising campaign. There is a full-page

advertisement run to assist senior citizens to organize themselves:

THE BUREAUCRATS HAVE SENTENCED
YOU TO DIE
Don't take it lying down.

And to help Vietnam Veterans do the same:

DID YOU RETURN HOME TO FIND A WAR
GOING ON?
And *you* were the enemy?

There is even an advertisement that ran in the *New York Daily News* for all the sad little hustlers who prey upon each other: THE TROUBLE WITH NEW YORK IS THAT SOME PUNK IS ALWAYS RIPPING OFF YOUR MOTHER WHILE YOU'RE OUT RIPPING OFF SOMEONE ELSE.

You sense that you are in the presence of a compassion that is broad enough to include old people, soldiers, petty thieves, even a bereft millionaire.

On the opposite wall are stills from a film Paramount made about Delancey for NBC. The actors are posed beside the real characters they portrayed. Walter McGinn played John Maher, Carmine Caridi of *Godfather* fame played Joe Sierra, John's lieutenant in charge of media liaison. All the film's locales were genuine.

Adjacent posters invite you to evening concerts by Mongo Santamaria and Cal Tjader. Another poster tells you that the women of Delancey will present a fashion show next Thursday, demonstrating what can be done with the donated clothes available at the warehouse. The opinions of prominent pundits and columnists are also displayed. You can discover that Nicholas Von Hoffman regards Delancey as a cross between the Mafia, the Communist Party, and the Little Sisters of the Poor.

So many certificates and diplomas abound that if these

are communists, they must be climbing communists. You will discover that Kenny Hepper, Delancey's first graduate, has reached superlative depths in underwater competence, returning to the world as an amphibian computer engineer-cum-diving instructor. Mon Singh Sandhu (Delancey's vice president) has been awarded a wine and beer license. A detail, perhaps, but he is the first ex-convict to whom the state of California has knowingly awarded such a license.

In fact, it is highly unlikely that you will be left alone long enough to read what is on the walls. At least some of the residents, whether black, white, Latino, Indian, male, female, young, or old, are likely to have introduced themselves. They are not shy about their pasts. Indeed, they wear the contrast between what they are now and what they were once with pride and some drama. They are ex-convicted existentialists, bearing witness to people's capacity to transcend their limitations. You keep thinking as you talk to them. Armed robber? Child prostitute? Twenty years in Vacaville? Surely not. And yet their friendliness is rarely formal or forced. The secret of their relaxed, courteous, and articulate manner is the "Games," a playful catharsis during which rage and hostility are discharged in a kind of psychic toilet.

If your humanism takes the place of religion, you may be in danger of going overboard in your initial enthusiasm. The sheer implausibility of people who had been locked away for years now being open, amusing, and gregarious was enough to render me euphoric. I thought I'd witnessed the raising of several Lazuri, the mass return of Prodigal Sons. Luckily John Maher put a firm damper on my glow.

"Silence please!" someone is shouting. "There is a special announcement. . . ."

A man in his early thirties, with the good looks of a faded cherub in an Irish cloister, has appeared at a microphone on the raised stage. It is John Maher, cigarette in one hand, coffee cup in the other. He has made a career of his own convictions—in every sense of that word. His stomach has recently embarked upon a career of its own.

"Okay! I just wanted to say a few words for the benefit of our guests here tonight, the squares." His voice is rasping but resonant, his accent vintage Bronx.

Don't be fooled by appearances! We got some classic weepers and whiners among our residents, people who still think this is Day-flop or some other federally funded program. Since we're getting close to Christmas and they're missing their mommies, some have started this Give-an-Armed-Robber-a-Break Week.

Trouble is, some of you squares are "nice" people, the kind who believe that the ex-convicts and dope-fiends we have here were "misunderstood." You have a tendency to look them soulfully in the eyes and say, "I know you've had a hard life to live." *What life?* They ain't *had* no life 'cept selling dope to kids or hangin' out with Scumbags Anonymous in East Oakland. They tell you, "No one here treats me like a human being." Question is, where did they get the idea that someone who mugs old women is a human being?

Oh, I know you think that Claud is *bee*-utiful 'cause he once stole the crown jewels of Poland and now he's reformed and *so dignified.* Well, Claud never stole nothing 'cept some food stamps that stuck to his fanny while he was sitting down on the job. So please don't take his bullshit.

And you *empathic* people with the Great Hearts, try the senior citizens of this town, or better still join our team of residents that's taking some Christmas to the crippled children. God knows they need all the love they can get, but there ain't no ex-addicts need your sympathy. Okay? 'Cause they aren't all better yet. They're still suffering from psychiatry and social work, which means they're looking to *use* you—socially, sexually, financially—every way they can.

We're thinking of having a Trick's Corner for all you squares that get took, who pay ten dollars for a dittoed sheet of that *ghastly* prison poetry, "The Psychotic Ramblings of Harry the Half-Ass."

So when you go upstairs to play Games, really *play* them! When some acne-ridden kid with an eighth-grade education says,

"Conceptually speaking, I would judge. . . ," will ya *stop* him, please, and say, *"Can you spell that word, punk?"* And please don't bring the refined and complex problem of your alienation from your second husband and lay it on Ray Flicks, 'cause Ray thinks that alienate is what you brew in the bathtub. You'll kill him by accident when you treat him like something he is not, and *cannot* become, so long as it is easier for him to pretend than to change.

On another subject, *we do not think that grass is groovy.* For the same reason alcoholics should not drink wine with their meals, or they will go home, drink whiskey, and beat up their wives. Please remember that many of our people here are still patients. If one of our women residents comes over to you with that scratch-my-crotch-I'm-sexually-liberated routine, then consider *her* future. She's here because she needs to be, and because most of her relationships have been so casual that she's close to despair. Odds are she doesn't want to fuck you anyway. She thinks *you* want it, or, with a face like Bela Lugosi, she knows she looks better with her skirt up over her head.

If you insist on fucking one of our women, and you do it after less than fifteen minutes of intense yearning over a dining room table, and she is so unmindful of our advice as to let you, then for God's sake be *honest* with her afterwards. Do not dignify the trivial episode by going through the Nobility Number that some of you reserve for your dealings with the oppressed.

"Dahling, I must go now into the night, but the memory of these few precious moments of intimacy and the passion of our meeting will be with me always as I wend my dark and lonely way. . . ."

Please spare her that, at least. Have the courage to speak the truth and say, "Ha, ha, ha! You silly cunt. I've got my wee-wee wet and I'm splitting!"

At least that way she'll learn. So help us all inject realism into our lives. If you're sitting next to a man in a Game, and he's got a face like a bubbling pizza, *don't* blame him for not having a girl friend, get him some Parmesan cheese for it! If you're talking to a gal who's nice but needs a nose job, don't pretend she's "really" a Beautiful Person. Tell her the truth. "I wouldn't take you out for an ice-cream sundae, 'cause with a hooter like that you'd knock the cherry off the top!"

Please remember that we invite you squares in here partly to be role models for our own people. I know that some of you are *cree-*ative, and that *cree-*ative people disintegrate to find meaning, but our people here just disintegrate! So if you come in here like brooding Hamlets or dressed as an artistic montage of recycled garbage, then some of our people could get the wrong message!

I have an announcement which is mostly for our people —although squares are welcome to attend. Next Saturday is the football game against the cops. We're gonna win, and we need a big cheering section. Some words of caution. Please watch your language. Remember they're mostly Irish Catholics, so any references to incest with their mothers are likely to be taken amiss. The more stupid of our residents should join that section of the crowd cheering for the cops—that way they'll be blamed for you. For example, anyone with an irresistible urge to discuss their own ethnic superiority, the relative whiteness of their skin, or the ineffable mystery of being black—all those would be happier with the cops. For our part, we are going to play fair, keep to the rules, and like the regular, clean-cut fellahs we are, we're gonna *knock the shit out of 'em!*

There are cheers as John leaves the microphone and walks to the coffee bar. Someone replaces John at the microphone and starts to call out lists of names and room assignments for the Games upstairs. Slowly the lounge empties as small knots of people depart for their mysterious rites. Ten minutes later only a couple dozen people are left.

"For those here for the first time, the Orientation will be held in the Red Room. That's to my right behind the coffee bar."

A videotape player has been set up on a dais, and a CBS television documentary on Delancey, a segment of "60 Minutes," is being played. As I enter the room, I can hear the voice of Morley Safer.

. . . and if conservatives complain that liberal judges and social workers are too soft on criminals and liberals complain that it is the nineteenth century approach to crime and punishment that has created an enormous criminal population, Maher has a third approach to criminal reform—criminals who have decided to heal each other.

The scene switches to Maher.

Ex-cons and addicts ain't nice guys—that's a myth! Are poor people and oppressed minorities wonderful, sensitive human beings? No! Problem is that x amount of it is their fault—because they let it happen to them—and a tremendous amount of it is society's fault. We gotta separate these two problems. So we come in here—and what we have in here is a *sane asylum*. You see, years ago, when only a few people were crazy, we used to have insane asylums. Now when it seems that everyone is crazy, what we have to do is start some sane asylums for ourselves and for a couple of years treat each other sanely. . . .

People have gotta understand that society is all screwed up. We're going to change it and that means knocking some of the bums out of the way. But *before* we do that, we gotta understand that we ain't nice guys either. Social victims are generally pretty dangerous, nasty characters because we're pretty twisted, and we gotta untwist ourselves, so we're human beings instead of animals. . . .

See we're really caught in this bind between right-wing nuts who want to beat everyone on the head and poor, weak-kneed, bleeding heart, vicarious thrill, radical chic creepos who wanna kiss your backside, until you're almost a schizo. A number of our people understand this, and what we want to do is get into a position where our problem, the oppressive nature of our relationships with society, is understood, but at the same time *we* are taking personal responsibility for our own change.

Morley Safer asks him how a man or woman taken into Delancey Street straight from jail, or coming there to avoid prison, changes to become a new person.

Simple! . . . It's craziness really. . . . If you go to a big house where there's two thousand people, five hundred of whom are totally out of their minds, psychopaths who belong in a mental institution, where there is a daily race riot between little Polish guys who think they're Nazis and Texans who think they're Africans, who keep grappling with each other all day long, while being encouraged by the administration to do this—then after a while what happens is you get a bit crazy. You start walking around with your blade, looking everywhere. When you come to Delancey, you have dinner. People yell at you to make sure you go to school. There are ladies; you can talk to ladies instead of having only drag queens on the next tier. You see civilized human beings, and the result is you get normal results from a normal environment.... It's not so difficult for me to understand [John taps his own head] if you put a dog in a cage and kick it once a day, at the end of five years you say, "Okay! I hope you learned your lesson. Come on out!" Then the first thing he does is bite you on your knee.

The program then turns to Delancey's various businesses, the flower and terrarium delivery service, the sidewalk cafe and restaurant on Union Street, the garage, the moving company, the advertising specialties sales force, and the construction business. Safer struggles to distinguish John's doctrine of hard work from Richard Nixon's, but John seems unafraid of the contamination.

Tell you who else said it! Mao Tse-tung said it, Lenin said it, Tom Paine said it, Benjamin Franklin said it. Get off your ass and work for a living, 'cause that's the only way we're gonna get productive enough to get the animals, the bureaucrats, the dingbats, the big politicians, and the corrupt cops off our goddamn backs! You don't get nothing without some work in this world.

There follows an account of Delancey's long battle with its rich neighbors in the Pacific Heights section of San Francisco. The Club or social center used to be in the sometime Egyptian consulate building, a mansion in Pacific Heights. Several neighbors banded together to have Delancey evicted for zoning violations. Eventually the Club moved to its present Fulton Street address after diplomatic relationships between the United States and Egypt were restored in 1974 and the latter joined the Department of State in pleading for the return of its consulate. But by that time Delancey had purchased, rather than rented, *two* additional mansions in Pacific Heights. The battle still continues.

Morley Safer asks John why it is important for the Foundation to locate in the best parts of town.

There's no need for all dope-fiend centers, veterans' centers, old folks' homes to be in slums, so that the muggers can come out and get the old folks, and the junk dealers can deal to the junkies easier. What has to be is that the whole spectrum of the community has to absorb its part of the problem.

"Do you think," Safer asks, "that society's been too soft, coddled criminals too much?"

No. Society's been too coddling of the [ex-] President of the United States, of the Mafia, of the corrupt unions, of the big corporations. Society ain't never coddled no Puerto Ricans, no black people, no Appalachian whites. Problem is this—criminals are not coddled who are poor criminals. Rich criminals are coddled—like General Electric got fined three thousand dollars for *beep-beep* with the electoral system. That's treason! They should be shot! Letting slumlords get six years in which to appeal injunctions on their Harlem tenements is coddling criminals. Letting bum Teamsters shoot farmworkers is coddling criminals. We should stop coddling those goddamn criminals and start helping the poor people.

Morley Safer asks John why he's doing all this. "What's in it for you?"

Well, when you're an absolute incompetent with no education and a criminal record, you can be either of two things. You can be a bum—or a great social leader. I failed as a bum . . . , so really I've no option.

The machine is turned off. Two men are running the orientation tonight, a square and a resident. They are Jack Webb, a retired police inspector who now has his own investigative agency, and Tommy Grapshi, an Albanian-American ex-shoplifter with close to twenty years behind bars. If Grapshi's face is familiar, it is because scenes from his Rip-off Seminar—or Thieves' Theatre—occupy much of the passageway leading to the coffee bar. He tours the Bay Area giving department store executives and staffs demonstrations of the multifarious methods of boosters (shoplifters). There are pictures of women in boosters' bloomers and of Tommy's climactic act in which he lifts the wallet of the chief executive, who rises and thanks him for the demonstration.

Someone in the audience asks about Delancey's income. Jack explains that the Foundation is almost entirely self-supporting from its own businesses. The economic "take-off" is achieved by the simple expedient of paying no wages. "If you have three hundred people bringing in an average of as little as two thousand dollars a year, that's half a million—with that you can live in mansions and exercise real power." It is estimated that Delancey now controls several million dollars worth of property—although banks *own* most of it—and the Foundation may yet make the *Guinness Book of World Records* for deficit financing.

Tommy now turns to the subject of Games, the one thing that regular visitors to Delancey Street *have* to do. He explains that the Games serve many purposes. They are a way of socializing squares into the more unusual aspects of the Foundation. They teach residents to assert themselves verbally instead of physically. They are a dumping ground for hostility. Delancey cannot being to deal with its "patients" unless their twisted feelings and values are expressed. The Game forces everyone to express himself or herself. Be silent and you will very quickly become the focus of the Game. Games should not be thought of as therapy for squares. If you are under psychiatric care, do not play without the advice of your shrink. Games should be fun, a form of verbal jousting with gross exaggerations. They are not necessarily true, although they may contain some truth. It is up to each player to discern the kernel of truth, if any, amid the verbiage of fun and fury. You may say anything in a Game, without fear of reprisal *outside* the Game. It is a moratorium, a place to test positions, try new techniques, indulge your prejudices, and "toughen your gut." It is a place where you can learn to take insults and to give as good as you get. Resentments should stop at the doorway of the Game-room.

At that moment John makes an unscheduled entry, picking up on the exposition.

"We got some squares here who think the Game is 'cruel' and 'hard' on people, 'cause we yell at each other and discourage sniveling. But there ain't nothing cruel about Games for someone who's lived in East Oakland, or for someone who's been in jail, where half the people are looking to cut you and the other half to fuck you."

John has made one circuit of the room and exits on the final words, a man from *Newsweek* hot upon his heels, and a cameraman in front of him, hopping on his haunches like a Russian dancer—perhaps to get an "authoritative" upward angle on the founder.

A woman in the audience raises her hand to ask Tommy about "Dissipations." She has runic symbols around her neck and holds her hands in front of her as if she were trying to levitate the audience. Dissipations, Tommy tells her, are weekend marathon Games, which last at least forty-five hours. They are much more intense and serious than ordinary Games, because people's deepest experiences and fears are explored as exhaustion wears down their defenses. Props like candles and coffins are used to symbolize death, while music and dramatic reenactments are used to create mood and to recreate traumatic events. You must play Games for at least a year before you will be allowed to watch Dissipations, since they concern matters of the greatest privacy. Most of the squares who work with and for Delancey, as lawyers, real estate brokers, and advisors, have been dissipated. You may volunteer to be dissipated, but acceptance will depend on your value to the house.

Jack takes over from Tommy to ask fellow squares not to

come into the Club after drinking booze or smoking pot. If either are detected on your breath, or if your behavior seems in the least way drunken or high, you will be escorted from the premises. Do not try to form intimate personal relationships with residents of less than one year's standing. Try to avoid listening to, or sympathizing with, some hard luck story that the resident has failed to sell to his brothers and sisters. You can "feed his sickness," unless you are careful.

Occasionally you will be approached by a resident who makes it clear that he or she should not really be at Delancey but instead should be working for, or living with, you. Consider carefully whether you want to find such persons with all their hang-ups and dependencies on your own doorstep one fine morning. You will not be welcome here if you aid or abet any resident to split.

Remember that any resident you invite out or to your home may not behave there as here. Play Games with any people you plan to trust. That way you'll learn about them first. Remember that Delancey is a big family. We know each other's business and personal lives. If you form an attachment to any resident, you must expect to hear it discussed in Games. You will be very quickly detected and severely Gamed if you try to play the field with more than one resident at a time. We frown on promiscuity. We encourage sex only in the context of mutual commitments. Our own residents have "relationships," then "trial marriages," then real marriages. Although the process can be terminated at any stage, all efforts at establishing intimacy should be wholehearted.

Tommy asks us to note that several male residents have bald heads. Delancey shaves the heads of all new male residents and of those who commit substantial offenses, e.g., shooting dope or being violent. We are asked not to fraternize with bald-heads. Women's heads are not shaved, but they wear no make-up or jewelry in their first weeks, and women who have offended wear stocking caps. If in doubt about the standing of a woman resident, one should ask. The shaving is done to help the individual commit himself. It symbolizes a new beginning and that growth must start from zero. It also tends to reduce the number of residents who split in the first few weeks, since they would look foolish to their old friends on the street.

The orientation continues for another twenty minutes. Afterward, it is easier to understand the full range of scenes displayed on the walls and pillars. The chieftain sitting against the background of tribal huts and surrounded by bushmen must have been photographed in Senegal. Delancey sent some of its most prominent black residents to Africa for a vacation and to search for their roots. They were "adopted by local tribes," according to the Delancey Street *Journal,* "who received them with great warmth and friendship, a lesson in civilized behavior lost on the more advanced tribes of Pacific Heights."

For the same reasons, Latino residents were sent on two month-long trips to archaeological sites in Mexico. Butch Hallinan, noted anthropologist and archaeologist, helped them trace their roots back to a proud civilization. The *Journal* notes that "it is cheaper *per diem* to send youngsters on an African (or Mexican) tour than to maintain them in the ineffective youth guidance centers and reform schools we presently operate in the State of California."

The smiling group dining alfresco must be seated at the Delancey Street "family style" restaurant on Union Street in San Francisco, where soup à la Senegal is a favorite dish. The excited children waving from the open top of an antique double-decker bus and peering into prison cells must be on one of the summer tours to Alcatraz Island that the Foundation runs for ghetto children.

There is the football team to which John was referring. (They beat the cops 13−0.) Next is the mountain climbing group, then the scuba diving group, the river rafting group, and the basketball team. There is a picture of the Pat W. Donnelly Memorial Playground built by residents on the grounds of the county jail, with Pat standing beside it, apparently alive. He is mysterious about the meaning of the memorial. "I buried one of my multiple personalities," he will tell you, "but I've still some to spare."

One large picture frame is full of news photographs, campaign buttons, and stickers. There are momentos of the campaign to free Bob Wells, imprisoned in 1929. "Forty-six years is enough!" the buttons read. There is a picture of Wells, an elderly black man leaning on a cane, surrounded by a cheering throng. He was finally released into the care of Delancey Street in 1974 after an intense year-long campaign, using a mobile prison cell to dramatize the tiny space in which the man had been confined for close to half a century.

Campaigns to free Wells had been run since the late forties. After years of furor and frustration, there in a corner of the dining room, taking a late meal by himself, sits "one of the most vicious and dangerous criminals in the history of California." He is a frail, dignified old man, with a white beard, prominent cheekbones, and a hawk-like nose that bears a deep scar down and across it. This is but one of the fifty scars that cover his body, according to the testimony of his lawyers. Rightly or wrongly, fellow inmates believed that the prison administration wanted him dead—and tried to oblige. He was on death row for seven years and was once taken into the execution chamber, only to be taken out again after news of a stay of execution arrived.

A group of residents pass through the dining room and call greetings. He waves his cane in acknowledgment. You can talk to him without finding any sign of the "viciousness" that California penal authorities insisted upon. You are likely, however, to have a curious conversation, for Bob is cranky. He seems to have lived his life by a very simple prin-

ciple: to find out what it is that people want him to do or say
and then to do something as different as possible.

But I am interupted by the Lady-of-the Runic-Symbols
plucking at my sleeve. I join her for coffee. She is obsessed
by the idea of Delancey's Dissipations. "Mark my words,"
she says as she gestures with a crimson claw, "the secret of
this extraordinary place lies there. You are writing a book?
Penetrate to the inner core!" I promise her I will. "Did I tell
you about my life?" she continues. "Christ!" I think, "the
Awful Confessions of Maria Monk." I look around for escape. Now that it's too late, I remember John's warning
over breakfast in the Fairmont Hotel on the occasion of my
exploratory visit.

"You think *we're* crazy? You should see some of the people who come to look at us . . . Bund for Bisexual Serendipi-
ty, Action for Auto-Eroticism. . . . That's why we make
them play Games, to keep the Sane Asylum *sane.*"

2

Desperate Games

THERE ARE TWENTY PEOPLE in a small room seat-
ed on an odd assortment of chairs placed around the walls.
Nearly everyone smokes and drinks black coffee. Wreaths of
smoke hang in the thick atmosphere. It is a Game night. The
Game is "on" Jake, a black resident whose short hair
suggests that he has been around only a couple of months.
Two directors are giving him a verbal "haircut," puffing,
sipping, and sitting forward on the edges of their chairs as
they talk.

Okay! Let's suppose that there's a reasonable explanation as to
why you were found in the men's room at three in the morning,
seated on a chair and covered in Magic Shaving Foam. Perhaps it's
a sheer coincidence that Freddie C. *ran* out of the bathroom as I
came up the stairs. Frankly I don't care. My curiosity about your
sexual proclivities is zero. Whether you're a transvestite, a sheep
fancier, or a sniffer of girls' bicycle saddles is, to most of us here, a
matter of swinging indifference. My complaint *is* that the energy
consumed in this house in gossiping about *your* sexual preferences
is enough to start a revolution—and that's the trouble. Your
bullshit peccadillos are wasting our time and draining our energies
from much more important pursuits.

24

A black director takes the action.

The brothers are not going to book your act. I want to know how this reputation you came here with—the Shaft of East Oakland, the only man alive capable of stealing thirty TV sets from the back of a parked truck in the sixty seconds while the driver took a leak—how did this fabulous reputation dwindle to that of a bogus faggot? You're entitled to be a homosexual, if that's what you want. Course we'll challenge your position to make sure you're not just scared of women, as a lot of guys are who've been in the slammer, but if that's what you want, we'll support you. But I don't think it *is* what you want. I think you're a shit-scared little nobody who would cling to *any* reputation rather than face the truth that your life adds up to zero.

I very much doubt if Jomo Kenyatta helped to free Kenya by sitting in public restrooms with his hand on his cock. So you have a choice. You can start to come across for your black brothers and the rest of the house, you can take your hand off your wee-wee and go to *work,* or you can stay a fuckin' *slave* and put on your Midnight Blackboy act for the benefit of the other scum.

The first director continues Jake's "haircut."

The point *is, you* are responsible for your own reputation here. If people lie about you, you can challenge them in Games, but instead a silly, satisfied smirk comes over your face when people do these soap operas about where you put your prick last night. You want to hold orgies in public restrooms, you do it *outside* this Foundation! So what we wanna know is whether you're gonna stop posturing, now and forever, or whether you're gonna degenerate into Wonderfoam—The Men's Room Exhibitionist!

Jake, who has been rumbling during this haircut, finally explodes.

FUCK YOU! Ah was *shavin'* man, that's all. The rest is *bullshit!* We was bad-mouthin' the house, Freddie and me, and Freddie ran 'cause he thought someone had heard him. That's *all,* mothafucker. Ah ain't your boy! Ain't nobody's boy!

That, by Delancey Street standards, is a mild response.

Indeed, you can distinguish newcomers among the Desperate, not just by the shortness of their hair or their lack of make-up and jewelry but also by the high volume, low quality noises they emit during Games. "Mothafucka," "scumbag," "asshole," and "bullshit" just about exhaust their epithets, while the phrase "like . . . you . . . know . . . man" is the basic organizing structure of all conceivable expressions. When they get angry, there is nothing left but to bellow their epithets at even higher decibel levels. It is not rare to have more than half a dozen people shouting fewer than half a dozen words at each other for minutes at a time. It seems to bring relief, however, for, when it is over, they will resume their chairs with an air of vindication.

In direct contrast, a number of senior residents have learned to marshal words with considerable wit and point. Delancey, in its Games at least, is less an autocracy or a democracy than a "rhetocracy." The impressiveness once sought through violence, theft, and exploitation is now skillfully conveyed through language.

It is a mistake to look for factual truth in Games. The feelings are usually true. The facts are rarely accurate. Jake probably *was* in the bathroom after midnight, but that is about all you can be sure of. Details are invariably "engrossed" (made more gross than they actually are), so that if there was a spot of shaving soap on his chest, it would surely cover the entire area of his loins by the time "the indictment was run" in a Game. That someone is unfairly castigated in a Game is not considered important. It is up to him or her to defend and later to heed that part of the accusation that was deserved. Since the Desperate are generally slow to blame and quick to excuse themselves, it is thought unlikely that they will ever suffer *too great* a sense of responsibility. The surfeit of mudslinging seems to assume that only a small proportion will stick to its targets anyway, so deft are they at dodging.

In fact Games make little sense when looked at in isolation from their context, and those who would borrow such techniques for use in a different context should pause and consider. I doubt if people are healed or grow *in* Games so much as they grow *between* the Games and the contrasting worlds of work, politics, and in-house socializing.

One gets a totally false impression of Delancey unless one understands that its various parts are in point and counterpoint. The Game ethic, the work ethic, the political ethic, and the Club ethic all pull in different directions, and the definition of good behavior depends entirely on the element in which a person is operating. The sharpest contrasts occur between Games and the world of work. In Games you are encouraged to be impulsive, imaginative, irreverent, outspoken, playful, anarchic, self-expressive, humorous, rebellious, informal, and egalitarian. At work you should be self-controlled, mundane, deferential, tactful, task-oriented, orderly, self-effacing, serious, authoritative, formal, and hierarchical. You can "dump" your doubt, despair, and rage in a Game, but you are expected to do your work with a cheerfulness and optimism designed to raise the morale of your associates and bring credit to the Foundation. Similarly, you blame yourself rather than the system in Games, but in politics you demonstrate what the system has done to you and the other prisoners of social forms.

In Games you can express racial, sexual, and ethnic antipathies. You won't be applauded for prejudice—but *that* you said it will not be held against you. You say what you feel, however ugly. But suggest on the floor of the Club that black and white couples should not cohabit, and you will be denounced within hours. You might even have to apologize publicly to the persons concerned. Hence, someone assuming that Delancey is racist or sexist because the Gameroom rings with "nigger" and "cunt" would be correct in a superficial sense but wrong in a more fundamental sense. These epithets are used as an ethnic group of "insiders" would use them about each other. The Game is a celebration and exposure of the collective unconscious where emotions seethe and hatreds slither—emotions and hatreds that are quite properly suppressed from expression (but not repressed from awareness) in all other spheres of activity.

Yet the opposed ethics act as important checks upon one another. When you cannot admit that you feel prejudice, you do in the end have to express it somehow, and that unacknowledged—and often indirect—expression can be insidious. If your authority is not to become *authoritarian,* if your power is not to corrupt you, then there has to be a "feedback loop." This is exactly what Games provide. For example, at Delancey a boss can give a direct order to his subordinates at work. The chain of command will back him up in any dispute with them, *but* the same boss can be "called into a Game" by his subordinates and listen for several hours while they tell him exactly what it feels like to be subjected to his whims. If the criticism of him is extensive, it becomes clear to him and his peers that his capacity to lead is wanting.

Authoritarianism, as opposed to authoritative behavior, refers to attempts by a leader to use his power to expunge the evidence of his own failure to create voluntary compliance. Games save Delancey from authoritarianism since they "engross" rather than hide a leader's errors. He will have his nose rubbed in any mess he makes, and while his subordinates preside, Games let rebellion qualify authority without destroying it. They let imagination illumine hard reality without ignoring it, make fun of seriousness, allow for informal discussions on formality, and elicit equal opinions upon the subject of hierarchy. Each polar opposite, having its own area of sovereignty, is safe from destruction by the other, and an additional rule forbids an authority to avenge himself *outside* a Game for what is said inside.

For some time I could not understand the compartmentalization. Why pure obedience in one place and pure insurrection in another? Why not a shifting situational synthesis of the two, as when you obey your boss but make it clear that you question his right to require obedience of you? After all, when Delancey Streeters graduate, as most aspire to do, they cannot go into a broom closet with their new bosses and shout "mothafucka!"

I discussed this problem with Mimi Silbert, who is John Maher's "wife" by a trial marriage as approved by the Foundation. She is one of the very few square residents and is Delancey's only certified expert in things psychological and criminological.

I complained that the values were held so far apart that they clashed like cymbals with one's head too uncomfortably close to the clash. Mimi explained it on two levels. First you cannot applaud fine moral syntheses unless your audience understands the basic components. Few people coming to Delancey can make even a simple moral injunction work for them. The bipolar value system and the bipolar structure (i.e., a "barber" who champions your need to grow and the managers of the various businesses who champion the need of the organization to prosper) both create clear definitions of the good. Each polar value is relevant in equally polarized situations, as residents learn to play contrasting roles in each sphere.

The second reason why these extremes are necessary is that most entering residents are themselves *in extremis*, e.g., exceedingly desperate, dependent, and angry. Part of the system has to respond to what *is*, while the other part seeks balance by emphasizing what *ought* to be. The tension of cross-purposes originates with a simple dilemma. If the

Foundation let its desperate depend and emote without hindrance, they would suck Delancey dry and break it up. If they were forbidden to lean for support and to show anger, they would collapse. The only answer is to hold them up physically and socially, while yelling at them to find their own feet. You must, in the words of F. Scott Fitzgerald, "see that things are hopeless and yet be determined to make them otherwise."

It is this counterpoint between "conservative" rhetoric and "radical" reality that often lends to Delancey its air of craziness. "We're all mad here," the residents will say, like the Cheshire Cat beholding Alice. With denunciations on every side of "freeloaders," "whiners," "pukers," and "snivelers," one thinks of Archie Bunker. But the social structure is one that Archie would abhor—a multiracial, multiethnic, nonviolent community and extended family where members commit everything to each other for no wages.

There is a fascinating contrast between the upper-middle-class Esalen-type encounter groups and the mostly lower-class Delancey-type Games. The first draws its participants from the isolated nuclear families of a competitive culture. The participants, all strangers, cuddle, feel, transcend, and celebrate each other noncritically as "beautiful persons." The second draws its participants from an extended family in a cooperative culture. The participants, all intimates, shout, spar, curse, and denounce each other in a circle as wide as the room allows.

Conventional wisdom would describe the first group as part of a "love generation" and the second as a pack of plug-uglies. But then one notices their *actual* social situations, more significant surely than rhetorical exercises, and the verdict is exactly reversed! Moreover, each group tends to use its encounter sessions to redress a balance. The first tumbles its lonely members into romper-room fusions. The second moves its structurally fused members toward greater individuality and personal responsibility.

If you are a "beautiful person" and find yourself scumbagged, it can be a shock. There is a story told of the idealistic young man who answered Delancey's advertisement for a teacher in its in-house, accredited high school. He made the mistake of coming to the Club and asking for "an interview."

"Bench!" he was told.

"I beg your pardon?"

"Siddown there and keep quiet!"

There he stayed for more than an hour, which is a short time considering who they *thought* he was. Then he was called to come upstairs.

"Are you speaking to me?"

"Naw, I'm speaking to the bench—always speak to benches—up here, punk, and stand there."

"I understand you are looking for applicants . . ."

"Wrong buster! Applicants look for *us*. Delancey's gonna make it. But I doubt you could make water. . . . Now *you* tell *us* why we should save your lily-white ass?"

"There must be some mistake . . . , I'm a teacher."

"Sure! An' I'm an astronaut and ol' Abe over there is His Supreme Ass-Holiness, the Arch-trick of Puerto Rico."

"But didn't you advertise for a teacher for your high school?"

There is a pause, then the room breaks into laughter. Someone crosses to the telephone.

"Education? We've found you a teacher. No, he *has* to have the job. Let me explain . . ."

In fact the logic of Games has almost everything to do with the situation of the Desperate and very little to do with the Curious and other squares, who will only become confused if they believe—like so many university students and graduates—that all experiences are produced to contain some special meaning for them.

If anything, Games are designed to mystify those who would "psyche out" the system. They insure that when residents meet outsiders, the former are playing on their home ground and can exercise their own special rites. It makes the encounter between different socioeconomic groups and groups of most unequal fortunes a more nearly equal one. Squares usually have strong inhibitions about cursing the disadvantaged. The disadvantaged suffer no such shyness about cursing each other *and* squares after they have been around Delancey for a time.

Games have certain recurring themes. A study of them suggests a pattern of strain in the system of rehabilitation. A perennial situation is the intimate-relationship-that-destroys. Women residents are the ones usually accused of this. The whole house may be working to shatter the preposterous self-image of a male resident and change his ways, but then a lonely ex-whore sees her chance and whispers sweet comforts in his ear. The results can be disastrous.

In the scenario that follows, Inez, a plump Chicano woman in her early thirties, is on the "dime," as the residents call the hot seat. She is tearfully concluding a story.

"And then he said, if I didn't go down with him, he'd split. He'd go back on the street and O.D., and it would be *my* fault, 'cause I'd only pretended to love him. And so I agreed . . ."

"But he split anyway, didn't he? Thanks to the dollar *you* slipped him. You mental basket case!"

"Yes, but you see I thought . . ."

"You *didn't* think. You did what you always do—roll over on your back like a spaniel and piss on yourself with doggie devotion whenever a man snaps his fingers."

The speaker turns to the rest of the room to explain.

"We found Inez in the back of the moving truck doing push-push with a shaved bear as the fog rolled in on Marin County! It was about forty degrees. She had her bare ass on the steel tailgate of the truck and a can of antifreeze beside her!"

There is laughter and a bubble of comment.

"Did you hear violins?"

"What romance!"

"Could they see you from San Quentin?"

"Try an immersion heater!"

"This is serious!" One of the women directors is concerned.

"You know you're not allowed to fuck patients, and now you see what happens. You're still doing your hooker-with-the-heart-of-gold routine, aren't you? You still can't say no. You couldn't turn to this man and say, 'Yes, I love you, but there are *convictions* in my love. I stand for something, and you will *not* hide between my legs whenever the truth scares you.'"

"What do you think about a grown man crying to get into your pants?" another woman resident asks. "How do you feel about a big bald sissy who buys courage in the form of white powder, browbeating you into fucking him? Don't you know moral blackmail when you see it? Why d'you think he chose *you* for a soft option? 'Cause he knew you'd sell your ass for fried ice cream. Well, now your big Oakie is going back in the slammer where you put him 'cause you fed his sickness. He has to be a big shot, and jail is the only place that will feed him while he plays *Oakie über alles.*"

"Über Inez you mean!"

There is general headshaking. One resident turns to the others in exasperation.

"What the hell are we going to do with her? She grows fatter every day until she resembles the Graf Zeppelin. She

cannot resist food or men or shaved bears. An Oakie calls
her into the back of the truck. 'Tell Mama to bring the
vaseline and the tortillas,' and she follows him like a trained
dog. . . . Don't you know yet, Inez, what a stool pigeon is in
Delancey? A stool pigeon is a person who sees a friend dying
and *doesn't* tell! It isn't 'love' to load the pistol of a potential
suicide. It isn't 'loyalty' to be the Latin slave of a white bigot
who's never managed an equal relationship in his whole
life!"

Inez blows her nose noisily.

"He was just a trick—I see that now."

"No, *you're* the trick! You come in here claiming to be
some fabulous thousand-dollar call girl, when in truth you
did it for $3.75 and two returnable Coke bottles behind the
Lady Luck Diner! And after you've put in a hard night's
work holding up some overweight postal worker from Richmond, don't you realize that *he* goes home in his car to his
wife and his kids and his regular job? But what did *you* do?
You slunk to your one-room apartment over the porno shop
on Post Street and handed over the $3.75 to your pet gorilla.
You were the trick, Inez, not your clients!"

"Her pet gorilla called for her the other day."

"Really?"

"Yeah, I was on the desk, and this creature—I kid you
not, he had a bone in his nose and bandaged knuckles and a
tail. He says, 'Ahrr want ma wooman. War's ma wooman?
Ah lerve ha!'"

"It wasn't a tail. I was by the desk and saw him. It was a
backward-facing erection. He looked like Godzilla with a
hard-on!"

"Calling all monsters! Godzilla versus the Graf Zeppelin!"

"The shaved bear was just a sparring partner."

"Who *was* he, Inez?"

"A dude I met in Berkeley."

"A *dude.* Why can't you sunkissed children of the Golden West speak plain English. This creature—Chimp-The-Pimp or whatever it is—does it follow you around?"

"Sort of . . ."

"Why? Are you studying its behavior for college credit? Anyway, I told it—as best I could, Dr. Doolittle not being available to translate—that pets could not see their mistress for at least five months, or until you grow up, whichever takes longer. Frankly it staggers the imagination how you could make it with *that!* I'm surprised you weren't locked up for bestiality."

"What's the freakiest trick you've ever turned, Inez, not counting Godzilla?"

Inez shakes her head and makes a gesture of dismissal.

"C'mon—ain't nothing we haven't heard already. Why Sophie G. over there was fucked by a Baptist minister in a washbasin in the Fairmont Hotel with her ass on the Gideon Bible."

"You got it wrong!" Sophie is enjoying herself. "The washbasin was full of hot water. The Bible was open and propped up on my tits while he read aloud about the whore of Babylon."

"Question is, Inez—'cause we've taken too long over this already—are you going to become a woman with purpose and integrity whose affections embody principle, or are you content to become a superannuated seminal pot for slaves?"

It is easier to understand the function of Games if we consider a resident's typical day. The resident of less than a year's standing, but who has survived the first sixty days, rises shortly after 6:30 A.M., has breakfast at the Club on Fulton Street, and attends Morning Meeting at 8:00 A.M. Here the day's announcements are read out, songs of cheer and uplift may be sung, and most statements are applauded. The mood is gung ho and sets the tone for the day's work, which begins immediately after the meeting is over, usually before 8:30 A.M.

The residents disperse to work in the War Department (the six businesses), the State Department (finance, legal, education, politics, media, etc.), or the Vatican (therapeutic and personnel activity). Regular jobs end for most people at 4:00 P.M., when close to a hundred residents attend classes of one kind or another several days a week, while others play a variety of sports. With the exception of the teen-agers and a few outstanding scholars, all those who study must also work a regular job.

From 4:00 to 8:00 P.M. most residents are supposed to be able to find time to relax, but in practice this period is crowded with activities that one person or another has thought up. There are continual voter registration drives, picketing activities, raffle ticket selling. There may be a "Cerebration" (an intellectual discussion of a political or social issue) or a protoculture class (to raise the consciousness of blacks and Latinos). Rehearsals for some event are usually in progress: a talent show, review, concert, fair, celebration, or demonstration. Few are the afternoons or evenings without an emergency meeting of some kind. Crises may seem minor—"Francine stuck her tit in my coffee!" is John's favorite characterization of the usual flare-ups. Yet the consequences can be major—Francine or the complainant could end up back on the street and dead of a drug overdose.

It is during these hours in the late afternoon and early evening that the tribes and minions meet. (Delancey is organized into six tribes, each with four minions, numbering twelve to fifteen persons apiece.) These are the primary groups, the most intimate parts of the extended family. If residents want comfort, support, and assistance, they usually find it here. Their minion leader will deal with minor problems and requests. Their barber or tribe leader will deal with major ones. There is a right of appeal to the Chief Barber and from there to Mimi and John.

Following dinner at 6:00 P.M. there is a social hour, which on Wednesdays and Fridays is an Open House. On these two days squares can dine and drink coffee and join the Games, which start at 8:00 P.M. Games usually include groups of peer residents, that is, those who have been around for approximately the same period of time. However, one or two senior members must be present in each Game. Squares are usually assigned to play Games with the more senior residents.

There are a host of particular Games adapted to the circumstances of the working day: Tribe Games, Minion Games, Work Games (e.g., the restaurant staff), Team Games, and Dormitory Games. There are also study sessions where Game moves are analyzed and plays catalogued. Special Games will be built around a resident who has been subjected to a traumatic experience, such as the death of a parent or the breakup of a marriage or relationship.

Games last three hours or more and can reflect the entire day's events. An unlucky resident could be "indicted" by a roommate for sleeping in dirty underwear, by his manager for dawdling at work, by a classmate for being late for school, by a friend for sulking through dinner, and by his minion leader for not seeking help in putting these faults to right. On these separate occasions he *should* have been by turns sweet-smelling, hard-working, punctual, friendly, and contrite. By 11:30 P.M. a resident should be able to retire, and if he does not take it all too seriously, he may even sleep.

At any time up to midnight a General Meeting may be called. This usually means that someone has been caught in nefarious activity. Typically those in authority will be beside themselves with indignation—a favorite position. The particular crime is enunciated with loathing and disgust. *"Tom-*

my Tucker turned his own sister on!" and this is followed by a public call for confessions. Those with anything to admit had better talk—NOW!

Although General Meetings must be terrifying for those of bad conscience and on rare occasions have led to expulsion from the community, I have difficulty keeping a straight face. My mood of levity is induced by the small hard core of compulsive confessors who inevitably rush to the microphone at *every* General Meeting. "I would like to apologize for the bad thought I had at breakfast about interracial relationships!" "I borrowed a ball-point pen from the manager's desk and forgot to return it!"

Delancey's marvelous sense of humor totally deserts it on these occasions. The presiding barber grimaces with horror as peccadillo follows on pietism. "Any *more* bigots around here?" he roars. "Who *else* has been stealing our property?" Sure enough a white-faced sinner stumbles to the mike. She removed four thumbtacks from the bulletin board and took them to her room to affix her photograph of Johnny Cash. The barber gasps, a cross between a high priest about to rend his garments and W. C. Fields doing a double take. We wait for a bolt of lightning to blast all thumbtack thieves. It remains only to denounce her boy friend, who *saw* her take the tacks and said NOTHING to save her from perdition. (It is not that the barbers lack humor or proportion. They dare do nothing that might halt the confessional flood.)

But, of course, the hardened deceivers rarely come forward on these occasions. This leads to a familiar figure in the Game scenario, the person-suspected-of-being-dirty-but-refusing-to-cop (cop meaning to confess).

Great store is placed upon voluntary confession to having broken rules. Even where there is hard evidence of someone's guilt, it may be withheld for a while to allow time to cop. That way you get many confessions *without* hard evidence, because the "dirty" will believe they have been detected and will cop. If someone sitting next to you in a Game looks somehow familiar yet strange, chances are that he has lost his hair since you saw him last and has descended from his spacious office to scouring pots and pans. Some fall precipitously. Others become clouded with suspicion and inch their way downward.

Bryant, a tall, middle-class, black youth with large sad eyes, is an example of the slow descent. He has sat silent throughout most of the Game. Then there is a pause, and he says softly, "I'd like to put the Game on myself."

"Did you hear an unpleasant noise?"

"Something's crawled out from beneath a stone. It's rattling."

"At least let me speak!" Bryant blazes. "How can you hope to do justice if you won't hear me?"

"Justice, ha! If you'd got what you deserved, you'd be fuckin' *dead.*"

"Let's hear him. Tell us why they shaved your head, Bryant."

"I *asked* to have my head shaved." Bryant is quiet again and contrite. "I have disrespected this house and lost its confidence. I have failed to convince my brothers of my innocence. I want to accept responsibility for this failure of communication. Had I not failed in several smaller matters, they might have believed me. Instead I mind-fucked a young woman, the secretary to one of our sponsors. I told her bullshit stories. I forgot to return a library book, and I went into the park and played my bongo drums when I should have been in the house helping my brothers."

There is a ripple of mock applause. Then a black director leans forward in his chair and snarls, "You're so goddamn sanctimonious you make me puke! Even now with your head shaved you can't come clean. You cop but you don't cop. I doubt you're *capable* of truth anymore. You know and we know that mind-fucking a girl and playing bongo drums are not head-shaving offenses. As for pretending that you have to be a martyr to our disbelief, that is such fuckin' hypocrisy that I'm surprised your nose hasn't grown clear out the window!''

"What's goin' on here?"

"Yeah, what's the background?"

Several people are asking for clarification. Bryant's "barber" reviews the events of the last year.

"Okay, you wanta hear the punk's progress? Bryant is one of our earliest residents. He was at Bush Street where it all began. About a year ago his two roommates accused him of being loaded. That's not an easy thing for a roommate to do. They said he was scratchin', he was nodding off, and he watered his TV set instead of the azaleas.

"Well, we held an inquiry, and Bryant swore on his mother's grave and with tears in his eyes that he was clean. He begged us to uphold the pledged word of a brother against circumstantial evidence. We decided to believe him. We do that with our senior residents. Someone who is not believed cannot become credible to himself or others. Soon after that the rumors started. A guy we know on the outside talked to a dealer, and he gave a description of Bryant that was dead on. Bryant began to fuck up all his jobs and his relationships. Another witness came forward who'd seen Bryant on the night in question and said he was *definitely* loaded. Finally his 'old lady' left him—couldn't stand the stench of lies around him, she said.

"So now we have this minicop, this utterly transparent pretense that he is punishing himself more severely than we would wish because he holds himself to higher standards. Trust Bryant to shave his head while trying to escape from the meaning of doing so!"

"Know why I resent you, Bryant?" One of Delancey's best business managers is into the ring.

"I resent the hell out of you college educated middle-class

fuck-ups. You're the *real* niggers, with your bongo drums, your tribal hats, and your protoculture, when the truth is you've maimed and crippled and worn down more black men and women than the biggest white bigot in this town. We uneducated slobs keep repeating to ourselves, 'gotta educate our children and ourselves and prepare for the day.' Then we look at you or Josh over there, and we think 'wait a minute! I could graduate from college and *still* be a slave. I could end up like Bryant—the most erudite liar that ever tied himself in supersophisticated knots and used his brains against his own life.' Ain't *no one* here believes you but yourself!"

"Wrong! His Lordship here believes him, don't you?"

I have unexpectedly become the center of attention.

"Really!"

"Charles? *You* believe him!"

"Christ!"

No conversation, however private, is safe from becoming Game material. A worry I had confided to someone I was driving home had come back to haunt me.

"What I *said,*" I hasten to explain myself, "is that the behavior of someone who is ostracized can become very similar to that of a person who is genuinely guilty. All the incidents cited as evidence of Bryant's guilt—the rumors, the additional witness, the end of his relationship, even his own moralistic pronouncements—are possible reactions to his rejection by this community."

"God, what a *bore!*"

"Save it for a lecture!"

"He thinks Bryant is beautiful! Don't you, Charles? *All* blacks are beautiful, especially when they stand alone, sad and dignified, surrounded by a mob! Saint Charles to the rescue! He gallops to the scene tilting his mighty pen at the ugly institution! Will His Lordship save his faithful servant Black Abstraction? Can he make the world safe for scrib-

blers? Don't forget to tune in to our next installment of
'Have Guilt Will Travel,' the saga of a solitary psychologist."

"No, no! You've got Charles all wrong. He doesn't
believe *or* disbelieve Bryant. He is open minded. His mind
and his mouth will be yawning open at the sound of the last
trumpet. His kind are never wrong 'cause they never
decide."

"Let *me* ask Bryant a question," I say, trying to stem the
flood of derision. "Now, Bryant, assuming your innocence
for the sake of this question, how do you feel about the
roommates who falsely accused you?"

There is a pause. Bryant is sitting alone, his bare head
bowed, hands clasped together, a suffering captive in an art
exhibition of socialist realism. He answers quietly,

"They both did what they thought was right. They acted
like brothers . . . trying to help me . . . , but they were mistaken . . . ," and he breathes a sigh.

"BULL!" roars his barber. "Are you *impressed,* Your
Lordship? Is that sentiment *pure* enough for an Oppressed
Person? You fuckin' liberals! Who else d'you think *taught*
him this crap?"

I shake my head. "You're right—it's too unctuous. I'm
sorry, Bryant, your last supporter is wavering."

Three weeks later in a Dissipation we heard the full confession: the price of the drug, the dealer's name. It all
checked out.

This incident with Bryant helps to explain much about
both the Games and Delancey's policy with Desperate newcomers. The Foundation's philosophy is *not* formalized; to
do so would risk mass counterfeiting, or "playing house" as
residents call it. The strict regimen, the confusion, the hard
menial work of the early weeks are deliberately designed
to precipitate explosive Games. The sooner someone's genuine anger and emotion have been registered and recognized,

the easier it is to deal with the incredible tangle of lies and self-delusion with which newcomers strangle themselves. Residents cannot begin to deal with each other's problems unless the habit of authentic externalization is quickly established. "Our greatest successes have been the actors-out," John remarked to me one day. "We loose the pouty-poohs and those who, despite all our efforts, hold it in."

The roars of rage are also, perhaps, the only possible introduction to the world of feeling. As residents develop, they are able to express many different feelings of great range and sensitivity. But for the newcomer, and especially the male newcomer with his *macho* image, anger is the only acceptable feeling, and it serves as an outrider for all the rest. The facts in Games are often crazy—even invented —but the feelings rarely lie, and even Bryant was eventually exhausted by the sheer effort of pretense.

Another rationale for the Games that intrigues me is that most residents in their early months are, in fact, consumed by self-hatred. Although sociopaths are often said to be conscienceless, Mimi Silbert contends that their guilt is, in reality, as strong as it is deeply repressed. The volcanic eruptions within the Games help to spew the guilt forth, while the name calling *actually makes contact* with the image that the individual has of himself in a way that the soothing assurances of most professionals can never do. For the person whose greatest fear is his own nothingness, the howl of execration is a desperate beginning to a new life, a fact he must accept before he can embark upon a new voyage.

I also get the impression that swearing and shouting wears itself out through sheer surfeit, for, though it is freely encouraged, it slowly dies out in the months following admission. There are, after all, only a small and finite number of ways in which human bodies can couple or relieve themselves. Where neither violence nor shock accompanies the use of such obscenities, their repetition loses power and languishes, although not their creative use in wit and imagery.

Verbal violence is also believed to sublimate physical violence. In prisons men kill and are killed for a single epithet. Angry words lead murderous deeds upon an iron chain in a system of compulsory intimidation. It is Delancey's real achievement to have severed this chain. Violence by words is encouraged. Physical violence or its threat is forbidden and leads to instant disgrace, even expulsion. As a result physical assault is very rare, even among residents with histories of violence.

It follows that Games among residents who are of long standing have quite a different atmosphere. The speed and wit remain, but the feelings include warmth and humanity. Mimi is still not satisfied that the present Game form is right for people of greater maturity. She plans to evolve "a second stage of Games," which will teach participants to reconcile the polarized values they have internalized. "The traditional Game does not *solve* problems; it *airs* them and the issues involved. We have to teach our senior members problem-solving skills."

The scenario that follows illustrates a transition from the "early" Game to the "advanced" Game. The point at issue, the-lovers-quarrel-between-square-and-resident, is all too common. The contenders are Jo, a white, female divorcee of around thirty, and Bernado, a Puerto Rican in his late twenties who did five years in San Quentin for armed robbery and has become one of Delancey's most valuable residents.

"I wanted to play a Game with Bernado," Jo explains, "because of the way he's been treating me. To be specific, we had a date to meet at the Club last Saturday at 5:00 P.M. By six he hadn't showed. I called him in Sausalito. He said he was in the shower—would be over soon. By seven he *still* hadn't showed. So sometime around eight I called again, and he gave some vague excuse about being tired. So I took the jitney over to his place and found him in his room polishing the andirons in his fireplace. He said he was too tired to explain and went to bed."

Bernado is not his usual self, which is fluent and assured, but is sitting on the low sofa smoldering with resentment as the tale unfolds.

"Okay!" he shouts. "We'll call it off. Finished! Forget the whole relationship. I'm just an ignorant punk from the barrio. No education. Not good enough for you!"

He crashes his fist on the coffee table. It strikes the edge of the ashtray, which hits and breaks a coffee cup. Ashes and dregs fly in all directions.

"The Creature from the Brown Lagoon is throwing a teen-age tantrum," someone remarks calmly. "He knows he's wrong and he's fresh out of excuses. Why d'you ask her out, Bernado? Why not beat on your chest and give a mating call? You can always break up our furniture if she doesn't come."

One of the barbers switches tactics.

"Look, Jo, we played a two-hour Game with Bernado last Tuesday, which included the way he's been treating you. He's had it up to here by now. If we go on, there's a danger you could win the battle and lose the relationship. Okay?"

Jo is obviously shaken by Bernado's outburst, and they seek to reassure her.

"This is just a Game. It doesn't count—you realize that? He has license to regress. This is what he was like *all the time* just eighteen months ago! We'd like to take this opportunity to talk to you. A crisis like this is a chance to ask yourself what you are doing here and why.

"Now you've dated three Delancey people in the last eighteen months, and we're wondering if you're not on some save-a-sickie kick. I mean you're already divorced. You've turned thirty. Your kid, even if she doesn't need a papa, needs a mother who's not anguished all the time. Why are you spending the twilight of your eligible years chasing after losers? You college educated girls—I'm sorry *women*—are always talking admiringly about 'prisoner's consciousness.' Are you sure it's not prisoner's prick? Is there something that *thrills* you about *macho* characters who used to point guns at people and do Jimmy Cagney imitations?"

Jo shakes her head, half laughing.

"No, I really don't think I'm after some kick like that, and I think a lot about my own motives. The fact is that Bernado can be tender, considerate, and fun to be with much of the time, but then suddenly I don't know him, like tonight."

A female square speaks up.

"Look, Jo, I've gone with Desmond for close to a year, and I've had the same sort of trouble. He's less educated than me. He's black and on some days when he's in a bag, he can't stand to have me near him. We talked it over and here's what we came up with.

"For Desmond I'm an adventure, something exciting, new, and strange. When he's feeling good, as if he could take on the world, he'll see me and we have a terrific time. But on bad days it's his fellow residents he turns to, and they lick each other's sores, sores that he doesn't want me to see. Now I'm just the opposite. I'm lonely like you, and I'd give anything to have someone I could rely on when I'm feeling low, and someone who'd turn to me before another to seek comfort. But isn't that the trouble for all of us who date residents? They lean on each other, then practice on us to see if they're ready for the wider world.

"You can easily use the advantage of your education to confront Bernado in this Game and leave him no way out, but you threaten his life line when you do that. The only friends he has who respect him are in this house. If they lose respect for him, he'll *never* find the courage to make it with you. This is the man who didn't like working in the

restaurant because there were too many squares! He spent
five years behind bars and without women; that's nearly half
his life since puberty. There are some days when he'll just
want to retreat and rub his private property."

"I agree with Cynthia." It's another woman speaking.
"There is an education gap, an ethnic gap, a culture
gap—and those are hard enough—but there's also a gap
between the tribe system they have here at Delancey, which
sometimes drives residents into a desire to escape, and the
lonely "escape system" we squares inhabit that makes us
long for tribalism. I sometimes think that square-resident
relationships are like ships that pass in the night, each
heading for where the other's been. I used to date Paul. He
split six months ago. He was furious, just like Bernado here,
when I once played a Game on our relationship. I think
what he wanted from me was privacy and a haven from the
endless scrutiny and criticism that bounces from these walls.
He told me he wanted to do something *ir*responsible for a
change. I was it!"

"Is this a Game or a fuckin' ego massage?"

The complainer is a slim black resident who works with
the sales team and likes his Games loud.

"I think we're being too soft with this lady. There's a
sweet smell of martyrdom around you, Jo. How come you
wait *four hours* for this punk? Next time give him fifteen
minutes or keep *him* waiting. Don't you know the junkie
mentality yet? We *always* want something for nothing! The
needle in the arm is so's we can get the sensations without
the emotional risks. So now he knows how much *you* care,
four hours' worth, but the creep hasn't exposed hisself. I bet
you're a guilty fatherfucker. You think 'cause Bernado's a
Latino you *owe* him something—like being humiliated? Bernado don't need to fuck up the lives of 'do-good' white
women—that's easy for him—he needs to care for someone

beyond hisself—that's hard! You want to help him? You demand respect, and when he learns to give it, he won't smash our cups no more."

Attacks made on Bernado while ostensibly talking to Jo are known as "carom (or c'am) shots." The rules of the Game oblige you to talk only to whomever the Game is "on," but with c'am shots you can reach anyone at any time. All you need is skill at combining aspersions.

John Maher's words, phrases, and epithets infuse all Games. Such terms and phrases as "push-push," "seminal pot for slaves," *"you're* the trick, not your client," and "I very much doubt if Patrice Lumumba/Benito Juárez peddled his sister's ass at the corner of . . ." are all sayings of the Maherishi. More than anyone he is responsible for the pace and wit of the proceedings. So faithfully is he imitated that it's sometimes hard to believe that he is not speaking.

However, John *did* play a couple of Games a few weeks after I arrived at Delancey. I was invited to attend. Most of the directors and prominent squares were also present.

As we settled into our chairs, John cast a baleful eye at my personal appearance. His appraisal began with my crumpled jacket—the surviving part of an old suit—took in my baggy English trousers, and settled finally on my sandals. These had been hurting my feet so I had put on some bright socks. I was just looking for something to slide my feet under when the room fell silent, and John opened the Game.

"Your Lordship! There's something that puzzles me. You're a purebred Englishman, educated immaculately I have no doubt. You must be at least familiar with Savile Row. Why, then, do you walk around in sandals and pink bedsocks looking like a seedy Bulgarian tourist in a Black Sea resort? There's some excuse for *us*. We have to wear manufacturers' rejects with two left sleeves or a crotch so high that you're goosed at every step, but you outdo us all.

Are you overidentifying with the People, trying to live down your English heritage, or leading a Slobs' Liberation Movement?'

The room breaks up, as I grin sheepishly.

"I'm just scruffy, I'm afraid. No special reason."

"I want to talk to Charles." It's Mimi's turn. Her eyes are twinkling. She is dark haired, petite, attractive, with a voice that bubbles with laughter as she speaks. You might misjudge her as girlish-dumb, but only for a few seconds.

"At the reception for Senator Bagley last night in the Red Room, I saw you take a slice of cheese out of your ham and cheese sandwich and slip it into your jacket pocket. Is that how a gentleman behaves? Is that how you treat your clothes?"

"Well, I hate cheese, and it took me by surprise. There was nowhere else to put it. Besides, I placed it with discretion inside my pocket handkerchief, which I always keep here . . ."

I grope into my jacket to show them.

"NO! NO!" Mimi cries in mock alarm. "DON'T PULL IT OUT! Two sardines, a dill pickle, some Bombay duck, and a garlic sausage. UGH!"

3

The Maherishi: Man of All Reasons

THE LAST CHAPTER explained that different aspects of the Delancey Street Foundation—its Games, politics, businesses, and in-house social life—were in point and counterpoint to each other. For the origin of this arrangement and a bristling array of additional opposites, we need look no further than to the personality of John Maher. He has created in Delancey a social system coextensive with his own personality. The departments of the Foundation are compartments of his thought.

John begins his definition of political oppression by recognizing that the system crucifies its victims between false dichotomies.

The Left and Right are two giant dinosaurs, both obsolescent, who fight *over* the issues of poverty and crime and trample the poor in the process of grappling with each other. Almost never does either camp argue for the workable—rather they spring to the support of the most easily configured and memorably publicized of alternatives and so purify each that they are quite unattainable by the great majority of the ordinary people.

For example, when I was in jail, the social workers and little old ladies kissed my ass and cried a lot and said what a hard life I'd had. The guards and cops kicked my ass, cursed a lot, and showed me what "hard time" was like. The system, so called, is the interplay between warring ideologies and opposed departments of the bureaucracy, a mock contest with genuine casualties.

Take a typical situation. There's a street in East Harlem where a dozen seriously malnourished families are discovered. Two blocks away on Ninety-eighth Street, frogs' legs are being served to gourmets at fifteen dollars a pair. Someone discovers this . . . Scandal! The Mayor calls a conference at which ten academicians arrive, who vote themselves onto a commission at generous salaries. The commission is picketed by the women because they've been excluded and then by the gays 'cause they've been excluded. It wrangles all day, coopts one of each, and adjourns to the restaurant to eat frogs' legs and is picketed by Friends of Frogs, and *essentially nothing changes.* The guys, the gals, the gays, and even the little fellahs in frog suits *think* they're being radical and progressive, but in fact they *are* the system—one of its many byplays and side shows.

John sees federal and state bureaucracies constantly *adjusting* themselves to become parasitic upon each polar pathology. There is one department to legitimize and to regulate (marginally) the greed of winners and another department to sustain the chronic dependence on losers. Each client group is a captor of, or captive to, a corresponding group of bureaucrats.

One way the bureaucratic state maintains itself is by isolating social problems as if they were not connecting. There's no solution to the problem of drugs until there's a solution to the problem of filthy slums. The social model that the medical people have used in their effort to make money and keep the grants coming is the "cancer model" as when sickness can be detected and cut out of the organism. But the drug-and-crime problem is more like yellow fever. The way you cure yellow fever is to get the patients out of the hospital and march them down the stream. You dig out the swamp and then come back and scrub the rooms and burn the mattresses. The ones left standing have licked yellow fever, saved themselves and the rest of the community.

If isolated opposites oppress poor people, what liberates them is to seize each horn of their dilemma and bend it to their will. Ex-convicts and ex-addicts only come into their own when they command the language in which they are described and shape the forces that have afflicted them. To this end John has reached in all political directions.

From the Right he has appropriated the work ethic, the need for strong authority, respect for parents, the need for self-discipline, an opposition to Big Government, contempt for welfare, a reliance on the local community, a belief in self-help, and the view of business activity as the mainstay of independence and group integrity. He casts a jaundiced eye on do-gooders, social scientists, hippies, and mental health. From the Left he has taken the idea of the community as therapeutic, has made the social ethic preeminent, and has scorned the personal accumulation of wealth or the display of consumption. He believes passionately in human growth, social justice, and the capacity of the system to change at his behest. He detests the prison system, regards the underdog as victimized, and struggles to save from their misery the very "scum" he scorns.

He has rewoven into a seamless web many familiar images. He has taken the idea of "the family" from the Mafia, the urban machine from Mayor Daley, nonviolence from King and Chavez, his existentialism from Camus and Sartre, his psychological humanism from Erich Fromm, his Irish rage from the Molly Maguires, his romance with roguery from Michael James Curley, his cosmopolitanism from the Kennedys, his stand-up comic routines from Lenny Bruce, his gamesmanship from Chuck Dederich of Synanon, and his claim to be a "pore ignorant boy" from Sam Ervin. Yet none seem like borrowings, so skillfully are they integrated, so completely has he made them all his own.

Only rarely will John display his parts in harmony. More often he resembles Proteus, emerging from the water in whatever guise best suits his current purposes. Foes find John entirely elusive. The "arrogance" they attack turns to charm before the eyes of a news camera, then teases them again the moment they are mollified. John similarly evades the fulsome praise of one-dimensional men. He will listen impassively while being decorated for "saving free enterprise," then retort, "Of course, we're all communists here." He will endure a delegation of student Trotskyites and muse, "What's really radical about us is we *work* for a living." In fact, he regards both capitalism and communism as passé—ideal types fit only for academicians to play with at taxpayers' expense. He uses his mastery of political polarities to bang their extremities together in humor and to upend them in irreverence. A fine example of his style was his pep talk to the teams of residents selling raffle tickets.

Today we're launching our raffle—'cept we're calling it a *drawing*. A drawing is a raffle of which the police approve. The Church of Rome has drawings and Sammy Slick has raffles. So we're having a drawing in the tradition of the True Church and its Cadillacs-for-bishops campaigns.

Ain't no one here shouldn't be able to sell *at least* thirty tickets a day. You could do it like Grapshi here, wear nothing under your raincoat and *frighten 'em.* You could do it like His Lordship over there. "I saaay! Would you mind? Thanks *frightfully!*" Or you can just plant yourself squarely in the path of an undersized accountant and his girl friend and say, "EXCUSE ME BUT WOULD YOU LIKE TO HELP A GOOD CAUSE?" Then there's other ways . . .

John looks around and beckons a young child over to his side. They confer. The child grins, walks over to a lady, and pulls at her handbag.

You leave that woman's bag alone! The kids today, madam, out of their diapers into your purse! Me and Delancey gonna save you from infant hoodlums. All you gotta do . . .
Never be ashamed!

Never be like Falstaff who was so humiliated no one could ever humiliate him again. When a man in white shoes steps outa the Fairmont Hotel, that's *our* five dollars he's got in his pocket. Two dollars more he should have paid to the maid who cleans his room, two dollars for the bellhop, and one for the desk clerk. You gotta get that five an' hold it in trust for the People. He owes it them 'cause he's breathing our air!

Now some of you'll be selling in Berkeley, and we hope that some of the intellectual types among our squares will be selling tickets, too. 'Cept I doubt it. They don't like to sell or to buy; they like to *advise* or *consult.* They'll come up to you and discuss the political ramifications of the color of the tickets and the aesthetics of the typography. Are the tickets *revisionist?* Should we have *etched* them? They don't like to sell things 'cause it ain't *bee-utiful* enough. "Oh, how *bourgeois* to sell raffle tickets!" they'll say. "I'd rather do *anything* than sell raffle tickets!" "Well," you could say, "in that case I've a few ideas about what you could do . . ."

Of course I don't want to put any of you here under pressure . . . [nervous laughter]. I don't want you to think that Susie can't graduate from college unless you sell raffle tickets. I don't want you to think that while poor old crippled Mo is in the hospital, his child is gonna be neglected. I don't want you to think that Booker will not be able to get his operation. I don't want you to think that . . . I want you to FEEL it! You gotta feel that GOD must want us to sell those raffle tickets, otherwise He wouldn't have permitted so many to be printed!

John sees his capacity to play with opposite approaches and pressures in terms of survival. While you seek the ideal, the real presses its claims upon you. He wheels and deals between ideas as between parties—but the end result is a growth process.

We develop *all* aspects of our personality. You're damn *right* I'm on an ego trip, but not that alone. What I want personally is the position and the satisfaction of helping to cultivate an organism that can change some things in this country. One of our long-range goals is the radical reform of penal codes. . . . The only fit work for adults in this country is to push the evolution of society and the human race as a whole, or you die of boredom and dillettantism. The real cure for us all is the development along many dimensions of some kind of character.

What fascinates me most about John is the long way he has gone toward reconciling those dilemmas upon which rebels and reformers in this country and elsewhere have historically impaled themselves. These dilemmas include radicalism versus traditionalism, social movement versus social science, creativity versus productivity, middle class versus working class, tribalism versus universalism, self-reliance versus social causation, suspicion versus trust, violence versus nonviolence. In the remainder of this chapter we will see how John handles each.

On the issue of radicalism versus traditionalism, John has grasped important truths from Martin Luther King and Cesar Chavez. As you try to change a social system, you must calm it *as* you change it, or it will go into shock and you will lose all control. Accordingly, you must especially emphasize tradition and continuity with the past in order to create a sense of movement *from* that past into the future. King did it with parables of mountain tops and promised lands, which were simultaneously *both* traditional, Judeo-Christian, and other-worldly *and* radical, secular, and political. Although different in style, John paints the roots of his thought and his Foundation in red, white, and blue to balance the novelty of its flowering. The name Delancey Street is part of an elaborate historical metaphor on immigration from foreign shores to share the promise of America. The American flag flies daily over Delancey's buildings, which bear the names of immigrant origins, "Russia," "Egypt," "Estonia," etc. It is typical of John that he would liken the ghettos and prisons of this country to Eastern Europe and foreign police states. It not only allows him to portray police and guards as KBG, but it dresses him up as America, the hope of millions encumbered by *anciens régimes.*

We are bringing poor people to America for the first time. In essence we are resettling America and doing it the way it was originally done. We are taking the outcasts of society and making them rehabilitate themselves through hard work.

John has taken on social science in the name of social movement, although he is not above utilizing the insights of social science *within* a movement context. "The Roman Empire was built without a single psychologist," is a favorite among his axioms. He refers to social scientists as "surplus population," part of the unemployment problem they are hired to deal with. They batten on the distress of poor people in a way that reveals their *own* marginal status. They must "save" to be saved. He can produce marvelous satires on how the social science bureaucracy will try to reduce a movement like his to the level of a replicable technique.

If Pontius Pilate had been a smart Brooklyn politician instead of a dumb Roman bureaucrat, he would have called in the Carpenter one morning and said, "Look, off the record. You keep leaving fish-heads and bread-ends around public bars after your revival meetings, which is a drag for the sanitation department. The Scribes and Pharisees are uptight—and they're people, too, you know! They pay taxes! And we got you running round the temple with your stick beating on the bankers. I mean, how you gonna get a home loan? Don't you understand, *you gotta let the system work until you can replace it?* Don't you see, the Scribes gotta make a living too?

"So, I'll tell you what we're gonna do, J.C., 'cause you got *great* ideas. Your ideas are right—it's your timing, buddy. We're gonna give you twenty thousand dinars—real pieces of the silver stuff—to start a boys' home in Bersheeba to try out your techniques and see if you can cure any of these Samaritans we have. If in three years you've got these Samaritans straightened out, we'll bring you to the Empire Conference in Athens, with the imperial treasurers,

Caesar Fordus and Rocchfelius Tertius, and we'll see if we can duplicate your techniques and this funding throughout the Empire—with the help of our friends of course!"

For John the controlling metaphors are organic rather than mechanical, and the organism flows rather than standing still to be counted.

Professionals keep coming in here, and they ask the question that clearly indicates a failure to comprehend what we're trying to do, and an attitude that we must be accounted failures unless we think as they do. [Here John mimics an erudite questioner.] "How many subjects, expressed as a percentile of your intake population, are currently leading constructive lives?" and I say to them, "That isn't the way history has been. It isn't the way communities grow or movements develop. We didn't build America by stopping the cowboys in Wyoming and asking them if their lives were stabilized! We just sent an avalanche of them. If you'd gone to Plymouth Rock with your clipboard and pencil a year after the Pilgrims landed and asked them, 'How many of you are leading constructive lives?' what do you think they'd have said? 'Well, half of us were frozen dead the first winter, and the rest of us are just thawing out.' But those who endured went on to found a culture that produced Hawthorne, Melville, Emerson, Thoreau, Paine, and Margaret Fuller. That's the way we're gonna be.

"On the other hand I don't want to seem to evade your question. We don't keep precise figures, but about sixty percent of those who come here are still with us or have graduated. Of those who split, a significant proportion are the better for having been here and are not, to the best of our knowledge, in jail or on drugs. But that estimate doesn't concern us very much because it isn't what we're trying to do. We are trying to create a cadre of people, resilient, resourceful, and sharp enough to change the prison system and the social system of this country."

John's analogy is apt, for there are very few survivors of the first dozen pioneers who set up the Foundation on Bush Street in San Francisco in 1971. The first women to come, the first teen-agers, the first homosexuals, the first older people, the first blacks, and the first Latinos all suffered disproportionate casualites. Not just Delancey as a whole, but each subgroup had to secure a beachhead and scramble ashore, and the women and the homosexuals still have a poorer chance of surviving. John contends that you cannot end prejudice by fiat. Before a minority can be included, at least one representative must be found whose strength of character visibly refutes stereotypes and defies prejudices. That person then becomes the spearhead for his brothers or sisters.

If John is accused of regarding his members as expendable, he will point out that they come to him already half-expended, and that their chances outside Delancey are considerably poorer than their chances inside. Talk to residents and you discover with some horror that close to half the young people they grew up with are dead, imprisoned, or institutionalized. "We ask them to turn upon their fates and fight collectively for survival."

John has good reason to deplore social science and its host of grantsmen—whom he calls collectively the Whittaker Chambers of prison reform. At Rikers Island from 1958 to 1962, John was a prime candidate for "psycho-lockup"—a punishment legitimized by hack psychologists as "rehabilitation." A less euphemistic age called it the hole or solitary confinement. On those occasions when the light was left on, he read omnivorously whatever the little old ladies sent in, which included obscure Russian novels, yellowing periodicals, and a dash of porn. He was once elaborately tested with ink blots, pegboards, and imbedded figures. "What d'you make of *that?*" they asked him. "And that . . . and that?" He finally decided that psycho-lockup was preferable and whipped out his cock. "What d'you make of *that?*" Later he made the mistake of confiding to a psychiatrist his plans for founding a movement of ex-cons and ex-addicts. The diagnosis? "Paranoid schizophrenia with delusions of grandeur and compensatory fantasies." As John has explained on Public Television:

It is conceivable that a man could graduate from Columbia in 1916 or 1917, fail in the rehab projects of the twenties, fail in the CCC camps in the thirties, fail in the debacle of the Veterans' Administration in the forties, fail in the urban renewal schemes of the fifties, fail in the ping-pong-paddles-for-the-people and community theatrics of the sixties, and on the basis of fifty years of failure be placed at the head of a government agency or university commission to clean us up.

It staggers the mind! No plumber who failed to fix pipes could get away with it for more than a few weeks, but these "experts" have gained control of the language by which their own abilities are evaluated, and they contrive an endless succession of "no-fail" definitions of their efforts, and then launch campaigns in updated terminology against the *same* old crummy problems decade after decade. When something goes wrong, they merely "find" more pathology among their clients than was ever previously estimated, blame it for their failure, and make that the basis for another grant proposal.

I mean it's amazing. They come over from Berkeley to speak to me, these forty-year-old men, going bald on top but with hair growing from the back of their necks down to their assholes, dressed like gypsies and covered in tin buttons and dingle-dangles. "And what happens when *you* get power," they say. "Won't it be just as bad as when they had power? We're against *all* power."

"Listen, creeps!" I told 'em. "You got twenty-two thousand dollars a year and tenure and three months vacation. *That's your power!*" If I hear one more of them complain of how they struggle up the ivy steps each morning, how the dean oppresses them, and how they earn less than construction workers, I'll puke. And sooner or later one of them will always say, "But isn't this all rather *fascistic.* I mean, what right do *you* have to lay your trip on the local drug dealer?" "'Cause I have to *live* with him and the people he poisons—that's why!" These fuckin' spectators, their tolerance and liberalism is a precise function of their distance from the problem!

John has also given battle to a major weakness of the New

Left and its attendant host of cultural "radicalisms"—the cult of creativity—the belief in every individual's right to spontaneous deviation. "No lasting changes in society were ever accomplished by a pack of prima donnas who exploit every injustice the better to express themselves and flaunt their sensitivity." John insists that every creative idea in Delancey must be pushed through to fulfillment via hard work, with no division of labor between those who conceive and those who act. It is a matter of community survival. It is also a matter of principle, for the pseudocreative slothfulness of the middle-class addict is a fat neck that John wrings with relish.

They got you tricked into this notion that first you're *creative*—it's this James Joyce trivia as an art form idea—and then you're productive. No, no, it's the other way around. . . . If you can draw a horse, then you can try to be like Picasso, throw some dabs around. But if you can't draw a horse, we don't wanna see your dabs. You can go down to Greenwich Village and play house.

John's quarrel is with posture of creativity, the claim to possess "potential" while indefinitely postponing its fulfillment. He denounces as existential cowardice of the first order the notion that one's sensibilities are too delicate and precious to be exposed to the system.

To academics and intellectuals what you *say* is far more important than what you *do*. Genuine action to help specific people is too morally ambiguous for them because they disapprove of the whole context. It's the Shriners and the Lions clubs who actually build hospitals for crippled children, but because the Shriners can't "express themselves" in the latest hip-humanism, they are ignored.

We were concerned last month that a candidate for a judgeship be defeated. As D.A. he'd withheld evidence from the defense that almost cost a poor bastard his life. I'm telling this to a group of intellectual women, when one jumps up and gives it to me. "It's a sell-out to the System!" she shrills. "You expect us to work for the *other* candidate, for that mediocrity? You call *that* a moral alternative?" "In that case I gotta problem," I said. "If shit-face gets elected, about twenty-five of our people could get locked away inside San Quentin for the best part of our lives—'cause he's *mean.* Now if fart-face gets elected, maybe five of us will have to go away. I realize that, in the macrocosm, in the universal scheme of things, that don't count; but it does matter to the twenty people who will be walled up unless we act. You have to decide whether you're gonna help us or go home and refine your moral alternatives."

We get squares up here who say they wanna help. "Right!" we say. "Can you drive our truck up to Napa to pick up some free cabbages?" No, they can't do that because it's not *meaningful.* "Well, it means something to *us,*" I say. They will not see that a community of people can *give* meaning to a job—almost any job. They all want to be *cree*-ative, if possible in *Mee-dee-ya,* as if you could change society by talking! And you know what their definition of *cree*-ative is? Some mind-boggling performance that mystifies the hell out of ordinary people and makes them feel stupid! The media people have been good to us and I shouldn't complain, but they make you so goddamned ashamed of being a human being who goes to work and does much the same job every day. *They* are superior, because they *explore, experience,* and ACTUALIZE themselves!

Turn on your TV tonight, and you'll see some representative of The League of Emergent Lesbian Mothers, a splinter of a splinter of Lesbos Unlimited, and while at least a third of the world's population is shadowed by starvation, this hurt person gets to "express herself" and argue with a grower of organic cucumbers, while a million viewers scratch their asses in sympathy with one object or the other. Tolerance is one thing, but beating the bushes to find ever more exotic forms of deviance, by ever smaller minorities, so that media people may seem ever more sophisticated is *crazy!*

Same with politics—we used to attend these "radical alternatives" meetings, but they were fuckin' unreal. Some creature with a face full of follicles would jump up and say, "The Socialist Workers protest the Socialist Citizens' vicious misrepresentation of Kropotkin's views of Rosa Luxembourg!" We suffer these idiots because there are not enough productive jobs to go around—and still less are there enough creative jobs. These pretend-revolutionaries and pretend-creators are really manifestations of mass unemployment in the middle class. But even those who fill creative jobs with distinction do not seem to understand that the Establishment controls the few jobs there are of this kind. A woman's cooperative that actually engaged the economy would do more for women's rights than the talkathons they all seek to join.

John has also been demonstrably successful in synthesizing middle-class concerns with working-class concerns. This achievement, at a time when the Democratic Party is threatening to come apart at its class seams, merits careful study. John begins with the thesis that many so-called middle-class problems, e.g., drugs, alienation, and crime, *originate* in the slums and spread from there. Slums are inevitable so long as resources are distributed so inequitably.

Take a simple analogy. If you have a whorehouse on the Lower East Side and the girls have clap, eventually some matrons in Scarsdale will get the clap. The solution is *not* to rush madly around measuring the incidence of matronly clap or running tests to show how similar East Side clap is to Scarsdale clap. The solution is to do something about the exploitation of the female prostitute and the terrible loneliness of her customers. It means you've gotta create jobs and provide education to the people who work in the whorehouse. . . . The entire history of the U.S. has been class warfare from its inception from the Boston Tea Party to the Molly Maguires to the Black Panthers.

That appears to have been in John's mind when he located the Foundation in three mansions atop Pacific Heights, in the temporarily vacated Egyptian consulate, the old Russian consulate, and the Estonia Hotel. His motivation was partly economic and partly an attempt to visit upon the upper middle class the problems of rehabilitation.

All social problems should move to where rich people live—that way the problems can receive attention from the sector which has most control over the system that produced them. For another thing rich people's space is a lot cheaper per square foot than poor people's space. Actually, *warehouse* space is more expensive than rich people's space, which is cheapest of the three. For the same price as you could keep fifteen crippled veterans south of Market Street at taxpayers' expense in subdivided rattraps, we could keep three times that number in a gorgeous mansion in Pacific Heights, with large, light rooms for recreation and assembly. The reason it doesn't happen is zoning ordinances wielded by people who don't want us there. All social programs are kept in ghettos to fester off the hopelessness. You can no more cure an addict or criminal in a slum than you could cure an alcoholic in a bar. How do you rehabilitate a person who gets up in the morning to see everyone lined up at the Welfare Office and goes to bed at night with everyone lined up for dope or a whore?

We say to the rich, no more! *You* own the hotels where the whores operate. *You* own the doorways where the muggers wait for the old people who've cashed their welfare checks at *your* banks. You got rich by this system; so *you* live with the results!

The bitter opposition to locating Delancey in Pacific Heights *also* owes its origins to the slums, the desire by those who escaped a bare generation ago to put the most distance between themselves and their origins.

Our eviction is pursued by a small group of recent descendents of horse thieves and robber barons who have pretensions to being San Francisco's equivalent of the Hapsburgs. The cries that we should move somewhere else never take into account that someone else lives somewhere else.

But it would enormously oversimplify John's character to portray him as "against" intellectuals, social science, creativity, hippies, and the middle class. The facts are that he is well-read intellectually; that in the person of Mimi he is married to a full professor, a social scientist, and an intellectual of outstanding ability and assertiveness; that he never ceases to urge his members toward middle-class qualifications; and that he himself is nothing if not creative! If he attacks the idolatry of "creativity" and "science" in middle-class society, he simultaneously attacks the "poorism" and narrow desperation of the oppressed. Like all healers, he represents to different persons and different groups that which is lacking in their perspectives, while blasting what is overblown.

What he seeks is a synthesis of tribalism with cosmopolitanism that has the virtues of both and the vices of neither. He wants the tribalism of cohesive ethnic groups organized street by street, block by block, as in Daley's Chicago, with economic self-interest as its permanent cement. But he also wants the internationalism of Eugene McCarthy and George McGovern, the knowledge that the persecution even of distant groups diminishes all people. His ideal is a residential community that is a microcosm of world-wide issues, which by solving racism, sexism, classism, and poverty in its own locality, becomes an exemplar, a laboratory, and a springboard for broader solutions.

Listen to what John says *inside* the Foundation, and as likely as not it will counterpoint his outside pronouncements. Here he is at one in the morning pleading with residents to expand their horizons and let in the world as sophisticated people know it.

. . . and they call Bill Toliver an Uncle Tom, too! Know why? 'Cause they want to keep all their black brothers and sisters *stupid*—so they can go on feeling like one of the boys, like a small frog in a small pond. So they keep the pond small by running those who aspire *out* of the fuckin' door. As soon as anyone starts to learn anything in school or excel in business, the punks and the bitches start in on him. He's an oreo! He's a trick! He's selling out to the honkies—*fuckin' birdbrains talk like that!*

One Billy Zant running a computer, one Karl McClory teaching school, one Sylvester Herring being a senator's assistant will do *more* for the black children of Oakland than a million motherfuckers who are too *scared* to stand up and be counted with the big folks. I suppose Malcolm X is an oreo 'cause he didn't say "mothafucka" every third word. Patrice Lumumba was Oxford educated, probably never used the word in his life! *Must* be an Uncle Tom! If he walked in here tonight tall and dignified and said, "I am proud to see that a black woman, Vivian, has become a competent legal secretary and plans to go to law school, because the Black Defense Fund needs her to help our people," some slimy cocksucker here would shriek, *"La-Mumba! La-mumba!* Who de fuck is he? Is you from East Oakland, baby? Can you do the boogaloo?" I doubt if Lumumba would have had much respect for five-dollar whores and three-dollar bag-sellers.

So when you hear this oreo shit say, "Listen, punk! Our people been fucked over for two hundred years. Ghana needs technicians. Congo needs agricultural experts. Senegal needs mining men and engineers. Black union workers who are treated like slaves need leaders. Black people need bankers so they can make their own money and not *beg* it off rich whites. All black men and women who've led the Movement and who've died for it were people who could speak and lead from knowledge. I don't think you'd find Angela Davis hanging out on Sixteenth Street in Oakland. Know who you'd find there? Scum-slaves who wanna *stay* slaves, who don't give a fuck what happens to their mothers or their children or themselves s'long as *no one else in the community makes it.* One thing about poor people, they're *always* ready to pull down one of their own. Same with some of the women we got here. Let just *one* distinguish herself in *any* way, and half a dozen bitches will *claw her fuckin' eyes out* and keep her crazy in case she takes something away from them.

The whites we have here are no better. [John is careful to spread his denunciations evenly.] "Nigger lovin' *Ma-ha!"* they say. "Ahm proud of bein' a *white* man!" Well they haven't consulted *me* on that subject. *I* don't consider 'em white men—white trash is more like it—poor terrified bigots who think *not* being black or Chicano confers something upon them. I've told you before, an' I'll say it again, you gotta go *beyond* the color of your carcass and stand in this world *for* something and somebody, or you'll *be* trash and *stay* trash all your days. If not being black is all you got, then hate is all you got, and you'll choke in it!

An' I'm sick of this Mexican folk shit, too. I had a lame-brain group of 'em in my office the other day. [He mimics their spokesman.] "I don' trust no one who 'ees not a Chicano. It ees becoz I um Spunnish that I um silent. It ees our culture to be tricked! You are a fuggot mun eef you paint. 'Ow you survive on Twenty-fourth Street as a pinter? They fuck fuggots! Only a mun can do that. I don' trust Chico, ee ees too smart! Ee sell out to the honkies. Ee's a trick!"

I told them, "It's your *silence* that makes you tricks, that lets the Teamsters steal your lettuce contracts. What you *really* mean is that I'm scared to fuckin' death that if I opened my mouth nothing comprehensible would come out. When you go to Mexico—as several of your people did last summer—you'll realize that there are Mexicans who paint great art, who've won Nobel Prizes for literature, who own oil companies, and build churches. You'll see the architecture of men like Perara and statues of Juárez. I *very* much doubt if Casals or Gerilla or Siqueiros or Orozco or Rivera or Paz would agree with any of you that artists are faggots." I can't imagine Salvador Allende coming into one of our meetings and saying, "I cunnot speeek to you, becoz I um Lutino, and Lutinos do not speeek! But buneeth my silence is graate courage!" Fuck that shit! Jails are FULL of Mexicans and Puerto Ricans, full of 'em! Know how they got there? Their "strong, silent friends" *ratted* on 'em! They don't talk to black groups, so they must be doing it to themselves.

And no one will say to these people, wait a minute, punk! Whores are not black women. Women who go to college and women who help to develop themselves and their children—these are black women. Latinos who sell dope to children and are drunk all day so's the white man can exploit them—these are not freedom fighters! They are foolish assholes.

Finally we have our middle-class fuck-ups—these Mama's boys who've had beautiful and precious feelings since the six*h grade—and that's *all!* We gotta *pretend* they're special and *cree*-ative, and then they *might* perform for us, with special privileges of course! These fuckers always *feel* more than you and me, they feel for flowers while old people don't get to eat, they *feel* like sitting on their asses while farmworkers are getting beat, but mostly they feel *bad,* 'cause their selfish little prick's so "into sensitivity" that everyone else can go to hell.

I had one of 'em come up to me last week and suggest a "moratorium." "Your *whole life* is a moratorium!" I told him. "You pretend to be original but you've originated *nothing* in forty-one years. How can you be 'into painting' when you care nothing for art and know nothing about it?" It is the lifestyle and the personal attributes of the artist which this bum wants to appropriate to himself, but he does not want to give the world of art or artists so much as his *attention* in exchange for what he takes. "Nobody ever asks me what I want to do," he says to me. *Still* he doesn't understand. The idea is that he *discovers for himself* what he wants to do, that he proposes it, molds it, builds it, fights for it, is rejected *with* it, revises it, makes it more presentable, and fights for it again. *That's* what this place is about—*that's* the only kind of creativity that helps your brothers and sisters survive and validates you as men and women.

John has also succeeded to a significant extent in resolving the dilemma of individual responsibility versus social causation. The dilemma has always been that telling truths about how the social system creates social problems can exacerbate the problems themselves by excusing criminal behavior and by dignifying every ugly tempered lay-about with a political definition. "Some nut pisses on a bus—and says he's doing it in protest against Western society's repression of his private parts."

John argues that convicts and addicts *are* indeed the products of social pressures. He searched in vain at Rikers Island for hoodlums of any skill or stature and has concluded that when D.A.'s are pressured to "fight crime," the police round up the most easily apprehended social losers as evidence of their efforts. So while it may not be "scientifically" true that criminals are principally to blame for their own condition, it is nevertheless *necessary for them to accept responsibility for their condition if the chain of causation is to be broken.* They must say to themselves, "I failed to survive with dignity. I colluded in my own oppression. From now on we will be stronger than the forces that victimize us."

John goes further and argues that so corrupting is the influence of society that it successfully vitiates among the oppressed any intelligent social criticism of itself. It is therefore essential to straighten oneself out first, in a sane asylum, before one can consider how society as a whole falls short of one's newly established standards. "You become a man or a woman when you put your energy back into society to right social wrongs."

It was on this issue that John broke with Synanon in 1970. It was at Synanon that John was persuaded, for the first time, that personal independence required personal responsibility. "You *got* your habit, sonny," Chuck Dederich told him, "you *kick* your habit." But when Synanon abandoned its graduation program and seemed to lose interest in altering the larger social system, John missed the experience of acting on his diagnosis. If you believe that drugs and crime are socially caused, you *have* to band together to fight those causes. It is the basis of John's existentialism.

There's no point taking in a man from 111th Street, therapizing him, and returning him to 111th Street. He'll be the only sane man on the block, which will drive him crazy.

John became a Synanon official, gained valuable command experience, and then split to found Delancey. He says of the contrast, "We're Jewish to their Amish."

Two dilemmas remain, which John has had much more difficulty in reconciling. If Delancey as a whole is vulnerable, its vulnerability lies here. He has some difficulty with suspicion versus trust and a related dilemma of violence versus nonviolence. Any weaknesses are less the result of character flaws than of particularly vicious cross-currents.

John's situation has to be appreciated. He must at one and the same time believe in the human capacity to mature through independence and self-regulation *and* remember that ex-cons and ex-addicts habitually cheat and betray, sometimes at the very moment they are giving virtuoso performances of "growth." He has sat up nights on end with residents to aid and comfort them, to see one inform to the FBI, a second complain to the State Parole Commission, and several distribute packets of heroin in deliberate acts of subversion.

Nor has John much reason to trust the white "liberals" of San Francisco. Virtually everyone claims to applaud what he is doing, but many strike in secret. Injunctions have stopped his trucks and tried to halt his businesses. The Permit Board made specific promises to postpone a decision in the event of a tie vote on Delancey's eviction, and when there was a tie, the chairman, Pete Boudoures, gleefully and publicly broke his word and moved to evict. Sixty persons objected to Delancey's wine and beer license, but not one of those sixty people showed up when a public hearing was called as a consequence.

To a considerable extent people stab John in the back because they know they would lose a duel face-to-face. Add this to the motives that his foes are loathe to admit—racism, fear, and anxiety—and you can easily see why John is shadowed by treachery, sniping, and sneaky forms of subversion. His problem lies in the fact that *dis*trusting people can be self-fulfilling. Sensing suspicion they embark on a duel of bluff and wits. Several political and social movements have historically eaten their own tails in fits of self-fulfilling paranoia. There have been *no* purges in Delancey, but if the pressures to distrust become much stronger, trust could snap. It is like a ship locked in polar ice—one can hear the timbers creak as the lock tightens.

Perhaps it is unfair to tax John with a dilemma that human civilization has yet to solve, namely that those publicly dedicated to the practice of nonviolence may unwittingly elicit assassination and the very violence they abhor. John has gone a long way, substituting political, economic, and verbal power for physical force, and severing violent *expressions* in Games from actual violence. But this latter technique, especially, has left him with some blood-curdling ways of speaking. For his attempted "solution" is not really viable. He *sounds* tough and truculent, while outlawing physical force for himself and his followers. For example, he has publicly advocated that drug dealers be warned: "First time you're a social victim, second time a cripple." But it's inconceivable that one can use such language for long, *outside* the Foundation, and not have to fight or back down on account of it or let his bluff be called.

John is right, of course, that you cannot flaunt gentleness near the bottom of the social scale and hope to survive. He is engaged in training the United Farm Workers in rhetorical skills and greater social presence to enable them to compete with the Teamsters, and he knows you cannot sound like a bruiser looking for a physical fight without making that fight more likely to occur. John even sees his own eventual departure as a variation on the bum's rush:

Thirty years from now when I'm an elderly fat slob with a cigar telling the kids how hard we had it, with luck a few of my best people will kick me in the fanny, take over the joint, and push the experiment a bit further. Delancey's no ultimate answer to human problems—but it's one hopeful step.

A final complaint sometimes lodged against John is that he lacks tenderness and genuine concern. I prefer to believe that he locks it away where "Mama's boys" cannot exploit it. A friend of John told me this story.

We were sitting in an all-night café. It was about 6:00 A.M., and this old stooped man with white stubble on his face was piling up his morning newspapers. He had a claw hand thrust behind him, but he could use it with grotesque effort by backing up against the papers. Someone made a crack about the old man, and John snapped back. There was an awkward silence, and we all watched the old man as he slowly and painfully arranged his papers. "That's one of *our* people," John said quietly, and his eyes were full of tears. That's the only time I've seen him cry.

4

From Mousism
to Maturity

You won't be long at Delancey before it is explained to you that the Foundation specializes neither in combatting drugs nor in aiding convicts *per se*. It is an organized cure for "mickey mousism," the disease of the self-destructive personality who uses drugs, and other people and himself, badly.

So while Delancey does not exist to evangelize the mob, rescue prisoners of conscience, or bring corporate embezzlers to repentance, it reckons to take in and take on some ninety per cent of those officially regarded as "the crime problem." That is, the armed robbers, prostitutes, forgers, shoplifters, con men, gang members, addicts, dealers, drunk-and-disorderlies, purse snatchers, and the merely desperate.

It is a fatal mistake, in John's estimation, for the mass media and the police to dramatize the war-against-crime. The portrayal of heroic policemen in life-and-death struggles with hoodlums only glamorizes the role of the latter. If the police can prevail only with such difficulty and danger, how brilliant and resourceful their opponents must be! The favorite television program in several California prisons is "The FBI." The less glamorous truth is that the police are mostly collectors of garbage, which Delancey is in the business of recycling.

"You are like grooms and stable boys in the age of the automobile," John Maher tells his people. "The age of gangsters is gone. The only 'big time' crooks are in politics, some unions, and big business. It is evidence of their power that they can define *you* as the 'crime problem.' *You* are just the symptoms. *They* are the causes. We organize the symptoms to fight the causes."

It is *not* true, however, that Delancey specializes in the less dangerous ex-criminals. Some among them have killed and many have used firearms to rob. Missing are the "masterminds" and Robin Hoods of so much fiction and so little fact. Everyone comes in as a "fuck-up" and a "stupid asshole" and "cleans up his act."

This chapter will examine four characters who tried to make the journey from mousism to maturity. In the chapter following I shall make some generalities about the process involved and introduce a number of additional characters.

Stephanie T., twenty-seven years old, is fair haired and conventionally pretty. The daughter of a neural surgeon, she was raised in Tiburon, California, and was educated privately before entering the University of California at Berkeley. A Mexican nursemaid was the principal object of her affection in early childhood. Her father was largely preoccupied with his work, and a coldness in her mother's attitude turned to revulsion as first one of her children and later a second was diagnosed schizophrenic. The atmosphere at home was characterized by a bitter, almost interminable sarcasm, with nearly every word of positive evaluation meaning its exact opposite. Stephanie escaped from this atmosphere at every opportunity, spending as much time as possible in the homes of her friends.

She emerged from adolescence with at least one obsessive craving—a warm, cozy nest, where a husband would look after her, and no bitter word would pass between them. To this end she joined a sorority and, in her sophomore year, married a member of an approved fraternity. Marriage, she believed, could guarantee her right to nurture. But her husband continued to drink nightly with the boys, while she weaned their baby son. She could not bear to reprove her husband and was hospitalized for ulcers at nineteen.

Stephanie dropped out of school and out of marriage to recuperate, taking the child with her. She returned to her studies the following year, switched to painting, and won a Regents' Scholarship to the Graduate School of Art.

It was heaven on earth—I just loved it. I painted myself out of a short period of realism into greater and greater abstraction, until I was painting single lines across a bright background on canvases nine foot by six. Sometimes I'd get mad and just strike out at the canvas. It was my own kingdom where I could be anyone and do anything I liked.

Even as her art succeeded, her peers and teachers applauding her every step up the abstraction ladder, Stephanie's social life was failing. She had several affairs—nothing worked. The child was ungovernable.

I was looking for a white knight. He would sweep me off my feet, control the child, and carry us off to a rose-covered castle and everlasting security. Instead I moved in with the guy who worked in the local cigar store, but it was the same story as my marriage with different symptoms. This time I got splitting migraine headaches and inexplicable fits of crying. I had no conception of *making* a relationship work. A relationship would make me work, I thought.

In the meantime my work was going wild. I spent every day in the studio, experimenting with three-dimensional effects on canvas. The shapes and lines would follow me out onto the street and back home. I was surrounded by this clique of brilliant artists, who were moving from grass to acid and were into Happenings. I was into this thing about the symbolic nature of the pyramid and must have painted a dozen canvases on the theme of the mystique of the vanishing point, an idea of utter clarity to me, which I couldn't communicate verbally.

One day I just flipped out. My art world was so preferable to my real world that I stepped out of the second into the first. I must have broken into that part of the art museum where all the modern jewelry was being exhibited, because I was arrested an hour later, pirouetting in the middle of University Avenue with a dozen gold bracelets on my right arm and a dozen silver ones on my left.

Euphoria turned to terror in the mental ward. Stephanie calmed herself by writing reams of poetry until her parents obtained her release. But she couldn't stay in the atmosphere of her home. She was still yearning for the quiet, warm place where some of her childhood friends had lived. So she rented another apartment and, with her child, waited to be found.

By then she was reaching the final year of graduate school. In each of her last two years she was given a summer teaching position. But it was one thing to lose herself in abstraction and quite another to teach basic art and deal with people. Each time she buckled and landed in the hospital.

Looking back, I think I painted myself into a box—or into a pyramid, literally! The metaphor took control of my life, and I could no longer tell the abstract from the concrete or the representation from the real.

In order to support myself and the kid I had to take a tiddlywink clerking job and sit and type and file and obey stupid orders. I was utterly miserable and so bored I would cry. My kid was in the throes of rebellion and walked right over me. And so I "disappeared" on the way to work one day.

I vaguely remember a ride on a motorcycle across the Bay Bridge, and I ended up in Ghiradelli Square. I was a kid again, in pigtails, laughing, singing, and skipping along. I set off a fire alarm, and, when the engines came, I did a "flower child" bit, sitting on the roof of the fire chief's car, swinging my legs and clapping my hands.

Later that day I crossed over to Union Street, went into the Co-op Art Gallery, and awarded bad grades at the top of my voice to most of the exhibits. "Schlock!" I shouted. "C minus! Fail!" I picked up a piece of sculpture on the way out and shouted "Kitch!" and heaved it through the window. Then I skipped off down the street. The police arrested me ten minutes later.

Again Stephanie was plunged into terror. She awoke in the general ward of a mental institution. There were large damp patches on the walls, the room smelled of urine, and roaches scuttled along the baseboards. The other patients were feeding themselves but could not seem to control their hands or heads. They must have been serving beets and squash because the old woman in the next bed dropped her face in her food and emerged with an orange nose and a crimson chin.

Only my father would deal with me now. My mother withdrew completely. I've rarely seen such horror in someone's eyes. I was moved to a private hospital and discharged a few weeks later.

Stephanie obtained a job and got her son back. Now she was teaching in a Marin County "Opportunity School"—a special elementary school for potential dropouts. The children were mostly from "problem families" with a lot of drugs and alcohol. She became enmeshed in her pupils' problems, much as she had in art, and for hours on end could not tell whose problems were whose and which were not her own.

She nearly married an Indian lover, but he stole a dozen hypodermics during their blood test, and, when she haltingly objected to tying the knot with an addict, he disappeared, taking her car and as many of her possessions as it could carry.

It wasn't much I wanted—just someone I could trust and a house better than a ticky-tack to live in, but it seemed that the more I yearned for safety, the more each man would take me for. I located a better house in Mill Valley, which I could just afford. I'd fallen in with a bunch of skids, bums, and dope-fiends who were into this "spontaneous love" bit. They all offered to help me move, but of course they never showed—flopped out somewhere I suppose. I found myself in the new house beneath a dozen boxes and pieces of furniture with the car they'd promised me nowhere in sight and my kid at the other house. Once again I buckled. When I came out of it two days later, the police had broken into my old house to rescue my kid. They'd found some drugs and my marijuana plant.

With the help of a lawyer, Stephanie drew a suspended sentence. She thought she could make it without the burden of the child, now lodged with her grandparents. But the familiar scenes replayed themselves with minor variations. She picked up a hitchhiker, who moved in with her the same night, to be followed by a couple of his friends and a prostitute. They all lived in liberty, equality, and fraternity on her paycheck while she calmed their quarrels and strove for a happy home.

A few weeks later she was driving some pupils from the Opportunity School when the police flagged down the vehicle. She scrabbled nervously for her license and produced some packets of grass instead. She was busted on the spot and resigned her position. Jobless and in the custody of her lawyer, she tried to evict her friends by telephone. This time they stripped the place bare, and she had nothing left in the world but the clothes she wore.

There followed a bout with hepatitis and surgery. She convalesced at her parents' house in Tiburon, where months of bills caught up with her, but her parents' silence was the only reproach. A few months later she was working in an architects' firm in San Francisco when two Delancey Streeters came in to sell potted plants. She ordered one to be delivered to her apartment.

It was Jack Behan and Louis Ferronato who brought my plant the following Sunday. In the interval I'd quit my job and was more desperate than usual. I'd visited Delancey a couple of times; so they knew me and we chatted. Suddenly I found myself gabbling at them—just on and on. I suppose I didn't want them to leave. I was so lonely. I saw them exchange glances, then Louis placed a hand on my arm to quiet me, and Jack said, "Be at the Club in an hour, okay?" It was an order, but I sensed a real concern. I packed a few things and was over there even sooner than they said. I've been here ever since—three years.

Twice since those days Stephanie has made formal application to the Foundation to start painting again. When she told me her story she was still reeling from the rejections. "John *really* capped on me. I don't think I can ask again, ever."

John shrugs when you tax him with this. "She *has* to ask and *keep* asking or she's not yet strong enough to be different from other people." In the meantime, Stephanie has done a stint in the publicity department, worked on the Delancey Street *Journal,* and represented Delancey in public speaking engagements, a process that would have daunted her only a few months ago. She is now in charge of all the Foundation's pictures and decor, and runs its framing shop. She plans to graduate when she has taught herself that business. Several months after our first interview, she drew me aside.

I *will* paint again, I know it. But this time I'll be ready and able to do all the other things that support a career, argue and bargain with people, be self-supporting in a business that helps art and artists, and build an emotional life based on reality. It's when you have a genuine grip on reality that you can afford to let yourself go and fantasize. . . .I know that now. . .and yet. . . .

Her brow furrows for an instant. "Yet what?" I ask.

I wonder sometimes if I'll ever be as good as when I was crazy. . . .

Josh P. is forty-three years old, the eldest son of immigrant Rumanian Jews who barely escaped the gas ovens. He combs his black hair forward in a coif to hide a hairline in precipitous retreat, and he sports a Vandyke beard without which his chin would vie for size with his Adam's apple. It is somehow symbolic of his entire life that he takes care of his head and lets his body go. He speaks as if he had spent a lifetime reclining on an analyst's couch discussing his own unruly flesh, without the slightest intention of changing it. His clothes are messy, his feet turn out, and his stomach is on independent suspension.

Josh's life is a trail of compost, which he has gathered lovingly, piece by piece, to pat into place around his personality to make it flower. And flower it does for a few short days, resplendent in its bed of muck. Driven by a sense of his own specialness, he has found a substitute of sorts. As Josh explains it, he is uniquely screwed up. Never were there complexes quite like his, so intricate, so fascinating, so exquisite in their disorder. Josh presents himself as the epitome of the human condition, sapiential man, tragically flawed. His own failures are similar to the Movement's, the counterculture's, the communes'. Let us learn from all who aspired too greatly and challenged a heedless world.

What remained of my family settled in a poor Catholic neighborhood in Philadelphia. There were three younger sisters, my parents, and my grandmother. My uncle and his family moved in next door. We were intensely devout, Orthodox, isolated, and conservative. My sisters were forbidden to wear any cosmetics, and mother found parasols for them to protect them from the sun! When our Irish and Italian neighbors weren't laughing, they were stoning us as we scurried to the temple in yarmulke and parasols. When I complained to my parents, they went on this trip about me being *the* Survivor, the first born, the-one-spared-by-God-to-carry-on. They had this thing about persecution, martyred destiny, and this at-least-we-have-each-other routine. I resented the whole rigamarole.

As a family we were haunted by memories of the apocalypse, and we'd go into long sessions of mutual torment about who should have got out of Rumania how, when, and where. It was like a play by O'Neill. Long *Night's* Journey into *Day*.

We had these crazy, familial definitions of reality. An object of reverence was my grandmother—our symbol of the old world, I suppose. To me she was a peculiarly obnoxious old biddy, and I could shock everyone by suggesting we poison the old bag. I could never forgive her for the night she feigned illness just as my aunt was going to perform in a concert. "Don't you see what she's doing?" I shouted to the whole family. "She's *faking,* and Auntie's been practicing for weeks!" But even my Aunt denied wanting to go. "Of *course* I'll stay with Grandmother," she said, and the tears were running down her face.

So from early on I was the Rebel. They call me "Reb" at Delancey, you know. But I sometimes wonder about the quality of that rebellion. I would find out who my family *didn't* want me to befriend—mostly Italians and blacks—and I'd bring them home. I brought a black whore home to our family Seder, just to shock them. We were both drunk, and no one in the family drank or smoked.

I used to get drunk on the way home from school and collapse on the doormat. I knew they'd be mortified. I wanted the neighbors to see, but I also wanted to be pulled inside to sleep it off in comfort. I'm a bit of an "armchair rebel." I register the maximum of dissent that can be combined with minimum inconvenience.

I was talking to a friend, a psychological novelist, and he pointed out that I was probably a *delegate* for the repressed rebellious instincts of my father. Tacitly he was "sending me out" to do these things and enjoying my experience vicariously. He was utterly dominated by my mother, who was a religious nut, and my grandmother. He was an old-style European romantic, kissing hands and making flourishes of gallantry. It was probably fueled by frustration. My mother had a never-on-weekdays attitude to sex, and her God would sit firmly on his ideas and squash them. He'd been trained as a teacher and intellectual but was running a small book bindery instead, specializing in old and rare volumes.

Surprisingly we prospered—perhaps the librarian at the University of Pennsylvania appreciated my father's reverence for books and the infinite care he took. In any event we moved across town to a big house behind Independence Plaza. I was just fifteen and hardly had we "made it" than my troubles redoubled. I would never fuck up enough to get thrown out or land in serious trouble but just enough to remain in the center of attention and on the margin of tolerance.

I have this lifelong penchant for cheap melodrama. I applied to three colleges, let the deadlines for final submissions go by, and then threw myself dramatically on the mercy of the deans. I was admitted to Cal Tech by the only one of three who gave me an audience. I went for my major in physics but could never work out the problems the way other students did, the way we'd been shown in class. I had to invent my *own* formula, like the physicist Maxwell, and redefine problems before I solved them. My grades went way down.

Socially I had a notorious reputation among the girls as an exciting date. I did this Brooding Hamlet number. Beneath a melancholy surface lay this noble, poetic spirit, raging against a rotten world. But I'm an actor without a real self. Strip the costume away and there is nothing. I fall into my own trap. So dramatic and scintillating are the early impressions I make on women that there is no conceivable hope of sustaining my performance. I could never follow through. Since I never persevered long enough to originate anything, I was left only with promising ideas and a vague claim to potential.

I had to run from any permanent relationship. I was engaged to a very intelligent, attractive, and wealthy girl; but I fled to the East Coast the night before the wedding and fired off anguished telegrams about caged eagles. A month later I arrived on her doorstep, without warning, of course, and offered to marry her within that very hour, a proposition she wisely refused.

In the meantime, I'd reached my final year at college. I was an old hand at "spectacular comebacks" just a few days before exams. But competition was toughening, and physics is a subject you cannot fake. I miscalculated and realized that I'd left it too late. But I had to fail flamboyantly. I went home, found a soft spot on the carpet, and made an epic collapse. My mother screamed. My father wrang his hands. My uncle came in from next door, pulled me bodily to my feet, slapped my face, and dragged me back to school. He even checked into a motel and escorted me to classes for three days. But all he really provided was an excuse. Now I could drop out of school as a protest against his tyranny! Besides, I hated him. Our family had a fatal schism between love and authority.

I got a chance to return to college a year later to get my B.S. I did okay for one semester, then began the same round of drinking and clowning. My nemesis was the biology exam. We had a practical that involved dissecting some broccoli. I knew I was going to fail and decided to go out in style. I came in with some mayonnaise and two slices of bread, made a sandwich of the sample, ate it, and belched loudly. Some female graduate students were running the exam. They giggled their heads off. One girl I'd been balling whispered that I was "marvelous," but they met next day and flunked me.

It was about this time that I met my wife. She had a Master's in Teaching at UCLA and was going for her Ph.D. when we met. I put a stop to *that!* I have this instinct for spotting a person's sense of inferiority, and I went straight for hers. How bourgeois to scramble up the success ladder! How safe and sterile could she be? Wasn't she an artist? (She was, as it happened.) Who could award a diploma to Originality or give a letter grade to Genius? It worked. A year earlier I'd persuaded a working-class girl friend that she was doomed to peasantry without a college education. I was a great crippler. Being miserable myself, I knew how to inflict misery on others.

You might well ask why I married after running from every other entanglement. After a brief flirtation with my wife-to-be, I discovered she had Hodgkin's disease. She reckoned to have four to five years to live, but with me the doctors were more pessimistic. It was closer to a year. It was amazing when you think of it. The Tragic Actor, who lacked even the guts to create as much as a comedy by his own efforts, had stumbled across a real Byronic tragedy. I was destined to be her Last Love, to clasp her to my bosom at the end!

But it wasn't as cynical as it sounds. I have this infinite capacity to delude myself at the time, and I spot my fraud only as it retreats into history. I remember being genuinely appalled at the prospect of her death. I prayed a good deal, and I had this recurrent fantasy of offering my right arm to Jehovah to spare her for a bit longer, and then my left, and so on. . . . I never thought to myself in so many words, "Well, she'll die before she finds me out." In one sense a genuine tragedy enabled me to act where I usually pretend. On the other hand, I doubt if I'd have married but for the aura of doom, the opportunity for histrionics, and the fact that my parents begged us not to. "Think of the children!" I hadn't thought of that—a child to immortalize our One-Summer-of-Happiness! We went to Europe for our Last Romance, and she bore a boy the following spring. However, she lived. That was seven years ago, and she's still alive. Her disease went into remission. We had to stop living as if each month was our last. The source of our crises dried up, and I was fresh out of dramatic material. It was then that I discovered that I didn't really love her—and a lot of the time I didn't even like her.

She had quit school, so we both painted, she very much better than I. I would force her to compare our abilities, and when she was gentle with me, I called her a patronizing hypocrite. I have a way with words. I even beat her up. It wasn't sadistic so much as dramatic. I'd tear the telephone from the wall, then pick her up and throw her down on the bed with more impact than injury. I once goaded her into leaving me, and the moment she began to pack fell upon my knees in contrition. That was supposed to stop her—but when it failed, I *did* become dangerous. I threw her down the stairs.

The great advantage of behaving so badly was that it enabled me to stage some virtuoso performances of Atonement. I had my basic repertoire of red roses, the same old fucking bottles of Cabernet, and my standby lines from Yeats.

> But one man loved the pilgrim soul in you
> And loved the sorrows of your changing face.

They usually went for it. When my wife wasn't going to die any more, I needed new scenarios. I took other girls to bed. Again, I *thought* I loved them at the time, but in fact I must have been using them as bit players for the climax of Act III, *in flagrante delicto*. I had to scatter quite a few clues before my wife burst in upon us. I was ready, of course. I sprang naked from the bed—all 240 pounds of me—the Don Giovanni of Rotunda. "You don't understand me!" I roared. Actually it was gross. The wretched girl was hiding in the shower stall, and our two-year-old kid was bawling. My wife left that night, and in the morning I realized, not without shame, that I didn't want the girl. She'd served her purpose. My "love" is for scenes and not for people.

I moved to San Francisco and worked in a book shop. I started sniffing mixtures of hash and glue which I hid in pocket inhalers. You just pretend to have a cold. On impulse I decided to look up my family in Philadelphia, and it was a shock. Everything had fallen into decay. Business had slumped with the competition from microfilms. The plant was locked, the workers gone, and my parents had aged exceedingly and were close to bankrupt. I had wanted to tell them that I ran a book shop, but the words stuck in my throat. If a book shop, why not a bindery? Ever since I was a child they had dreamt that I would take over. The business had probably foundered because they weren't able to trust anyone beyond the family—and anyway why bother? The business *was* the family.

I talked about this to my shrink in Sausalito. He had an interesting insight. "Your rebellion," he said, "was always against the *content* of your parents' beliefs, never the form. You rejected the myth of the survivor, but you still regard yourself as special in some indefinable way. You tore up the script that was written for your life only to invent your own, which is just as false and restricting. You laugh at your father's romantic submission to women, yet your own domination of them is no less romantic and cowardly."

The condition of Josh's parents appeared to sober him. He decided to make some money for their support. He helped a friend make some displays for a children's museum to illustrate laws of physics. Some of the effects were visually intriguing, and he began a business building moving sculptures and mobiles to order. His media caught on in a number of artists' colonies, and soon he had a sixty-thousand-dollar house and a workshop in Monterey, California, and orders worth a quarter of a million dollars. He basked in the atmosphere of the avant-garde, employed

three people, and wined and dined up and down the California coast.

Once earlier his family had "made it," and Josh, age fifteen, had cut loose. Now he repeated his performance. His
wife's fifteen-year-old brother was staying at their house.
Josh came down into the cellar and found the boy about to
mainline with heroin. He fumed and lectured. The boy ran
out into the garden, leaving Josh with the full hypodermic.
For several minutes Josh stared at the instrument; then he
shot the heroin into his own arm.

Within a month his habit was costing him thirty dollars a
day. When his wife began to have an affair with another
man, Josh's habit doubled. He confronted her; she left. For
the next month he inflicted himself on friend after friend in a
traveling road show of *The Cuckold.*

My newer friends were too "liberated" to be shocked, and they
even intimated that I was a fucking bore. So I concentrated on the
one person who'd always booked my act, my wife. I began drafting
suicide notes into which "genuine" pathos would creep after the
third draft. When she failed to respond, I began to think of ways to
kill myself in her presence. I had designs on the Golden Gate
Bridge, but there was no way to make sure she would be watching.
I had recurring visions of falling into her arms covered with blood.
I went to a theatrical supplier and got one of those blood bladders
which actors squeeze beneath their clothes to simulate gore. I rang
her front doorbell and wasted two shirts on baby sitters before giving up.

It sounds crazy, I know, but once having chosen a woman who
would agree to foster my illusions, I would drive her further and
further until she recognized me, at last, as a fraud and a bum. You
know the climactic scene in *The House of Wax* when the girl strikes
at the face of the proprietor and his wax mask breaks to reveal the
mutilation beneath? At some level, I *wanted* that. I had to go on
and on to see how much I could get away with before my audience
turned on me. I have this compulsion to test the limits of credulity.

Now that he was hooked on heroin, Josh had to push the

limits out of economic necessity. He persuaded the people
who worked for him to forego their wages, as he strung
them along for six months. He rushed up and down the state
getting cash advances for orders he would never fill. He
barricaded his house and hid the cash records to stop his
wife's divorce lawyers from discovering his desperate ex-
travagance. When they became suspicious, the siege was on.
He abandoned his home and hid out.

Josh made the rounds of his remaining friends, falling on
their thresholds to sob and beg, "Just a hundred dollars to
get me to Synanon!" "I have this job offer in L.A.!" He
would take the money straight to his connection and shoot.
One aspect of this slide to total degradation has affected him
more than the others.

I used to take my kid out on Sundays. I couldn't even spend a
day with him without having to fix. I'd drag him away from
Golden Gate Park down to the Mission District in search of my
connection. He started crying once, "Why are we here, Daddy? I
don't like this place!" "Daddy's sick," I explained. And he looked
at the junkies and whores and winos and said, "But these aren't
doctors!" I'd try to lose him for a few seconds while I shot up, but
he'd panic and start searching for me, and more than once he
found me, crouching obscenely in a doorway or beneath the stairs
with the needle in my arm.

I finally overdosed in a restaurant and was arrested. I was given
the option of Delancey but chose a drug program in Kensington
instead. For a while things were fun again. The program was run
by two young women fresh out of Vassar, Masters of Social Work
whom I resolved to make my mistresses. I was their star convert.
They'd set up speaking engagements, and I'd play the part of
Reformed Addict, bringing down the curtain with now-I-can-look-
my-child-in-the-face-again. It was a huge success. On the nights we
were on the road, I'd get to ball whichever of the silly bitches was
presenting me. We'd always agree that her love had healed me and
made me whole. My main problem was getting her the hell out of
my bed so I could shoot up and nod off.

Josh couldn't stay off heroin, even for the periodic urine

tests. After a few weeks of frantic bottle switching, he fumbled his act and ended in a mess of urine and broken glass. This time it was Delancey or jail.

For a time it looked as if Josh might make it at Delancey. His work with mechanical sculptures had made him a skillful construction worker. He offered a seminar in physics to which many came. But he could never see why John did not promote him speedily to his brain trust. John, a consummate actor himself, saw in Josh, perhaps, a counterfeit of and a satire on his own dramatic style. To John, Josh was the personification of the middle-class cop-out and the desertion of the poor for "artsy-fartsy postures."

In Games, the other residents would cover their ears whenever Josh became more-insightful-than-thou. "Don't TALK about it," they would chorus, "DO it." But he never would. He stood up his physics class at the third session. It was the addition of "teacher" to his personality profile that he wanted, not the task of teaching. When he left one morning, he was only making physical that perpetual psychological divide.

"Is it true Josh has split?" I asked in the coffee bar.

The three drinkers barely turned their heads.

"Josh *is* split," said one.

"He never *was* with us," said the second.

"So how can you tell?" asked the third.

Bill Toliver was born in the black ghetto of St. Paul, Minnesota, to working-class parents, although his grandfather, with whom he strongly identifies, was a minister in Kentucky. His parents separated when he was eight years old, and he spent the rest of his childhood in four foster homes, which took him in for a profit and turned him away as a liability.

For many years Bill had the dubious distinction of look-

ing almost exactly like his sister, and he spent much energy
pointing up the chief difference: she could sit still and he
couldn't. He would dash about aggressively to establish his
gender. His high school principal was a staunch believer in
"open air activity" for ill-disciplined boys. Every time Bill
misbehaved he was sent to the farm, to camp, or even to the
zoo. Since he infinitely preferred these trips to sitting still at
his desk in the vicinity of his sister, he misbehaved as often
as possible. Eventually he won an athletic scholarship to the
University of Minnesota. But he broke his leg while emphasizing his masculinity on a motorcycle and dropped out of
school.

Next he joined the Army, and his younger brother joined,
too. They did things together whenever possible. Bill was
sent to Fort Hood, Texas, and wandered into the Fort
Worth Hotel with some white companions. "We can't serve
this boy," said the waitress. Bill hadn't noticed any children
behind his chair and turned completely around before
realizing she meant him. This and other incidents of racism
made him angry. He began to drink heavily and fight.

He served for a time in Germany where he learned to play
the drums with GI bands, engaged in scotch-drinking tour-
naments and chug-a-lug contests, and learned to look sober
while totally intoxicated. Whatever his friends did he would
try and go one better.

In California, following his discharge, Bill worked com-
petently as a medical orderly, fell in love, ruptured his
kidney in an automobile accident, collected the insurance,
and followed his love to the Sorbonne. It must have taken
courage for a kid out of the ghetto who didn't know a word
of French to fly to Paris. Bill's courage took a characteristic
form, however. He downed two bottles of scotch and a half-
bottle of rum during the flight and had to be helped off the
plane and through customs. He holed up with his girl for
three weeks with a bad case of culture shock.

Then he began to haunt the cafés where the Americans hung out and soon got regular work as a drummer.

One night before a concert a friend took me into his room. "I'm gonna *do* something before I play," he said. "I'm gonna shoot up maxitone, speed. This is outasight, man! It's wild ass! I can't explain it to you. You gotta *feel* it to know." He shot this clear liquid into his arm and began to say "Man!" "Wheeew!" So then I, who have never done *anything* by halves 'cept grow up—and being my reckless, carefree self and wanting to be one of the boys and afraid of being a scaredy cat—took the works and mainlined it. It's an amazing feeling, like a rush of heat rising through your body. It's never as vivid as that first time when your system is virgin. I began to talk and talk and talk, and everything I said was immense in its wisdom and acuity.

That night I drummed as I'd never drummed before. All my insecurities and inadequacies vanished, since I *knew,* beyond any shadow of a doubt, that my performance was masterly. It was better than booze because that slows you up. This was speed—the elixir of my hyperactivity.

I couldn't sleep for the next thirty-six hours, so I grabbed a book, a masterpiece, and read it in two hours. I cannot remember the story—not even the title now. It is the *process* I remember, of grappling by turns with issues of immense significance and ambiguity. "Wow!" I thought. "That's it. That's the answer!"

It was easy to get the stuff. All one needed were prescription blanks from the American Hospital. Bill would sign them "Dr. Benny Goodman" and "Dr. Miles Davis" to amuse himself. With speed he could be anything: artist, barber, carpenter, philosopher, and mystic. He only had to go into himself and conceive the perfect image, and it would spring from his head fully armed and qualified. He made "beautiful" furniture, gave immaculate hair cuts, dispensed the sagest advice, and distilled the wisdom of the ages in a single phrase. There were rarely fewer than twelve people in his hotel room every night.

A friend would come to me, and I could tell his problem at a glance. My intuition was uncanny! "Be a *lawyer!*" I told a friend who was hesitating between law and writing, and that's what he is today. The several images I had of myself gradually gained coherence and pointed to one larger truth. I was the Good Samaritan, a black angel of mercy, the Rejected One whose love redeems his tormentors. I lost all concept of day and night in these reveries. I would turn up for a 7:00 P.M. appointment and wonder why the sky was growing lighter. I was twelve hours late! I forgot to eat and went below a hundred pounds and would munch handfuls of sugar to gain energy.

A not unnatural consequence of Bill's self-annointment as The Great Giver was a following of freeloaders and great takers. He became "paranoid" about his "friends." Could there be another reality beneath their love? Were their motives at times on a less than spiritual plane? Was he being secretly subverted? He attended a performance of *The Prodigal Son* and decided that he himself was no less than the subject of that play. So he gave up speed and joined the troupe of players. If they did not at once offer him the lead, they at least let him open each performance with a prayer.

The troupe toured Holland and Belgium before returning to Paris, where Bill began shooting again. One night the theatre manager refused to pay the cast, and there was a sit-down protest on the stage. The police arrived, and the theatre manager appeared to Bill to be roughing up the director, who was a woman. Bill decided that, since most of the players were gay and therefore unable to defend themselves or the director and since he was the only *man* present, not to mention the only embodiment of divine wrath, he must hurl himself upon the manager and twenty gendarmes. That he did and woke up in jail.

He was released at the behest of the American Embassy to which he confided his discovery that the Paris police were infiltrated by communists. He then hurried home to place cardboard on all the mirrors in his rooms to foil the cameras concealed behind them. To sharpen his mind against the plotters he mixed maxitone, hash, amphetamines, heroin, and lighter fluid, adding various colors of chalk to identify his "cocktails." To insure that foreign agents could take advantage of neither his euphoria nor his relaxation, he mixed uppers with downers in speedballs. But the plots seemed to thicken with his mixtures.

Not surprisingly perhaps, since they were shooting his concoctions, his "friends" began to behave in mysterious ways. They would wander in and out of his room in the small hours with nary a word and no evident purpose. One night a book on LSD appeared mysteriously on his pillow, and a man said cryptically, "Billy, they are stealing your spirit," and then staggered out. On another occasion a voice said, "*Think* of the clear light," and less than an hour later someone came in with a flashlight! All of which was either a communist conspiracy, vastly more sinister and extensive than he had imagined, or it was basic dope-fiend behavior. It depended on your perspective. As for Bill, he had no doubts.

He left for a vacation in Italy, but the communists followed him. They seemed to be *very* interested in his speedballs and would appear every time he shot up with his clients. He returned to Paris to find communists everywhere. Under the transparent pretense that he had paid no income tax and had struck policemen, they were after his secret power. He rode to the airport on the floor of a taxi and with brilliant subterfuge boarded a plane for the United States as if he were an ordinary passenger. Only he was hooked. . . .

Shortly after Bill's return his younger brother was killed in an automobile accident, and Bill's morale collapsed completely. The two brothers had been devoted to each other. Bill settled—or rather unsettled—himself in San Francisco at about the time of the decline and fall of Haight-Ashbury. He acquired a long, black leather coat, a large flop hat, a cane, and a goatee at the tip of his narrow chin. He was super cool and developed a special walk appropriate to this status.

His new posture was one of worldly wisdom. He had traveled the earth and returned with the Message, "You cannot be *too* good in this world!" For some time he made this sorrowful sagacity his Epistle to the Street People. At least he was one step ahead of them, but then, as his concert partners had complained, he was *always* ahead of the beat.

As the environment began to decay and his habit became more expensive, Bill decided that preaching worldly wisdom was not enough; practical demonstrations were necessary. Tourists, too-good-for-this-world, who came belatedly to the Haight to see flower children or enjoy a psychedelic experience, would discover Toliver instead. Provided they put their money "up front," they would have the experience of seeing him vault over walls and dash down alleyways, coattails flying, in the full possession of their money if not his own wits.

One time one of Bill's many mixtures proved too exotic for his own nervous system, and he suffered a seizure during which he bit three holes in his tongue. The doctor, who barely saved him from choking on his own blood, speculated that he might already have injured his brain beyond repair. Bill was warned that on his present diet he wouldn't last a month. His reaction was to throw a Three-Weeks-to-Live party where he passed out under a table. At least no one could call him a scaredy cat now or fail to distinguish him from his sister.

It was his sister who heard of his condition and alerted his surviving brother. He met Bill outside his lodgings, offered to drive him to the liquor store, and drove him to Delancey instead. Bill was such a mess by then that John hesitated to take him in. As it was he had to be carried across the threshold.

John shook me in that first interview. He didn't talk like social workers. I used to have *them* for breakfast! He said, "You have nothing in the richest country in the world. And you are in the process of killing yourself. That makes you the stupidest asshole we got—and a disgrace to the black race."

These words and Bill's total exhaustion triggered the memory of an experience five years earlier in Paris. That experience with its death and rebirth motif told Bill what he had to do now. He had been walking alone in the Cathedral of Notre Dame, high as usual, when he heard a voice tell him that his time had come. He walked across the square to the Della Hotel, and the voice repeated, "Billy, you're gonna die."

My ego, or whatever it is that protects you, was whispering back, "Ignore it! It's the drugs." But the voice was authoritative, implacable. "Billy, you gotta die! Go into the hotel, undress, go up to the roof and jump." I walked into the foyer and began to undress but became embarrassed. Two men were sitting there. I was wondering if they'd try and stop me, when the voice said, "Sit down where you are and remember everything you did wrong. Let your life pass before you—then die." And I sat there on the floor, and the men were watching from their chairs. We must have talked that night, or sometime earlier, because they knew my name.

It was hours later, almost dawn, when the voice said, "You thought I'd let you jump? Confused as you feel, crazy as you think you are, bad as you know yourself to be, *this is your hell,* to stay just as you are. Hell is a summary court in perpetual session. This is how you'll be from now on, unless you *believe.*" Then the voice said softly, "The others are leaving you now." Moments later I saw the men rise. "Well, Billy, you're not speaking, so we're going to bed." "*Ask* them!" hissed the voice. "Please stay," I said, "You know what I'm going through." "You call *that* belief?" said the voice. "You call that trusting people? You think that will make up for your bullshit martyrdom, your manipulations, your lies. *Beg!*" And I cried out, "*Please don't leave me! I can't make it without you!*" And the two men paused, then settled back into their chairs.

So when I came to Delancey I knew I had to shed Supercool and all that crap. I knew I had to reach out for help and plead. It was like finding a place I'd dreamt about, that I'd always known was there. I *had* to believe in a force that transcended by own, one of which I could be a part.

Bill is now one of Delancey's outstanding success stories, a director, a pillar of its black community, and a vital force in the cohesion of the whole. Scores of residents owe their lives to his help and strength. He is especially interesting for having changed but not changed. Nearly all the original predispositions of his personality remain intact, but a new configuration has produced a growth pattern in place of the former pathology and has altered the meaning of his existence.

For instance, his messianic fervor finds its outlet as Delancey's unofficial "minister" and master of its ceremonies. He now stars as The Prodigal Son except that the drama is real and the sons are legion. The mysteries that engage him now have to do with human growth, and there may be a dozen people in his room till way past midnight, seeking his help and counsel.

As head Barber at Delancey Bill now cuts hair both literally and figuratively and has done better work with the construction company than the ineffable carpentry of his Paris days. He still stirs exotic mixtures, but they form compounds now of ideals, organization, and action. Where members of the band once complained that he was a half beat ahead, his colleagues now tease him for clapping the loudest, smiling the broadest, and singing the lustiest. Though he now has periods of meditation to balance his furious pace, he still has the reputation of being the house hyperkinetic. He still drums—now in the company of Mongo Santamaria on his many visits to Delancey. He led the group of black residents on their trip to Senegal. He is preparing to run for San Francisco's Board of Supervisors.

Bill credits John with much of his transformation.

I told him I had to be great to someone and for something. I told him of my admiration for Martin Luther King, that I'd seen black kids hungry, desperate, and infested—and that before I died I'd help to change that and that death held no terror for me now. I'd been there and back. I remember John told me, "The key to your future is dignity, or self-respect if you will. Your flaw has been that you never really believed that you had it within yourself, and you were driven to flaunt it and act it out and obsessively wrestle others into validating you. Learn to be comfortable with yourself. Have it quietly within yourself to know who you are. It is only in its falsity that others can steal your manhood. Risk your life for others but do not squander it. The genuine martyrs of history laid their lives on the line, but others exacted the penalty."

In a sense I still manipulate, but it has a different quality. Where once my entire energy was consumed in molding people and events, now I need only touch them "with my fingertips" as it were, and some force stronger than mine or theirs takes over. I believe in God. I believe He made people to grow, and that growth is the underlying principal of the universe. I first met Rhonda, my wife, on New Year's Day in the Club. I asked God for her.

But let me give you an example of how I "manipulate" now. There was a young woman in my tribe. Her father had died quite unexpectedly. She cried by the hour as we sat with her, and when I sensed the grief was almost out, I said to her, "But there must have been good times . . . Will you tell us about those?" And she thought for a moment and began to tell, and with every passing minute her eyes grew brighter and her voice strengthened and her face shone, till at last she sprang to her feet, embraced each of us, and turned to leave. "One more thing," I said, "you told us your father was dead and in a sense that's true, but we've seen him in your smile, in your bearing, and your voice. Now you know what you have to do here in Delancey. You have to live with this family and whatever family you create, so that when *you* die, your brothers and sisters here, your children and their children, will grow in strength even as they recall your ways." She stood by the open door and our eyes met. You know something? All the speed, all the uppers, all the heroin I've ever taken can't beat that moment—and we weren't even touching.

Ted Williams was born to Greek immigrant parents relatively late in their lives. His father was over fifty when he was born. His mother was in her mid-thirties. He grew up in the small community of Napa, California. He is good looking in a rough-cut way, like a classical Greek profile that looks as if it had run into a sucker punch that depressed the nose and raised the chin, so that he grins full across his face.

Until recently he was never close to either of his parents, and when he or his brothers used to raise a ruckus to attract attention, they were soundly thrashed with laundry sticks. As a result he kept out of his parents' way and ran pretty wild.

At eleven he stole a gun from a pawnshop and took it along when he and some friends wanted to camp out for the night. They became frightened as darkness fell and decided to go home but felt the need to vindicate their courage. Ted took dead aim at a cow and fired.

They were arrested three weeks later while shooting at gulls. The gun was confiscated. The "cow" turned out to be a bull, a prize bull to boot, and it was dead. It cost the boys' parents $570 and several broken laundry sticks. Ted was in Juvenile Hall by the sixth grade and was sent from there to Faith Home Teen Ranch.

I had a good time and came back yelling "Hallelujah!" and "Praise the Lord," but no one was into that back home, so it lasted about two days. I was married at seventeen to my high school sweetheart, and by eighteen we had a baby. That's when the fighting began, 'cause the baby was getting her attention and I had a hard life! I was neglected, rejected, disrespected! No, seriously, we had no conversation. She was incredibly naive, and I was working at the local sugar refinery, loaded most of the time on bennies, speed, red devils, yellows, or Seconal. For some reason I didn't get her loaded. I wanted her pure perhaps, but if one person is using and another isn't, that's a real barrier since drugs become your main thoughts, your conversation, and they "solve" the problem of what to do with most of your time.

I practically deserted them both and spent most of the time partying; so we separated. One night my wife crashed a party and begged me to come home. She'd taken pills to break through to me. I took her home and we made love.

One of the worst scenes of my life happened three months later. I was sitting in my apartment with this new girl, ready to go out to a dance, when my wife walks in with baby Gina. I could see at once she was pregnant. She looks really *beautiful* when she's showing. I knew it was mine. She was scared of other men. "I gotta talk with you!" she said, and she asks the other girl to leave. "No, you don't," I yelled. "*You* leave! We're going out." I was real cold. I'd taken speed, and it makes me narrow and hard and excited. She started crying and telling me what I could already see, but I turned my back on her and walked into the bathroom to take a shower. I was being real *cool,* I thought!

I saw my wife's shadow through the curtain as she grabbed something from my medicine cupboard. I jumped out of the shower but she was gone, through the living room into the bedroom, and baby Gina was hammering at the door crying "Mama! What you doing?" I shouldered open the door and she'd cut her wrist. She'd botched it, luckily, and cut the bottom of her hand. I strapped it up with Band-Aids. She said, "I hate you. I'll kill the baby." And I said, "That's cool, 'cause I'm going out now."

Ted wipes a hand across his forehead. His eyes are watering.

Hey! This is *awful*—I'm beginning to feel it again. What a rotten bastard! Anyway I went off to the dance and I was beginning to come down and I felt terrible, and my girl was looking at me and probably thinking, what if this creep dumps me like he did his old lady? So I go to the telephone and call my brother, and he went over to my apartment and got my wife and my kid to their home.

I went back to my wife a few days later out of sheer fuckin' guilt and stayed with her till after the baby was born. By then a "friend" and I had begun to burglarize houses. It was the "in" thing with the crowd I hung around with, and I'd do *anything* for acceptance, pills, and LSD in that order. We got caught shortly after the birth, and I drew nine months because they found some stuff from other burglaries in my house. In jail I got a "Dear John" letter from my wife.

When Ted got out of jail he could only get a job collecting garbage and soon turned to dealing drugs. But he "got greedy," started using drugs himself in large quantities, and ripped off his connection. When his connection came looking for him, Ted beat him quite badly. This was the apex of his gangster period. He dressed in a fancy cowboy outfit and did his dealing from the front of an antique car. Someone turned him in, and in lieu of jail he was sent to a drug program called The Family, an annex to the State Mental Institution at Napa.

It was a federally funded program inspired by some ex-Synanon people with a penchant for the frivolous. Ted was obliged to wear a conical hat inscribed with the words "Big Bad Ted." Others had hats with similar inscriptions, while the most recalcitrant members were obliged to crouch in garbage cans wearing curious attire.

For fomenting a dispute between "No Consideration" and "Manipulates Everyone," Ted was forced to wear a sign saying "Toasted Marshmallow" (a little crisp on top but mushy underneath) and had to walk around the grounds with his clothes on inside out and worn backward.

I felt like an asshole at first, but the other patients in the hospital grounds were as nutty as fruitcakes and noticed nothing unusual. When I settled in, I began to enjoy myself. We didn't have to do any work except sweep the day room and our bed spaces, so we did therapeutic exercises at taxpayers' expense, and these expanded to fill the time available. My favorite was "The Music Encounter." We would lie on the floor with our heads on pillows, and I'd play my favorite records, telling the others to imagine they were walking in a wood and had come to a house, and in the house was someone dear to them. Then we all listened to music some more to get into the mood; then we'd each say who the dear one was—as I say, it beat working.

Then there were "Blind Walks" and "Trust Walks." You'd blindfold someone and have 'em walk over rocks and down steep places, and they'd trust you—they'd have to. I walked this fellow along a bench and told him to jump off the end. "Go on! *Trust me!*" And he jumped right into this big muddy puddle. He was *furious!* I led another person on a "Touching Textures" exercise. I can't remember how it was supposed to stop him being a dope-fiend but never mind. I lead him up to some deer shit in the woods. *"Feel* it," I told him. *"Experience* it. *Be at one with nature!"* He held it in his hands, rubbed it against his cheek. Then gave a sniff and let out this *roar* of rage! We couldn't stop laughing.

After a few months they let us out on weekends. I had my disability check, and I'd drink, cop dope, and even smuggle it back in. It took forever until they noticed I was high and threw me out, but my parole was nearly over by then and I wasn't violated.

I moved in with my old girl friend, but I had a habit and was un-employable; so I began stealing her roommate's personal checks and forging her signature. I split when I thought they'd discovered me, and then things got really bad. I was living in a flea-house hotel at two dollars a day, with a filthy bed and five days' growth of beard. I'm breaking into the rooms, stealing off winos, and tak-ing the very little they had. I was in a real self-pity bag. I'd no checks left and was down to my last five. I spent it all on one fix and felt nothing and began crying. Then I went down to the police station and turned myself in.

But the police put me in a holding cell. They hadn't got anything on me! "Christ!" I said, "I've forged over fifty checks; there *must* be warrants out for me somewhere. What's the matter with you guys? I'm a fuckin' menace!" And I began to confess to everything I could think of, and the names of banks, stores, hotels where I'd passed these checks. "Get on the phone," I begged them. "That place is *sure* to remember me!"

So Ted came to Delancey but continued his old tricks for a while. He told the house about one disability check but pocketed the proceeds from a second check, split, shot dope, and tried to return the next day. He was barred from entry and told to return the following day. He spent a miserable night with the skids at The People's Church and a long day on the bench at Delancey.

It was terrible. John was white in the face and shaking with rage. He called me a thief, a creep, and a punk. "You got nothing in this world but your own word, and that you've just debased. That makes you a *slave*. You'll shine our shoes for sixty days!" So that was a couple of years ago.

How did I change? Well, let me say first how I *was*, 'cause I wasn't always the warm, lovable, sensitive guy you see before you today!

We are in the Delancey Street Restaurant, and the manager is passing our table as these words are spoken. He gives a snort of derision. Ted leans toward the recorder.

This is Ted Williams! I'd like to report for the record that I am being subverted by one Harvey Stone, notorious ex-dope-fiend and well-known purveyor of pig-like noises. When are we gonna get some service here, Harvey? I *built* this place, man! . . . Now, where was I? Oh, yes, how I *used* to be. Well, in my dealing days I wore a Stetson, black leather pants and jacket, cowboy boots; and I drove a '36 Plymouth with suicide doors. I talked like Edward G. Robinson. I would nearly kill people driving after dark, 'cause I wore these real small shades. It was part of the image, though I couldn't see thirty yards in the dark with 'em on. What an asshole!

I adjusted quite easily to Delancey after that first mistake. That's because I've *always* adjusted to the people I was with. When I was with people who ripped each other off, I ripped too; and when I was with people who showed concern, I showed it. It was *when* I did what the house wanted that other things began happening, too.

The first thing I discovered was that they didn't want me to pretend. "You're a kiss-ass!" they told me. "Stop brownnosing all the time." And that's when I discovered I didn't have to turn myself inside out to get people to like me. I'm just myself, and they *do* like me, and that's an amazing discovery!

Delancey's like a garage—a stopover in life. They check you for everything that's defective. They tune you up—till you're operating on *all* cylinders and they're firing in sync and the whole is balanced. It's a beautiful feeling. Do you know I could never stomach certain social situations, like someone's crying or lost a kid, or they're going to pieces? I'd get so *embarrassed.* An' if they wanted affection from me, I'd run, or I'd push 'em away! Not because I didn't need affection; who doesn't? It was because I couldn't handle the emotion.

Well, that changed pretty soon after I got here. Now I can handle just about anything that's thrown at me, and I'm using those skills in my personal life. I met Vicky on a blind date about a year ago. She's a farm girl, drives a tractor. That doesn't sound romantic I know, but God is she a beauty! She's very warm, sweet, naive in a way, needs a lot of affection—guess I'm projecting. But it's wonderful when you're learning to love to know someone whose face registers every possible emotion. I can tell what she's feeling, if I've pleased her or hurt her and how much. My first wife would stuff her feelings and so would I. I mean, Vicky really wires me up! I ask myself if it's infatuation or just wishful thinking or the fact that she's good in bed? But it isn't any one of those things or even the three—it's everything!

We go on walks together. We work together on the farm or on my carpentry. We have these heavy conversations until late at night, and the things she tells me are *vivid*, like it happened to me! She doesn't know about a lot of things, and I can tell her. She asks me why her parents want something or say something, and we try to work it out.

We're going to get married, soon as I graduate, sooner if possible, but I have to get a job 'cause I owe my first wife child support, and she's married another loser, and he can't support my kids from jail. Vicky asked me, "Why all the formality? Marriage is just a word, and we're making it together anyhow." And we discussed it, and I said, "Let's do it for our parents, yours especially. *We* don't need a service; we're getting each other, but they are giving you up after twenty years, and this is one way to show 'em I wanta do things right. I'm making this promise in front of them and my whole Delancey family."

I'll never forget the day I first met Vicky's parents. I knew they were rural people, conservative. I couldn't have handled it in the old days. I'd have got angry, punched someone out. But I'd been through a lot of heavy stuff in the house by then, and I thought I could manage this. So we went upstate to the farm her folks run, and I swallowed, and I looked 'em in the face and said, "I'm sure I'm not the kind of person you dreamed of for Vicky to marry. I've been a low-life scum. I've been in jail. I'm divorced and I've been a dope-fiend, and anything else you want to know about me I'll tell you, 'cause you're entitled. But I want you to know, I've changed. I've got a large "family" with dozens of friends. I'm getting a contractor's license, and I'm in charge of my life. But most important, I make Vicky as happy as she makes me."

Well, they stood there for a second, and no one said anything. Then Vicky's mother opened her arms, and we hugged and she kissed me and her old man shook my hand, and it's been that way every time we've met. It was mellow, real mellow.

But you asked me if there was any one moment at Delancey when I knew things would never be the same? There was something like that, in a Dissipation. You know, those long Games that last two nights and three days? It wasn't *my* Dissipation. It was Gerry McGee's. He's my best friend. We're gonna graduate together and try to set up a business together. I was supposed to be called into the room to talk to him. Well, his turn didn't come for hours, and I slept as I was entitled to. Some fool forgot to wake me. Then there's a hand on my shoulder. It's 4:00 A.M., and they want me to talk to Larry J. I was still half-asleep and had no idea that Gerry's turn had come and gone.

Suddenly everyone's shouting at *me*. "Where were *you* when Gerry needed you?" And Gerry was yelling, "Fuck *you*! Go back to sleep! Who needs you anyway?" And we were screaming at each other, and then we both fell silent. All the rage was out, and there was nothing left but this feeling we had for each other. "I'm sorry I slept," I said. "I'm sorry I didn't sit up with you. 'Cause I love you more than my own brothers. I never knew what a friend was till we met." And he said, "The shit's out of me now. I love *you*, brother," and we held each other for close to twenty minutes. Then I went to the bathroom, washed my face, worked the rest of the Dissipation, and really helped some people, 'cause tears are cheap unless you act on what you feel.

The next day Gerry and I went for a long drive, and we had this heavy, heavy talk. We agreed that what had happened was important, and we wouldn't let it go.

I should also say that I've been head carpenter here for fifteen months. I make estimates, draw up blueprints, present them before the Planning Committee—and John's gonna get us in the union. I know it! I get this fantastic fix from something I've built myself. I'm so proud. I think, Wow! I *did* that! I thought it. I drew it. I made it and now it's there—created out of my head. And there's people, hundreds of 'em, seeing it and using it, and they'll be doing it years from now. I get a lot of compliments, and people want me to teach them.

So that's it, I guess. I've been here over two years, and this is what I've done. I've developed insights I never had before. I've developed a skill I *love*. I've found a creativity in me that I never dreamed I possessed. I've discovered I can love someone—and be *proud* that other people admire her, too, 'stead of threatening to break their legs. I've discovered that I can deal with an entire range of human situations.

When I look back at the people I knew on the street, I wonder how I could ever explain it to them. We were always looking for the highest high, the greatest sexual climax, the biggest score. But my pleasure now is sort of scattered, in what I used to think were all the "little" things. Playing with the kids on the carpet, finishing a job, seeing Vicky swing herself up into the seat of the tractor, walking with her in the countryside. It's like all moments like those are filled with life now, and before they were dead.

It's funny that it should come from all those *square* values, dignity, independence, hard work; and I was looking for something new. John said something about that . . . wish I could remember.

"John says," I prompt him, "that there are no *new* values. It is the illusion of the age. The right values are the ones we always knew about, which were there all the time. It's when we fulfill them that they are renewed and come to us fresh."

"Yeah! That's it! You do it, and it blows your mind!"

5

Up and Down on the Misery-Go-Round

LISTENING TO THE STORIES Delancey Streeters tell of the times before they arrived there, one is struck by the circularity. It is as if their lives had been spent in a run-down amusement park, resonating with canned laughter, riding up and down on the misery-go-round in an endless succession of highs and lows. They were like children in their incapacity to tell the gay from the garish. They went for the raucous music, for the color-added hotdogs made of goats' intestines. Their romances were like huge balls of cotton candy that evaporated within the hour and became sticky little messes. All this has about it an air of bilious falsity, blotches of rouge on the face of rapacity:

> *Then turning to my love, I said,*
> *The dead are dancing with the dead.*

This chapter is about the generalities we can make about the life patterns of residents before they came to Delancey and how these patterns alter after entry. We shall draw on the four stories in the previous chapter as well as from additional interviews which were typical of many more. What,

then, have most of these varied individuals in common with
one another?

*From infancy onward they have lacked the opportunity and
have failed to develop the capacity for intimate personal
relations with parents or partners.*

Ray's mother remarried when he was five and dumped
him on his grandparents. His grandfather took him on a
fishing trip to a coral island in the Gulf of Mexico. Their
boat slipped its moorings, and his grandfather swam after it.
He never came back. Ray never cried that night alone on the
island, and he didn't cry when the Coast Guard came the
next day and told him his grandfather had drowned. "I
didn't know what I was expected to feel."

Ray's aunt went to court to get custody of him. His
mother contested it. Not that *she* wanted Ray, but she did
not like her sister horning in. He lived with his aunt until she
threw him out. She then called the police and reported that
he had run away. He took refuge with his uncle, but his
uncle was wanted for auto theft and took to his heels one
morning. Finally a young couple who were involved with
the Hell's Angels befriended Ray. The wife seduced him.
Meanwhile this ménage à trois combined to deal drugs.
When Ray dealt with a narcotics agent, he was arrested,
convicted, and sent to the California Youth Authority. Before he had finished his term, the husband was shot twice in
the back of the head, an incident the authorities contrived to
call suicide. Ray decided, wisely, to curb his curiosity and
stay away from bikers. He still speculates in his dreamy way
about who shafted whom, how, when, and where.

Susie was born to a black alcoholic mother and a white
transient. Her mother referred to Susie's mulatto origins on
every possible occasion. It was her favorite joke. Both her
white and black visitors thought it was funny. A black man
friend began to beat her mother so severely and continually

that Susie called the police. After that she was shifted to her aunt and uncle, who were heroin addicts. They taught her how to use. She was just in her teens. *Six* foster homes later, she became attached to an affectionate hippie couple who lived down the road. They made the mistake of making formal application for guardianship and were indignantly refused. Officialdom had its standards!

Tad's mother did not want to have him. Nine years earlier his baby brother had been crushed in the ambulance on the way to the hospital, when his mother went into convulsions while giving birth. She blamed his father for that and for Tad. She was a department store buyer. Her husband was a used car dealer. Both were "hard as nails," Tad remembers, and they quarreled all the time.

One day when Tad was eight, his mother stopped in the street to talk to a tall woman in tweeds, with close cropped hair, a deep voice, and a cigarette in the corner of her mouth. He was indignant to hear his mother complain to this stranger about his father. The stranger came to dinner the next week, and when his parents began quarreling, the stranger took his mother's side. His father seized the woman by the collar and the seat of her pants and threw her out the front door. But she returned several days later, and Tad's father moved out.

Tad went wild when the woman moved in. She thrashed him with the buckle end of her belt, threatened him with the kitchen knife, and knocked his mother about with her fists. But his mother had changed. She became "sweet" and "feminine" and totally submissive. She cuddled Tad a lot in private but failed to sustain him in a single dispute with the woman of the house.

One morning after a late-night barbecue party, which may have kept the woman awake, Tad missed his most precious possession, a German officer's hat that his father had given him. Tad found its remains, burnt to the metal ring in the

barbecue pit. "You did it!" he screamed at the woman, crying and trembling in his fury. "Say something, Mother! Tell
her it's wrong. You said plenty to Dad!" But his mother
only cringed and tried to comfort him. They sent him to a
detention home for boys.

He had trouble with his sexual identity in adolescence, but
that was nothing compared to what happened his first year
in junior college. He had picked up a girl at a beach party.
She agreed to go up the mountain in a car he had borrowed.
They were to make love. He gunned the accelerator and
roared away, one arm hanging nonchalantly from the window. He was going to score! He eyed her appraisingly in her
bikini as the car gathered speed. What a chick! But the chick
screamed. They were approaching a right hand turn at sixty
miles an hour, and she had seen the other car. Tad's hanging
arm was broken in three places. The steering wheel crushed
his throat, shattered his jaw, and knocked several teeth into
his windpipe. Both kneecaps were lacerated. His companion
broke her ankle and cracked her pelvic bone.

Tad's father had never been able to show him affection
or reveal tender emotions—and he could not now. He did
spend the night in the hospital chapel, where one assumes he
told God what he could not tell his son. Tad would not have
known of his father's vigil if a nurse had not mentioned it. A
week later Tad's grandmother left a newspaper clipping at
his bedside. There had been two families in the other car.
The two husbands in the front seat had died. The little boy
between them had lost an eye. Tad was being held, the paper
said, on two counts of involuntary manslaughter.

That night I was looking for some way to die. I had no right to
kill fathers and bereave families and survive. My only comfort was
that my mother was due to visit that evening, and there was
someone to share my hell. It seemed forever, and I was in great
physical pain, too, with my limbs in traction and my neck and
lower face in a cast. Then the nurse brought a telegram, opened

it, and held it above my head. I can still remember the words. SORRY CAN'T COME TONIGHT. ITS RAINING AND YOU KNOW HOW MAMMA HATES TO DRIVE IN THE RAIN. LOVE. The nurse had to wipe my eyes and help me blow my nose.

A few months later the physical pain ceased but not the mental. Tad feigned physical pain to maintain his habit of morphine, Demerol, Percodan. . . .

One final episode stands out in his recollection. He was nineteen years old. His father had come to fetch him for their occasional weekend outing. A few days earlier Tad had suddenly lost control while visiting his aunt and buried his face in her breast weeping in sheer loneliness and desolation. He had been encouraged by her response to try it with his father. For a second he teetered in front of him, then fell forward only to bang against his father's forearm. The man was reaching into his breast pocket. "Here, Son, I don't have much time this weekend. Why don't you take this twenty and have a *real* good time!" Tad spent the money on heroin.

Prior to their drug addiction or imprisonment most residents were already "addicted" to the stereotypes of mass culture.

Where socialization and intimate rapport break down there are only the crude stereotypes of human virtue marketed by the mass media. In the last chapter we saw Stephanie juggling her incongruous dreams of Brilliant Artist and Love-Nest Wife and fumbling both. We saw Josh, existential hero, the labor-saving Sisyphus who with simulated anguish rolled his papier mâché rock up the mountains of our discontent. Bill Toliver was the speedball mystic looking for a short cut to the mountain top, while Theodore of the small shades was cruising around Vallejo after dark, as menacing in his myopia as Mr. Magoo.

There is, indeed, a cartoon quality to much of their activity. Ray of the ménage à trois held up a gas station with two fingers in his coat pocket. Like a sight gag in a Marx Brothers movie one waits for his fingers to appear through a hole in his pocket. He was apprehended a few miles down the road still carrying his concealed fingers. There are malefactors around Delancey who would have failed to confound the Keystone Cops.

Jerry was a tower man on the Pennsylvania Railroad on the Newark side of Hoboken Station. High on hash, he got all the switches mixed and tangled up three trains in the meadowlands for three hours on a late Friday afternoon in July. "The drivers must have told the passengers whose fault it was, because when the trains eventually passed my tower, the passengers were leaning from windows of the car, purple in the face with rage and with the heat, shaking their fists at me."

The masscult stereotype is extended one-dimensionally and run into the ground.

As H.R. Haldeman was leaving the Senate Watergate Hearings, he ran into Dick Tuck, the political prankster. "*You* started this," said Haldeman. "And you ran it into the ground," answered Tuck. Delancey is full of ex-runners-into-the-ground. Without satisfactory interpersonal relationships, they are prey to egocentric fantasies and comic-book heroisms. Like neighborhood Nixons, they cannot conceive that Strength extended one-dimensionally becomes brutality, Manliness becomes macho, Courage becomes foolhardiness, and Brilliant Subterfuge becomes basic dishonesty.

At this point it may help to recall John Maher's multidimensional social philosophy, discussed in Chapter 3, wherein each human value was qualified by its opposite. This is John's antidote to the one-dimensionality of most entering residents. Toughness must be joined to tenderness, self-interest married to social concern, while creative and abstract conceptions must be followed through to concrete realities. A true radical conserves key American traditions and maintains continuity from past to future. While criminals *are* socially caused empirically, they change developmentally by breaking those chains of causation.

It is easy to see where the one-dimensionality comes from. It is quintessentially American. When millions compete along a few simple dimensions, the minority of winners produce the mass of losers. One of the privileges of affluence is precisely that of filling out one's value system and personality with additional dimensions and becoming "liberal" toward poverty and "sensitive" toward beauty. You must *first* maximize self-interest, make yourself a pile, for only *then* can you (or your children) be selfless and aesthetic. The New Left and the counterculture were flower gardens on the roof of the stock exchange, and they declined with the Dow Jones. The philosophy by which wealth is accumulated is the *same* philosophy that spawns crime-in-the-streets. It merely manifests itself differently at different points on the social register. For losers *can never cease in their self-interest.* The financial resources necessary to the cultivation of the tender sides of their personalities always elude them as they claw each other to ribbons.

Typical in this respect were Tad's parents. His father was frustrated-Tough (without tenderness), and his mother was beaten-Tender (without toughness). The schizoid nature of the family left its mark on the personalities of its members. The patterns formed by the fragments vary from case to case, but the *fact* of fragmentation is constant.

Even the schizoid nature of America's foreign policy has left its mark on the psyches of Delancey's veterans. The same Super-Toughness that escalated to woo the "hearts and minds" of peasants in Southeast Asia had several

Delancey Streeters running themselves into the ground, in lock step with our best and brightest (for whom the ground was cushioned). A good representative of Delancey's veterans is Foster Brandt, an articulate, ebullient black man in his late twenties.

Foster was the "white sheep" of a middle-class professional family. His father died when he was eleven, and he laughed at the funeral because Uncle Horace wanted the children to kiss the corpse and Foster's brother panicked. In fact, Foster was as revolted as his brother, but he habitually laughed when grieved or horrified and swaggered while deathly afraid.

He was not sure when it began. He remembers as a child, crying and clinging around his father's neck as the man swam out into deep water. He remembers a night in the Catskill Mountains in New York. His father sent him out alone in the dark to beat the bushes. The child was supposed to drive some suspected bears into the range of the car's headlights and his father's gun. The experience was traumatic. He remembers coming home from tap-dancing class and, at his mother's insistance, performing for his father. The latter shook his head in sorrow and disgust, for Foster was not a robust child. He suffered from asthma and skin rashes and was small. His mother felt that he needed protection. His father left such things to her.

Foster was picked on at his school on New York's Upper East Side. He had more pocket money than his classmates, and they would relieve him of it. Distrusting his emotions, he would back down and back down, while the slights accumulated, but periodically he would erupt. When Cory, another pupil, took fifty cents from him one day, Foster rushed into his home, got a fully loaded gun, and began shooting. A bullet broke Cory's finger, and while he lay on the ground and screamed, Foster tried to kick him unconscious. A friend of Foster pulled him off. Foster attacked another boy with a large piece of wood for similar reasons. His mother felt her son was misunderstood.

Growing into adolescence without a father, Foster set out to prove his manhood through a series of escalating exploits. He climbed up the George Washington Bridge in the fog and jumped the spaces between the girders. With a group of older companions, who strung him along for his pocket money, he played "chicken" by jumping from rooftop to rooftop. This was in the Sugar Hill District of New York where the houses are six stories tall. He missed his footing one night and fell five feet to a fire escape platform. Rising half-stunned, he staggered around before tumbling down the steps to the platform below. There a girl friend's aunt opened her window and hauled him inside.

The girl friend's brother had just joined the Marines, and this inspired Foster's friends to form the Young Marines. They would drill, do calisthenics, wear officers' insignia, organize route marches, haze recruits, and assemble weapons. A test of manhood was to climb the 155th Street Viaduct, which runs beside Yankee Stadium. One initiate was hung by his trouser legs from a thirteenth floor window. When the trousers ripped, he narrowly escaped falling and has a nervous condition to this day.

We did everything together. We drank our first wine together, smoked our first weed, shot our first dope, and ultimately joined the service. Most of us went to Vietnam. It was the logical culmination. Now we are all dead or fucked-up completely.

It was Foster's money that paid for the dope. Heroin made him sick, but he would shoot up with the others and then vomit somewhere privately. As the youngest and weakest he was generally the lookout on the robberies they pulled, but when their leader Johnny was arrested robbing a liquor store, Foster leapfrogged to higher status by electing himself The Avenger. He tried to kill the owner of the store with a rifle, while the old man rocked in his rocker in his living room. The bullet smashed his glasses and broke his nose. Foster escaped.

But still he was not content. After a summer spent counseling Boy Scouts, Foster and his friends held a rip-off contest. Each was to try to steal more than four hundred dollars during a single afternoon. As the shadows lengthened, Foster was still short of his goal. In desperation he ran into the 163rd Street Subway Station waving two guns, robbed the cashier, and fled *through the tunnel* to the 161st Street Station, where he emerged to rob a surprised lady on the platform. He won!

In the days following they stole from an uptown boat basin a yacht in which they cruised around Manhattan. They also stole a helicopter, which they crash-landed. In the meantime the wheels of American justice were turning at their customary speed and might never have caught Foster but for his habit of running toward approaching wheels. Two members of the gang were caught in Caledonia Park and fingered the other members, who all broke in three minutes flat and begged for the opportunity to inform on everyone else. After all, their courage was not of the moral kind, and what else were their exploits for but to buy the friendship none could give to the others? Foster always strove to cement his membership within the gang, but the price in sheer hazard never ceased to climb.

He was in plenty of trouble. The charges included aggravated assault, attempted murder, and grand larceny (three counts). His bail was set at $55,000. He was placed in maximum security at 275 Atlantic Avenue, on the ninth tier with the murderers. He had arrived.

Enter Foster's mother, who quickly saw that her delicate boy was in danger of being seriously misunderstood. She hired top lawyers, who had the bail reduced, and she put up the deeds of her own house and her restaurant as collateral.

Later Foster's case was separated from the other bad influences. Delays, legal maneuvering, and plea bargaining whittled it all down to one charge of assault in the second degree. When the judge learned of his desire to volunteer for military service despite being married, which would have saved him from the draft, he was put on probation, on the tacit understanding that he would shoot up Asians instead. To the rescue of the pitiful helpless giant in the Asian quagmire came the undersized, misunderstood masher. The system gets the soldiers it deserves.

Foster was gung ho. After jungle training in Panama and parachute training stateside, he joined the First Cavalry in Vietnam. His training coincided with the maturation of his physical frame, and he grew prodigiously around the chest and arms. Things were exciting at first. He whizzed over tree tops in a Huey transport helicopter on which fifty-caliber machine guns had been mounted. The guns were too big for the craft, which careened sideways each time the guns were fired. It was a metaphor on Foster's life, and he loved it.

The maximizers of single dimensions are subverted by the characteristic within themselves opposite to the one they are trying to maximize. A "latent self" betrays the "manifest self."
Foster construed himself as Tough and repressed his Tenderness as "weakness." Besides, his mother and now his wife served up the Tenderness unconditionally, so why bother developing it in himself? But he was away from home now, and his Toughness became a tiger he dared not dismount.

Foster was a member of a ground patrol, which drew fire from a Vietcong bunker complex. The bunker was located in a clump of trees and bushes surrounded by open space.

We had 'em pinned down, so we called in the C.H. 37's, which dropped fifty-gallon drums of kerosene, followed by napalm. The whole shrubbery was a furnace. Then figures began breaking from the bushes shouting, "Chuy Hoy!" They would run several yards towards our position, human torches with blackened faces, and fall a few yards short. You ever smelt human beings burning? It's incredibly sweet and pungent—like a curious brand of barbecue sauce at a cookout. I just watched and vomited, but I couldn't rid my mouth and nostrils of that smell.

It was about this time that Foster's nightmares began. One, especially, recurred night after night.

I dreamed I was on a long-range reconnaissance patrol, which is what we *were* actually doing at the time, Junior, Sparky, Evans, and me. Except that in my dream, I was unaccountably alone in the jungle. Jesus Christ, was I alone! All the equipment was there, the flakjackets, the M-79, the radio, but there were no people. My dream would begin with the radio going dead in my hands, and there was stillness. The jungle, which was lush green, would gradually turn black, the color of the Vietcong's black pajamas.

I know what you're going to ask! Whether being black bothers me? The *hell* it does! It always has, from the day my father told me I was black and always would be. Along with my small size and my skin rashes, it was one more barrier in the way of people liking me. That's why I had to be Superman and have more material things than my friends. And the weird thing about my dream was that I'd got my wish and that was just the trouble! Superman had survived. He was indestructible, but he was alone with his weapons in a jungle.

In the days that followed it often seemed to Foster that his dreams and his days had intertwined. Junior was shot and evacuated; then Sparky was killed. Finally Evans tripped on a "bouncing Betty," and the booby trap sprang from the grass and blew him apart. Now Foster began to dream of his mother, aunt, wife, and children—dreams of such vividness and intimacy that the real horror was waking at dawn. He would creep silently away from his companions at first light, hide a few yards away in the jungle, and abandon himself to fits of weeping.

But his secret desolation seemed only to add to his public violence. Most of his companions were content just to kill VC. Foster would empty his entire clip into them or use a machine gun and watch them come apart.

I had to kill *more* than others killed. I had to obliterate a man's spirit, and after he was dead, I'd hack off appendages.

But the experience that brought Foster to the end of the road was when a friend standing beside him in a bunker was struck by shrapnel that sliced off the top of his head.

There was this explosion and I ducked. Suddenly I was covered all over in these *red Cheerios*—you know, the breakfast cereal, only swimming in red sauce? They were Freddie's brains. I realized then that I was not a tough guy . . . and if this was toughness, it was not for me.

One image stuck in Foster's mind. He had found the body of an American Marine in full kit. But there, crawling among the insignia and the magnificent equipment, were maggots. The imposing military surface, the inspiration of the Young Marines, was rotting from within. His dream had putrefied. He was on drugs now. He knew he was not a tough guy but didn't know what he could be instead.

Tender-minded dimensions can be run into the ground as surely as tough ones. They, too, are subverted by their opposites.

It is far too easy to equate character disorder with militarism. If Delancey has its share of disillusioned patriots, it also has their opposite numbers, the Love Generation degenerated. A flamboyant example of the latter was Ed Walker, a black Hawaiian, son of a sports celebrity, and former part owner of The Black Cat, in its day a famous San Francisco night club. He is not typical of most Delancey residents inasmuch as he never touched drugs until his late thirties, and he enjoyed a stable home life. But his splashings in the milk of human kindness until it curdled and soured are very familiar.

It all began for Ed one midsummer day in 1967. He had sold The Black Cat and was engaged, for the first time, in humdrum business in order to support a growing family. His occupation was a far cry from the sports heroism surrounding his father in Hawaii and from the show business world of celebrities and night life he himself had moved in. His life space had narrowed. He felt driven. There was a hippie celebration of the summer solstice at Golden Gate Fields, near Berkeley. Fifteen thousand people and twenty rock bands filled the stadium. Ed was entranced and jumped around singing and shouting joyfully. This was rejuvenation, a second coming for the not-so-young! The next evening saw him in the Haight-Ashbury, a well-preserved Peter Pan searching for his Wendy. Sure enough a fifteen-year-old child with flowers in her hair and dressed in filmy raiment skipped happily toward the man who grinned, and still grins, so delightedly at the world. They hopped, stepped, and jumped to her apartment on Oak Street, where they both shot up and made beatific love.

Wendy was blessed with middle-class parents from Montana every bit as substantial as the Darlings of *Peter Pan.* Every week they sent a check, which she shared with lost boys. Ed did not believe in being kept, and so considered what he could do. Some of the older men in the community sported white beards and mountain staffs and lived off their flock of children for the price of a cryptic saying or two. Ed decided to deal drugs and help organize the community instead.

Even in its heyday the Haight was a carefully cultivated illusion. Beneath the playfulness were gang leaders, war lords, and territories. Superspade was running much of it

and was reputedly grossing $250,000 a week before some-
one murdered him. There were innocent children all right
with mummies in Montana and elsewhere, but they were
protected as they gamboled. Ed organized "the sidewalk
commandos," who would move in on any drunken lout or
on anyone who threatened to take a flower child to bed un-
beautifully. If the children asked sweetly and spontaneously
whether Superspade and his gang could "spare some
change," well they certainly *could*. They scattered dimes
among their geese and gathered golden eggs, and everyone
loved everyone for a season.

Ed became a dealer astride a white horse, with dueling
pistols, spurs, and a riding whip. They called him "Cowboy" or "Wild Black Hickok." He alternated as a World
War I flying ace in scarf and goggles, "a thousand feet high
with my feet on the ground," or he would appear as D'Ar-
tagnan in a high ruffled collar and sword. He was surrounded by Admirals, Hessians, Moors, and Crusaders. Vietnam
was a long way away. On Sadie Hawkins Day five thousand
screaming women ran after a greater number of men. The
metaphors mixed freely as Minnie Hahas vied with Little
Bo-Peeps to roll in the hay with Li'l Abners and Holy Men.

But it all soured of course. The sanitation department un-
horsed Ed, and the police took his pistols. Peter Pan had
become a speed-freak, and Wendy caught serum hepatitis
and turned yellow. The nursery tale deviated from its happy
ending when the crocodiles came out of the sewers to eat the
lost children while avoiding the Captain Hooks who could
defend themselves. No one believed in fairies any more. The
upper-middle-class kids, who had been playing at self-
abandonment, took off for fresh fields and postures new,
leaving a mostly lower-class residue of the genuinely abandoned, who had never realized until too late that playing
charades was a class privilege. Ed was reduced to forging
prescriptions and selling pills. He was caught, jailed, and

further reduced to repossessing property bought on credit. He would pull television sets from pleading families and drag away their beds. It was better to be high till busted, and high till busted, and high. . . .

Nearly all those interviewed had behaved in their past lives as if they wanted to be caught.
The idea of wanting-to-be-caught-and-punished is an old one. Perhaps it is nothing more than the projection of the observer. Anyone who takes "excitement," "risk," or "courage" to their extremes will be caught or crash or get killed anyway. Do we need a subconscious desire for punishment? I think we do. There has to be some explanation for how the manifest, maximizing self is prevented from destroying the individual. To some extent the society at large will intervene to stop escalating violence or to exploit provocative vulnerability and invitations to violation. But at another level there is considerable evidence that the opposite, latent self pulls the plug on his overblown brother.

Consider the case of Patrick O. McGillycuddy. He stands over six-feet tall with straw-blond hair, a thin frame, piercing blue eyes, and sage advice that points in three directions like the Straw Man in *The Wizard of Oz*.

Ever since my childhood I was convinced that there was something medically wrong with me—some terminal malignancy within. I would go and see the doctor, only to be struck dumb in his presence. I couldn't explain why I was sure there was something wrong. I'd say, "It's my ear" or something, which it wasn't, and get out as fast as I could.

When I look back on my life and my crazy career as a criminal, there's one principal theme of explanation. I wanted to get caught so that I could be examined physically against my will. I mean *what* was I doing selling stolen stereos from the trunk of my car at 11 P.M. at the junction of Fillmore and McAllister? It's a black district, a high crime area, and there I was, pale white in the gloom, hustling passersby from a stolen car, with stolen plates, forged identification papers, burglar tools in the back seat, and a set of works (hypodermic needle, etc.) on the dash. On top of that my partner was a police informer.

But there always came a time when I *had* to be caught or do something crazy. It was because I was obligated to my own rhetoric. I'd say to some fellow, "Burn me and I'll kill ya!" And if later he burned me, I had to save my reputation for following through on my word. So unless I was caught quickly, I'd become dangerous. Then I'd always promised my friends I'd go legit when I'd made my stake. But I really didn't believe I could make it in legitimate business, so I'd get caught.

Yet the other part of me was paranoid about being subverted. "Why pick on *me*!" I shouted as the police closed in, and I became convinced that my thoughts were visible and the police could "read" them.

Notice that Pat's "illusion" is a parable on the facts. There *is* a "conspiracy" of sorts between his latent self and the police. His maximizing, manifest self has provoked both of them in concert to do him in.

The effect of drugs on these preexisting social and personality dynamics is to make them worse.

Most of my informants were messing up their lives *before* they went on drugs but became considerably worse when they started to use. It is not difficult to see why. A favorite of Delancey's "actors-out" are the stimulants, the amphetamines such as bennies, crystal, speed, and dexies. They also like coke (cocaine). All stimulate the central nervous system, alert the attention, increase activity and render it at times euphoric. If you *already* have the tendency to run particular ideas about yourself into the ground, these stimulants drive you to do so with greater energy and obsessiveness. Long after the extremity of your action has stripped it of social rewards, stimulants can impart to you an aura of success.

Should you require an occasional rest from this frantic activity, the sedatives, such as yellow jackets, red devils, phennies, and goofers, can bring you down. They do so *without* the requirement that you modify the outlandishness of your life style and without resort to human affections or relationships. In effect drugs are counterfeits of, and reductions-into-pieces of, successful human relationships. Such relationships have their highs and lows, euphorias and withdrawals, tensions and relaxations, illuminations and concentrations. But all these effects are indissolubly linked and wedded to social intelligence and interpersonal skill. You endure tensions to relax in reconciliations. You discover you are lovable by granting another the right to reach an opposite conclusion. The illuminations of LSD, the euphorias of heroin, the loosenings of alcohol, all invite one-dimensionality. All can shatter the natural rhythms of relationship, and by replacing particular human endowments, they can cause these endowments to atrophy. Delancey does not condemn chemicals for those in whom the arts of loving are strong. It insists, however, that even the smallest amounts are lethal to Delancey's mice and can trigger inherent tendencies.

A great many people have never had a human experience that compares in pleasure with a chemical high. When Bernado, whom we met in Chapter 2, was asked by a prison psychiatrist in San Quentin why he shot dope he explained:

It's very simple. I *like* it. Nothing in my experience has ever improved on it, and nothing in my future is likely to. If I could build myself a cozy pad, with a girl, food laid on, and heroin, and not have to scramble and fight for them; I'd be high *all the time!* You got anything better for me? You gonna employ me? Of course it's killing me—I ain't that stupid! But I'd prefer to live high for a few years than low for a lifetime.

The psychiatrist shook his head. "You are one hell of a sick person," he said.

Ann Dowie

John, Mimi, and the twins, David and Greg.

The old Mein mansion, one-time Russian consulate and now Delancey's business office.

Ed Turnbull

All through the summer months when school is out they take parties of ghetto kids on tours in their double-decker bus.

"... I know you think that Claud is *bee*-utiful 'cause he once stole the crown jewels of Poland.... Well, Claud never stole nothing 'cept some food stamps that stuck to his fanny while he was sitting down on the job."

Ed Turnbull

The Club.

The Morning Meeting. The mood is gung ho with messages and songs of uplift.

Pool at the Club. In the background, the current raffle has reached $75,000.

The accredited in-house high school.

Bob Wells after his release. "He seems to have lived his life by a very simple principle: to find out what it is that people want him to do or say and then to do something as different as possible."

Delancey Street 13, the Cops 0.

A victorious team hoists Willie Bonin, who scored the only touchdown of the first season.

"Notorious dope-fiend" Harvey Stone at the time of his admission to Delancey Street. . .

. . . and Harvey two-and-a-half years later as the Restaurant's manager.

The Moving Company School.

"Wild Black Hickock," alias "Blazing Saddles," welcomes a customer to the Restaurant.

The terrarium shop and delivery service. Carol Mendell (left) and Lena Kizart. (Lena split shortly after this picture was taken and died of a drug overdose.)

Rip-off Seminar. Nancy Murphy and Vivian Neal demonstrate shoplifting with a 'Christmas package.'"

Ed Turnbull

The Sausalito apartments.

S.T.D.Lancaster

Clare and Jack Behan at their wedding on Alcatraz. "Against the 'House of No Relationships' they celebrated new commitments. . . ."

Bill Toliver (left) dressed as his Old Self in long coat and flop hat. The scene is from the NBC movie-for-television *Delancey Street*. Bill and other residents played minor parts.

Delancey's Bentley — one up on the upper crust.

Of course it is not that simple, because part of Bernado, his latent self, did *not* want to die. In fact he would not have been in San Quentin if the latent self had not earlier prepared a *gotterdammerung* for his ostentatious opposite. Bernado is a Puerto Rican in his late twenties, with dark curly hair and a handsome if mournful expression. The waitress in the restaurant called him "hot lips."

I would keep company with the craziest in my community that lived off thieving. The successful thieves were quiet, but I had to prove something. We chose to hold up the big liquor store in our neighborhood that cashes the welfare checks. I was *known* there—perhaps that's why I did it. The owner's been ripped off before and pulls a gun on us. The bullets are flying everywhere, and we get the hell out. A couple of hours later there's an all-points bulletin out for me by description *and* my full name!

My girl, my kid, and I are hiding out in another part of town. She's been complaining I'm never in, so I'm in tonight. It's a scene of rare contentment. I'm propped up on pillows on the couch, half-undressed. My girl has her head on my shoulder. My kid's snuggled on my chest. Then bam! The door crashes in with such force it tears from the hinges and falls flat. The *whole* fuckin' window frame busts inwards with this bull behind it. I got five cops coming at me from all directions, and I don't even have my pants on! The baby turns white and screams, and my girl just stands looking down at me with this sad, sad bewildered expression as she shakes her head—it was like my mother.

When the latent self is publicly appealed to, the individual suffers an agonizing choice between denying one of his two selves or dealing with the contradiction between them.

Bernado's mother died while he was in San Quentin. Like Foster's mother, she had loved him unconditionally, or perhaps more, as he fell deeper into trouble. Certainly she suffered, endured, and forgave more. Her funeral was exquisite torture for Bernado. His accustomed style of showing his toughest facade to his neighborhood and drinking secretly from her infinite tenderness was unworkable now.

He was being expected to show contrition publicly in the face of his detractors, to deliver himself into their scorn for her sake. He could not do it.

He came from San Quentin with a guard on either side. Maximum security was the watchword. On the way to the church he sat next to his father, who uttered the only words any member of the family or the neighborhood spoke to him that day.

"I hope you're satisfied." His father glared balefully through his tears. "She always said you'd be the death of her, and now you've succeeded."

Bernado recalls a glow of triumph. *He* had not broken like his father—nor would he!

What I remember most in the church was this glaring conspicuousness. As the coffin moved, I walked behind it with my handcuffed wrists before me and my leg irons clanking at every step. I had two guards at each shoulder and a sort of invisible barrier around me—so that wherever I walked there was empty space. You've heard of "charmed circles"? This was a cursed circle, with eyes around the edges fixed on me as if I were afflicting the funeral.

I'd been closer to my mother than anyone, and she'd loved me after everyone else had stopped. Now she was gone, and I couldn't give her a tear. It was my sense of machismo. I was being tested. They'd staged this thing to break me, and I would *not* break. I would be stronger than my sniveling relatives. *That's* how sick and stupid and desperate I was!

So great was the sense of guilt among many residents that it had to be formally "dissipated."

The conventional wisdom about Bernado and his fellow residents is that they are "sociopaths"—men and women without conscience or fellow feeling. The truth is otherwise. The feelings are very strong indeed, but they are "stuffed down into the gut" where they fester to cause a heart-burning guilt. Bernado's public denial of his mother was part of his public denial of his latent self.

One reason that newcomers have their heads shaved and are so roughly abused is to make common cause with this latent self-hatred against the posturings of the public self. Only negatively toned evaluations can break the habit of one-dimensional extremism and the drug habits that accompany them. To speak of Courage and Sacrifice is to set no clear limit on their maximization. To speak of machismo and reckless stupidity makes it clear that the limits have been passed. Typically residents will be attacked from *both* sides, for their public machismo and their private self-pity, while the standard of *integrated* moral values is held before them. "A man of real courage shows *feeling* for his parents and his people."

So in a Dissipation they took Bernado, and they put the handcuffs and leg irons on, and they set up the coffin and the candles and had him reenact the scene. This time he roared with rage and wept with humiliation and begged his mother's forgiveness.

"Too late!" they told him. "She's dead. Besides you cannot be forgiven secretly for public failures—that's the game you *always* played, the Macho and the Mama! You have to give your concern, in *her* memory, to the other members of the family."

Pepé ran with the Barracudas, a Chicano street gang in East Los Angeles. They spent most of their time fighting over neighborhood territory against the King Cobras and the White Fangs. A couple of Barracudas were jumped, and Felipe, their leader, was in the hospital with a four-inch cut on his face and neck.

A few days later Pepé and some friends went drinking at a lodge in the mountains. Returning home through a public park, they spied three Cobras on a bench. They parked their car down the road and crawled through the trees, with guns at the ready. Pepé had a shotgun given him by a thoughtful uncle. In the fusillade of fire two of the Cobras were wounded, but a little boy playing a couple hundred yards beyond the bench was killed.

There was not enough evidence to convict Pepé, but they got him on parole violation and gave him six months to fifteen years. He fought so often in prison that he might have served the longer of the two, if Delancey had not offered to take him.

"Latinos do not cry!" Pepé snarled at his tormentors through an entire forty-five-hour Dissipation. Bernado and others tried to help him but to no avail. They put him in a second Dissipation. They played tapes of gunfire, made hail to little Caesar, charged him formally with carrying a concealed rattle (he'd been in trouble at the age of five), and brought a friend of the house from L.A. to curse him on behalf of the community. They had blown up a picture of the little boy and made him look at it. What a worthy opponent for a macho kid! Just about his size (Pepé is small). At last Pepé's face fell into his hands, the tears trickled from between his fingers and didn't stop till dawn.

The sense of guilt and the experiences attached to it are first expressed then made into a gift of sympathy, sharing, and help to others.

So when the brother of Manuel, a recent resident of Delancey, was stabbed to death in San Quentin, it was Bernado and Pepé who tried to help him. "You will never get over the death of that child," John told Pepé, "until you've helped other people live and get over their pain."

But Manuel, too, sat sullen through a whole Game put together for his benefit. Bernado and Pepé went with him to the funeral, but he could neither show grief nor comfort his mother. A few weeks later in a Dissipation he complained:

What could I say to her? I haven't no conversation. When something's important I just lose all the words. I *did* say, "You'll be all right, Mama," and she turned to look at me and began crying. I know what I *wanted* to say. I wanted to say I was clean and I'd changed, but how often have I told her that, and it wasn't true or didn't last? I just couldn't say that again.

That night JoAnn Mancuso was running the Dissipation. She is Delancey's first woman director. She speaks quietly.

"I'd like you to imagine what your mother was thinking. What was going through her mind?"

But Manuel is silent, so starting with JoAnn they guess.

"Perhaps she was thinking, how many more are going to die. Two of them are junkies, another's in jail, how long before we go through this again, and where does it end?"

"And when you said your five words of comfort," Bernado says, "I bet she thought, my youngest . . . how long before I bury him too? . . ."

A voice comes out of the well of the dark room. "She was probably thinking, I wish I'd died first so I didn't have to watch this. Please . . . let the next funeral be mine."

Suddenly a dissipant throws himself forward into the circle around Manuel . . .

"And I'll tell you what's gonna happen, 'cause I've seen it! Every time you see her she'll look older and more tired. Me and my brother were two dildos—fucking her to death—and she'll be so lonely! . . . Oh, God, she'll be so lonely!" And he falls on the carpet doubled up in his own grief.

Soon Manuel, his eyes streaming, is rehearsing what he will say to his mother.

Ray-of-the-armed-fingers had to take care of a gun while some bikers he was with gang-raped a girl.

"She was screaming," he sobbed, "and I had one of the guns. I could have stopped them."

The audience is skeptical. "They'd have killed you. Better not kid yourself with imagined scenes of bullshit heroism. Your failure was less dramatic. It's that you ran with, or rather ran *after*, those punks and acted as their errand boy—that's your trouble. So long as you wear that sheepish-creepish smile and want that everyone should love you, you'll find yourself in just those sort of situations."

The personalities of residents do, in time, grow along multiple dimensions, which integrate their values and their community at one and the same time.

It usually takes at least a year before residents find themselves growing in dimensions they had not dreamed they possessed. Often these virtues are exactly opposite to those they once maximized so frantically.

For Bernado it was the discovery that he could help the inarticulate—all those whose feelings were too big for words.

I know who *you'll* be writing about, the super-dramatists with their horror stories. But those people are already half-recovered. They can get attention, impress people. My people are those who don't have the vocabulary to say what's so unbearable. It's like you're in a case of thick glass, and people see your funny gestures and your mouth working but no words. That's the worst feeling in the world—and I can help them out from behind that screen, 'cause I've been there.

For Tad it was the discovery that telling his story in all its horror had set him free of its clutches. He had friends, now, who could share their experiences, and that made them stronger than their pasts.

I went to see my mother and the woman. They were just two old people. I was amazed! It was as if they'd lost all their powers to haunt me, and what I saw were not monsters but a rather sad, worn couple.

But there was one day about a month ago when I knew I'd

changed completely. I'm in the advertising specialties sales force. I was trying to sell a year's supply of decorative matches to this small restaurant chain. I was trying to tell this guy about Delancey—'cause matches are just matches—when he says, "Yeah, I know! Another of these drug programs. Saw your boss on the tube—big mouth!"

On impulse I put my samples away, and I said, "Let's forget the sale, okay? 'Cause I want to tell you something." So I told him about Delancey and what it meant to me and how it changed my life. You know, I've never talked like that! I mean, I was *eloquent!* All my life it's been me, me, me. Was I making a good impression? Did this person like me? And I wanted that so much I didn't get it, like my wants were tripping me up. But for half an hour I forgot "me"—and *wow!* Then I realized I'd got carried away and began to pack my samples. "Wait a minute!" he says. "You're not going yet." And you know something? He bought enough matches to last him till 1985! I've always fantasized about being a great talker, but I could never learn the trick. There's no trick; I know that now. You have to have people and ideas you care about—*then* you can talk, because you have subject that goes beyond yourself.

Foster began to change before he came to Delancey. In his final days in Vietnam he had been shot in the chest. As a result he spent six months on his back.

I'd never been forced to be still and *think,* but that's all I could do now. The bed next to me was a transparent plastic airbed. It was full of some clear jelly substance, and suspended in the jelly was this pinkish colored *human* jelly. He'd been hit by napalm, ours, and he had no hair and no skin, and I could see right into him. I'd known him before, and he'd been *mean,* as bad as me or worse. Now I watched this pink protoplasm struggle for its life and slowly organize itself back into human shape.

It was a horrible-ass thing to watch but awe inspiring, too. This incredible will to life, this long painful struggle to come back, a struggle like my own. It was like an X ray of my soul in purgatory.

And I watched and thought as I lay there, and I knew I'd been on the wrong side in this struggle. I'd tried to stamp out these amazing, intricate beings, and I'd done it blindly in a frenzy, while those who'd once tried to lock me up sanctioned it all. I'd never looked inside myself or into the depth of other people. I'd manipulated surfaces. I swore to myself as I lay there that if I came out of this, I'd be on the side of healing and life.

But when I got back on my feet, all my resolutions melted. My marriage died. My mother virtually had to drag me into the land of the living, and I was on drugs. She got me into Synanon, but someone hurt my feelings and I split. I think I'd have split from Delancey, too, if it hadn't been for Susie. Everyone was yelling and cursing at me, but she smiled for just a moment and whispered, "We're all doing this because we care, remember that." And that startled me because my mother's caring hadn't been that way. So I stuck it out here, and that's how come I got this chance to go back to school and do biomedical engineering. It was then that everything I'd sworn in that hospital bed came back to me, with no excuses not to act on it. I was in a Dissipation, and we went through everything . . . the desecration of those bodies . . . the lot. I saw that this work was something I had to do, not for others so much as for myself. I had to *use* the suffering I'd inflicted and the suffering I'd seen to make me better in my work.

Just last month an amazing thing happened. Dr. Richards, the head of the chemistry department, took me aside. He said, "You're a very humane person. You really *are* concerned to reduce people's suffering." And we discussed my going to medical school—that's an additional four years—so I've not decided yet. But that's the first time anybody said anything like that to me. I remember he used the word "tender," and it's funny because it made me feel strong, and when I think of all the people I've blasted and taken apart and after each episode I was still the same scared, weak person I'd been before. Healing is a wonderful process. Just to be a part of it gives me everything I once tried to grab.

Louis helped to found the Delancey Street Moving Company. Those were desperate days, and the residents lived hand-to-mouth.

I used to come into the Club late—past 8:00 P.M.—and all covered in sweat. And people would say, "Hi, Louis! How much you make today?" And we'd say, "$250!" or whatever it was, and I'd look around and I'd think, Christ, I, Louis Ferranato, fuck-up, gun-freak, and dope-fiend, I'm *making this place!* There's people going to school, 'cause I'm working. There's even people wouldn't be *alive* but for what we're bringing in. That's a real charge to my system. That's a new experience for me. And John would turn to me in general meetings or Dissipations and say, "Louis there buys the time for us to therapize each other. He *works for us* and don't let's forget it." I'd get a real fix when he said that!

For Susie, who'd been in seven different homes by the time she came to Delancey as a teen-ager, it came as a staggering realization that there were people—so many people—who cared if she made it.

John asked me what I wanted most in the world. I was fifteen. I said, "I wanta go to school—but I'm years and years behind—a real ignorant slob." He got me and Maria into The Drew School, that's private and very exclusive. The high schools wouldn't take us, and John says Special Education is a slave system to support surplus teachers. The Foundation paid our school fees by painting the school. If we glanced out of the schoolroom windows, Maria and me, we could see our people slapping on the paint. That really concentrates your mind on school work—no gazing absent-mindedly into space!

Then one day Maria splits—and John is shouting and cursing. But I see his eyes, and there's real pain there. I think to myself, I gotta see this through—'cause this man cares—I don't know why he should—but he cares. So last week I graduated, and guess who my class chose as a commencement speaker? That's right, John! And he gave this rousing speech, and when it's finished, he comes down from the platform and kisses me, and everyone's hugging and exchanging presents. That was a wonderful day . . . so now I'm going to go to college.

But some people have to grow up in a hurry. Pete O'Farrell's father called the Foundation late one night and explained that he had perhaps two weeks to live. All he cared about now was Pete. Would he split and shoot drugs when he heard the news? Was there some way of telling him in a controlled setting?

They built a Dissipation around Pete, and he ran his life story for laughs, with his father the butt of many. Then they told him the news and asked him to rerun his story, and it was as if he had stepped through a looking glass—everything was the opposite of before. Pete went through the whole cycle: incredulity, resistance, rage, grief, and giving. By Sunday morning he was busy helping the "hold-outs," and it was then that he gave way to words that epitomize much of what Delancey is about.

You keep grandstanding and posturing and bullshitting and playing house. Don't you know what's at the end of the line? DEATH! You think you can fool *that?* That's *real!* So why don't you start loving those who love you while there's life left in them? And why don't you wake the fuck *up* and LIVE the time you got left!

6

The Waterhead Hearings

IT IS FRIDAY EVENING in the assembly room at the Club. The directors sit behind a long table, with Hal Fenton, a director, in the chair wielding a gavel. A large placard inscribed "The Waterhead Hearings" dominates the wall behind the table.

This is actually the opening exercise of a "Dissipation," a forty-five-hour, nonstop marathon session of group attack-therapy. Dissipations often begin with humorous interludes, which solve the problem of what to do until exhaustion begins to erode the defenses of the "dissipants." John is pacing the floor between the long table and the rows of chairs, making one of his extemporaneous introductions to the purpose of Dissipations. He may speak for five minutes or two hours. It depends entirely on the mood he senses in himself and in the audience. He casts his eyes slowly over the twenty or so dissipants in the room.

I've got a feeling about this group, a gloomy feeling. It's a dog-turd-on-the-funeral-parlor-steps feeling. Not that they're bad people. There's few in this group with anything really vicious in their background. It's more a matter of futility and waste, of emptiness,

131

silliness, and pretension. Some of the men here make like real Damon Runyon characters. I mean, they're Trojans—wet, used Trojans on the cold tile floor of a public urinal at three in the morning! That's the sort of feeling one has ... looking at them. ...

When I was in jail, I used to feel so sorry for all those other pricks locked up with me. Poor boring motherfuckers, I used to think, what the hell's gonna happen to them. Then one day I snapped. *I* was one of them. For *ten years* I'd been one of them. You see, the way you learn, the way I learned, is to get humble. You have to take a long hard look at yourself and know what you are. Forget who you are, and straightaway you get fucked. ... Men or women who steel themselves to truth are free of all that pressure and that miserable compulsion to maintain their fraud. *Recognize your fraud,* the silly armor you have constructed to save yourselves from pain, that now constricts every move you make and stifles every breath.

We see the poor, stupid lames every time we pass the neighborhoods where we once hung out. Some asshole in a "leather" coat dragging along the ground, a huge, wide-brimmed flop hat that must have come from an outsize shop for farmers in the Australian outback. He holds an "ivory" cane from Thailand that cost $57.00 and is worth every bit of $3.50 and dreams of a candy-striped Cadillac. And this poor excuse for a man will tell you, "This is how I feel! This is me!" *That* isn't how he felt when his mother dropped him on the bed full of blood and scum. *That* wasn't how he felt at school when the teachers gave up on him and the world called him stupid. *That* isn't how he'll feel minutes before they haul him away in a cheap box, a few months or a few years from now. His stupidity—a word that comes from Latin meaning stupor—is just a mirage of self-delusion that occupies the short time between his birth and death.

As John says this, the lights dim, as if the lives of every poor lame from Santa Rosa to San Jose were being snuffed out. The effect is probably an accident, since the lights are sharing current with the tape recorder, and as John lowers his voice, the technician increases the recording level. I think of a line by Beckett: "We give birth astride a grave, the light gleams an instant and it's night once more."

John continues:

When we emphasize truth, there's always a few who think they have to tell their best horror story. The counterpart of the Australian hat is the Australian Girl Scout who was fucked by a kangaroo and so became kinky! But the *real* truths are usually less dramatic—like Mo over there who has perhaps ten, perhaps fifteen, years to live, who's used up most of his life in stupidity and who can't get it back now—and *that* enrages him! If he gets mad at you, it's because history is repeating itself before his eyes. He *both* envies you *and* desperately wants you to wake up before your lives dribble away, too.

A stranger in this room might well think that we get fucking self-righteous and moralistic with each other. It may sound like that at times; so remember, *no one here is pure.* There isn't anyone here who hasn't fucked up long periods of their lives, and who isn't yelling at the inner self they seek to change while they're yelling at you. We do this for ourselves to cement the changes *we've* made. Madison once said, "The evil I try to stamp out in another I dimly perceive in myself." Mo over there was a poor, half-assed nigger who'd spent most of his life in jails. Now he's clean, got a young wife, a child, and a good position with dignity and meaning. He has got *at least* a hundred of you out of jail. Hal, here, was a con man until well into middle age. He turned around, and so can you.

You see we trick ourselves into believing bullshit, 'cause it's comfortable to be dumb and painful to become smart. In a cancer operation, there has to be some blood. We have malignancies inside of us—in that quaking protoplasm we call a soul—and you have to cut yourself open, cut it out, and sew yourselves up. And because it hurts, you'd rather believe in the horse-piss cure, or the bed-rest cure, and if you do that, you'll die. Recognition is pain.

But why are we here tonight and for the next two-and-a-half days? We come here to get away from the everyday world and the pettiness that usually crowds in upon us *and* to get away from the private fantasies that afflict us in our trundle beds with the covers up over our ears. Here we do what every tribe, family, and culture has done all through time. We examine, we feel, we investigate and explore the depth of our existence. We don't parade around carrying statues of Saint Sebastian the Snake Sucker, and we don't dance around fires waving spears. Incidentally I've heard that some of you have got interested in some reincarnation doctrines.

Don't count on it—that's my advice. You've wasted enough vitality in *this* life without building hope of another. Ain't none of you coming back as a long-dick alligator in the Okefenokee Swamp. With *your* luck you'd come back as flies on horse shit in North Dakota!

No, we haven't time for that, because we have to ready ourselves for an intellectually advanced society that fucks poor people as a way of life. We have to explore and discuss the things that are locked deeply in our bellies during most of our working lives. They live down there to give some people ulcers, to drive others nuts, and make the rest into phonies. Either we learn about these things —or they'll control our lives. But if we learn, then we become free to choose. Then we play God and shape that kind of person we want to become. Existence precedes essence—perhaps that's too heavy for some of you, but never mind. Basically what I'm saying is that the shattering of the silly, stuporous games we play, the re-cognition that behind the armor we erect is *nothing.* This is what frees us to become *something,* to others and to ourselves; that is what existential validation *means.*

You see we have to be tough on ourselves to get all this psy-chological, sociological, liberal garbage out of our heads. There are whole professions who live off of us. They have a vested in-terest in what they call our "sickness." And because the emotions are strangled by all their professional bullshit, they live off us emotionally, too. They get their *thrills* by kissin' ass. You program freaks have heard it all. How convicts and dope-fiends are too *sen-sitive* for this world. They *feel* too much. That's *bullshit!* Ain't nobody who steals from his own mother can say he has feeling. Ain't no two-bit dick-suckin' whore who spends her kids' milk money on dope can call herself sensitive. We don't admit this to outsiders, but *most convicts are scum.* Of course, social conditions *made* them that way. They've been fucked over, and they fuck each other. Point is, that's never going to change, *until we take respon-sibility for our condition.* To see that we're scum is to realize that we don't have to be! Recognition clears the way for change.

That "sensitive" shit is put out by lonely creep graduates from Stanford who gotta a Ph.D. in social work and want to get their in-sides wet while masturbating over someone else's lie-filled story, 'cause their own lives are all impotence and professional peeping.

So you're in here to work—to lose the snake-oil image, to

become dignified black men and women or white persons or homosexuals, rather than loudmouth jiggerboos or redneck shitkickers or faggots. Resolve in these three days to add to the sum knowledge of genuine human experience. Express feelings so you know what they look like outside of yourselves. And don't give us the "I-am-what-I-am" routine because most of you aren't *anything,* and, after years of pathetic pretense, *that's* where you'll have to begin. Because I'm fed to the teeth with getting letters from men rotting in prison, pleading over and over again for us to save them—only we haven't the resources, and the reason we haven't is that some *lame* is in my office whining, "Aw, I wanna fuck Agatha, and they won't let me!" So grow up or get out. We've got work to do.

John disappears from the room, leaving the floor to others. Perhaps an hour later or two or three, he will walk back into the room talking, as if only seconds had elapsed between manifestations. There is a buzz of conversation for about two minutes before Hal gavels the room into silence. Now all eyes are upon him as he sits—or rather perches —tall, gaunt, and hunched forward.

The most current trend in the United States is to try to clean up the government from the President downwards. In honor of the lately concluded Watergate investigations and trials we have launched our own Waterhead Hearings to see if we can do some cleaning up of our own. Our two able committee investigators, Jack Behan and Ray Figueroa, have spent the last few hours gathering information on the activities of known Waterheads, several of whom are being called before us this evening to testify.

Our enemy is not crime, because there are few real criminals left outside the boardrooms and legislatures of this country. Nor are we principally concerned with dope-fiends. We are here to root out and cure mickey mousism, which is why we have collected some mice samples.

During the next two hours you are asked to stay continuously seated in this room since you may be called upon at any moment. Those wishing to pee—or make one last effort to drain their heads—should do so now.

There is a rush for the door. A few minutes later the first witness is announced.

"Call Delia Dobson!"

Delia, a pretty twenty-year-old, comes forward nervously and sits down in the brightly illuminated "hot seat." Her complexion is mysteriously darker than her hair, suggesting that either the latter is dyed or the former needs scrubbing. There is a gale of laughter as Hal leans forward and affixes a small, chrome faucet to her forehead. She grins sheepishly as he begins.

"Your name is Delia Dobson—I mean your *real* name?"

"Yes."

"I ask because we've had people here who call themselves Blue-tooth Louie and Snake-oil Seth. How old are you?"

"Twenty."

"And how many grades did you complete in school?"

"I finished the eighth grade."

"What happened to the ninth?"

"I just never went to school."

"Where did you go instead?"

"To juvenile hall."

"Why were you sent to juvenile hall?"

"For not going to school."

"And how long did you run in this circle?"

"Until they sent me to Napa."

"The funny farm?"

"Yes."

"Were there any subjects at school that interested you at all?"

"Not really." Delia shifts uncomfortably.

"You can read and write?"

"Some."

"In the whole wide world, Delia, is there *anything* that engages your interest?"

Delia considers for several seconds.

"Music," she says at last.

"What kind?"

"Country and Western."

"Who's your favorite musician?"

"Hank Williams . . . Johnny Cash . . ."

"You know anything *about* them? I mean, suppose you could get tickets for the Cow Palace, would you go an' listen to Hank Williams tonight?"

"Sure!" Delia is enthusiastic. "I'd do that!"

"You'd have difficulty," says Hal dryly. "Hank Williams died in 1953. Tell me, do you know anything about geography or history?"

"Not really. . . ." Delia seems to be in mourning for Hank Williams.

"What country do you live in?"

"United States."

"United States of *what?*"

Delia furrows her brow and bites her lip with the sheer mental effort.

"California?" she says with more hope than confidence.

The room breaks into laughter, but Hal cuts it short with a formal discourse on the sadness of such ignorance and the immensity of the task facing all of us. Then he continues, "Delia, we have information here that at the age of sixteen you turned a trick with four men, all parolees, in the apartment of your parole officer in Vallejo."

Delia feels that "it wasn't really a trick." The four men had threatened to beat her unless she acceded. Afterward, because she was crying and the parole officer was expected back momentarily, they promised her ten dollars. This they subsequently borrowed from the parole officer and gave to her.

"Makes you wonder who's the trick," Hal muses.

"Are you telling us," another director pursues, "that you have never since turned a trick? Our information is that you were so widely sampled and in such variety that you became known as 'Delia-catessen.'"

"Well . . . I never turned a trick . . . for money."

"For drugs?"

"Yes."

"Ah, these fine distinctions!" Hal shakes his head. "They will swear on their mother's grave that they never stabbed *anyone* at Eighth and Geary—then one-and-a-half hours later you discover it was *Ninth* and Geary! Which brings us to the next allegation." He adjusts his eye glasses.

"The said Delia Dobson did, on the twenty-seventh of June, 1972, prostitute herself in exchange for three small bags of baking powder, assuming the same to be heroin. Correct?"

Delia shrugs.

"I don't really remember. I was burned several times that summer." She is blinking now, and a solitary tear breaks loose to wander past her nose. It is decided to call the next witness. The mood is still humorous, and they do not want to spoil it. Poor Delia has two more days and nights for atonement. Her time is not yet.

The next witness, Grover Phillips, is a slim, six-foot, black Southerner with a natty appearance and an air of poise. Under questioning he tells of moving from Georgia to San Jose at ten and landing in juvenile hall by the time he was seventeen.

"In 1965 did your elder brother move into an integrated neighborhood?"

"Yes."

"And did you celebrate this brotherhood of man by arming yourself and five companions and breaking and entering the house of your brother's next-door neighbor, a white family?"

"Yes."

Hal smooths out a piece of paper that has just been passed to him.

"I read you the following allegation: 'Grover Phillips upon entering the aforementioned premises did climb the stairs and there see a ghost. Whereupon he ran out of the house and into the back seat of the car where he lay crying until joined by his companions. He later sought the advice of his preacher, who said, "Repent brother—dat was de Holy Ghost!"' Correct?"

"Yes and no."

"Which?"

"Well I did see something like a ghost, but the preacher bit is invented."

"How did this ghost appear? You sure it wasn't a member of the Ku Klux Klan?"

"It wasn't like that."

"Was it like Casper?"

"Yeah . . . and dragging something . . ."

"Chains! Clanking!"

"Sort of . . ."

By now the room is convulsed in laughter, and someone has gone to the bathroom to fashion for Grover the "Order of the Chain." Hal has another sheet of paper.

"It says here that Grover lived with and kept for a period of three years a woman seven years his senior, who had nine kids, none of them his own. She finally tired of him and ratted on him to the fuzz. He was arrested for possession minutes after he'd handed her his final paycheck. Earlier that same week he had told his friends 'Love conquers all!'"

There is a burst of clapping at the nobility of this sentiment. Grover grins ruefully.

"True?"

"Yeah . . . mostly. She had five kids."

"I see by your probation report that you have committed

twelve burglaries and got busted for all of them. Other sources have told us that during your last caper you crawled through the skylight of a bathroom, attempted to support your weight upon the ring that held up the shower curtain, but that you, the ring, and the shower curtain all fell down into the tub. You were there apprehended by an angry householder who menaced you with the bathbrush until the police arrived. True or false?"

"It's substantially true."

"A bathtub is the true repository of a Waterhead. We have here for you not only 'The Order of the Chain,' but a water faucet for your head so that you and the bathtub may be truly joined." Hal affixes to Grover's forehead a small faucet.

"Call the next witness!"

"Buzz Coleman!"

Buzz is an amiable, hefty white man in his late twenties.

"You were a native of Vallejo?"

"Yes."

"Information has been laid before this committee that for a considerable period of time you were, if not the best paid informer in Vallejo, at least the most compliant. So much so that you became known as dial-the-fuzz Buzz. Have you heard that name?"

"No."

"Perhaps in order to smoke you out, a dealer sold you a packet of Cremora Coffee Creamer, whereupon you injected it into your arm, swaggered around with the needle still hanging there, shouting, 'Boy! What a high! This is the best I've had.' For which reason you are also known as 'Bullshit Buzz.' Are these allegations true?"

"No one called me those names to my face. The thing with the needle is true."

"We have a note here that while at Napa State Hospital you were found in woman's attire crouching in a garbage can and later described it as an escape attempt. It says also that Buzz stole a color television set from his next-door neighbor and left it on his doorstep while he tried to steal another. There it was discovered by the neighbor, who had come to see his mother about contributing to the March of Dimes. Is that true?"

"The woman's dress thing was someone else in the ward. It's true about the TV."

While flash bulbs pop, Hal affixes the faucet to Buzz's forehead.

And so it goes on, with Volga Mack fiercely denying that she made it with five men in the back of a Volkswagen car, with a sixth breathing on the window to steam it up. She will, however, admit to three in a different location and to statements made at breakfast that morning including, "I will take it in the ear or anywhere with a hole."

"What do you think of such statements?" a female director asks her.

"Pretty desperate," she admits. "Guess I don't respect myself or other women or anyone, really. . . ."

In fact, Delancey is filled with the adventures of Mickey's Mice, and many more stories could be told if these hearings were not being confined to the twenty persons being dissipated.

A golden-haired teen-age resident is notorious for having confessed to burglarizing a large house in the Berkeley hills, while she was high on pills. After breaking in, the full drug reaction hit her, and she was found fast asleep in the master bedroom. The Dissipation christened her Goldilocks, and she was presented with a stuffed baby bear.

Brad was expelled from his Catholic elementary school for an alimentary epithet carved so deeply into a school girl's desk that the desk had to be thrown out. He was *nearly* saved by a young nun who suggested a conversion of the epithet to read "mass holy."

Then there was Brick who boasted of many daring robberies. Careful inquiries revealed a less impressive record. He stole two thousand cream puffs from a local bakery but took so long to dispose of them that he poisoned a substantial segment of his community, who vomited for several hours before turning him in.

He next staged a daring night robbery on the local movie house. Having overcome the cashier in her glass booth, he and a companion emerged into the foyer with their arms full of money only to find that the movie had ended at that precise moment, and three hundred people had burst into the foyer.

The listeners to this tale assumed he had suffered the ignominy of a citizen's arrest.

"Hell no!" he explained. "The crowd was all grabbin' at the money, an' I was kicking left and right with my feet. Then a policeman comes through the crowd, and his night stick slams across my arms so the money flies everywhere, and *more* people is grabbin'. Hell, they arrested ten of us!"

Among the directors investigating the waterheads is Jimmy. Jimmy recalled to me that he once had forty caps in his left-hand pocket and one hundred dollars in his right when the fist of a narcotics agent came right through the panel on his door. He rushed to the bathroom as the fist began grabbing to unhook the chain. In his panic he flushed away the money by mistake! The two agents, arriving only in time to see the toilet complete its action, contented themselves with knocking him down, leaving all the stuff in his left-hand pocket.

So the Waterhead Hearings give way to the main part of the Dissipation, which will last until late Sunday afternoon. The fun is mostly over. Delia, Grover, Buzz, and Volga have had barely a glove laid on them, compared with what is coming as sleeplessness takes its toll and defenses begin to crumble. With sixteen others they will live through the dragging hopelessness of people's lives with some vivid episodes of horror.

Before Friday and Saturday nights are over women will be keening over dead and neglected babies, a black Southerner will be screaming with rage as a savage beating by a sheriff and his deputies is reenacted in mime (take that, boy! An' that!), and a Puerto Rican youth will be kneeling by a lighted coffin, begging his dead father to forgive him for the pain-killing drugs he stole from him during that last illness.

But perhaps it is Delia who will seem the most pathetic of all, not because she has suffered the severest traumas, but because she can find in her whole life not the smallest adventure or even feature with which to regale her listeners. Her words will come in the broken, stilted jargon of a scatological confession, which is the standby of Delancey's hardcore inarticulates.

"Oh, God, I'm such an asshole. I've fucked up everything. I'm not a worth a shit."

Her shoulders will heave as she retches and sobs on her emptiness. John will be standing over her talking more with weariness than with animosity.

"What do you do with *it?* What *can* you do with it? It has no conversation. It cannot sew or cook. It has no skills. Marry it, and you would be insane with boredom before the week was over. What would you *say* to it? Change the channel? Make me a peanut butter sandwich? I suppose you could put your wee-wee into it, but after a couple of days *that* would bore. It's frigid anyway. It starts to take its panties off after three minutes' conversation, only because it cannot think what else to do and it is afraid that you will leave it."

Then he changes his tone, becomes gentler and speaks to her directly, his hand on her shoulder.

"You are not a prostitute, my dear. Prostitutes make money. You are not an addict, because they have habits.

You are a child *playing at being a hooker* and *playing at being an addict*. You are a child in a woman's body. The world out there will destroy you unless you grow up."

Much later still as Sunday dawns the room breaks up into small huddles of people whispering urgently to each other. The "Patch-up" has begun. Someone cradles Delia's head and speaks to her.

But don't you see—John was right? That we, you and me, don't have to pretend any more, don't have to shove our feelings down and sit on them—that means we're free to be anything, now and tomorrow. . . . You have friends in this room—real friends. You made them tonight and last night because you were honest, and there's not one of us that doesn't feel or hasn't felt like you. We'll help you . . . and between us we'll become real women with pride and dignity and purpose. But you know what you have to do to start . . . right now? You have to help Cindy here, who let that kid she was sitting with drown . . . okay? Now what can you say to her?

7

Ex-Convicted
Existentialism

IT IS ONE OF THOSE FOGS that roll down the hills of Marin County like billows on the sea—long rolls of white with ribs of deep green between. For a few moments you can see your way; then another bank of mist envelops you again.

Out of the fog bank and into a sliver of sunshine comes a sinister procession: three black Cadillac limousines with tinted windows. Within sit surrealist figures, their fedoras pulled down, their collars turned up, dark glasses reflecting the walls of mist. A small knot of onlookers gawk at the sight. The transfiguration of the mob? A scene from a Fellini movie? Neither. It is the Delancey Street Foundation coming to San Quentin to claim a released prisoner.

The procession halts by the main gate to the prison. A single mustached figure slips out of the lead car, looks shiftily from side to side, and strides to the front gate.

"Git our friend out here, quick! We ain't seen him in some time, and we wanna take him out ta lunch!"

"Yes, *sir!*" says a voice from behind the grill. Moments later a somewhat bewildered young man, clasping his few belongings in a cardboard box, steps out of the gate.

"Lefty!" says the Mustache, "da Boss wants to see ya!"

They approach the lead vehicle. Five blondes spring from the back seat of the second vehicle and entwine themselves one by one around "Lefty," each raising a heel daintily as she kisses him. Now "da Boss" emerges and gives Lefty a mysterious handshake.

"Good to see ya, boy!" His mouth is distorted by a large cigar that sticks from between his widely spaced teeth like a cannon from its battlements. Now the entire "gang" has appeared—tiny, tall, fat, and thin, some in spats, some in zoot suits, some in shiny leather coats. There are bulges in their pockets, and they hold their hands menacingly within their coats as if about to draw. One by one they shake hands with Lefty; then "da Boss" jerks his thumb. The group slips back into their vehicles, and the procession melts into the mist.

It is fun, of course, but Delancey rarely does anything for one reason alone. Their displays have none of the sledge-hammer moralism of guerrilla theatre. They are closer to parables, with something there for everyone and a couple of points to think about. For the benefit of residents, they are spoofing their own discarded gangsterism, while deriding its projection by the media. For the benefit of prisoners, they are demonstrating the usefulness of having friends "on the outside." For the benefit of everyone, they are showing that guards have a knee-jerk deference to anything that sounds authoritative—no matter how illegitimate. (Lefty's real moment of triumph came when a worried guard muttered, "You shoulda *told* us you were a big shot!") Finally, John is trying to manipulate the symbols that evoke immediate awe and then flip them over to show that Delancey has influence, too, but of a different kind. Delancey will not threaten the families of those guards who give mob members a bad time. It *will* use the mass media to publicize complaints. A few months later John would confront the warden of San Quentin on the "Merv Griffin Show," and the discussion would get to specifics. Delancey marshals its array of forces with one general principle in mind—to surprise and confound everyone except its friends—and sometimes even them. Ex-convicts are not *supposed* to be moral authorities, teaching San Francisco's wealthiest the lessons of Christian brotherhood. They are not supposed to be community benefactors. In a town where old people are poorly protected, you do not expect ex-muggers to provide escort from the bank. You do not expect to see them cruising in their own yacht on the Bay, relaxing by their own swimming pool, serving wine they do not drink themselves, entertaining governors, running credit unions, and preaching nonviolence.

John is an avid student of the existentialist philosophers. Mimi Silbert once worked as Jean Paul Sartre's private secretary. John and Mimi have made operative in their Foundation a central tenet of existentialism. If you accept your basic human predicament—that you have been convicted, stigmatized, truncated in the only life there is, that you cannot handle chemicals, that you need others to keep you sane—these *limitations* are the springboard for a new *freedom*. Being an authentic Irish street kid with the accents and expletives of your origins makes it all the *more* amazing when you fashion those basics with the artistry of an orator. The very contrast between prior "fuck-ups" and their present achievements jolts the audience into admiration. Hide your origins, pretend that you were never a loser; and you slam the door on the fingers of would-be emulators, while confirming the prejudices of the ruling class against all those you once resembled. Only those persons prepared to keep alive the glaring paradox between their own present freedom and their past slavery, *only* they, hold open the door for others to follow.

It is typical, then, of Delancey that Jack and Clare Behan chose to celebrate their wedding on Alcatraz Island, against the backdrop of the prison, and that Mo and Laurie Hodges christened their baby there in a joint ceremony. Dick Kirchman, a "humanist minister" and early square supporter of Delancey, presided. Against the "House of No Relationships" they celebrated their new commitments to each other and to a better life for the child. In the background was sterility. In the foreground was fruition. Delancey had traversed the path between.

Jack admitted to the press that he had spent eighteen years of his life in prisons—ten years for armed robbery in Sing Sing. Mo had served twelve years. After their respective ceremonies they toured the cell blocks to remind them all that in commitment to each other lay the escape from imprisonment of every kind. Mo went into the solitary confinement cell and sat there in the pitch darkness for a minute or so. Jack went down to the dungeons below.

It was spooky. God, I thought, if walls could speak! If there could just have been someone to count all the lives that dribbled away down here in the cold and the darkness. How many just banged their brains out on the rocks and went mad or died? It doesn't leave you, you know. The doors clanging, the whistles blowing, the shouts of the guards, the endless small circles in the exercise yard. I visited Carson State Prison last month to interview some prospective residents. I found them walking around and around a concrete exercise yard in 110-degree heat. There they melt you. In Alcatraz they froze you below ground.

Over my years in prison I must have done at least eighteen months in the hole. Most of it was following a "riot." I was considered a ring leader—although no one led. We all went crazy together when they cut the automatic remission of sentence and told us about it later. The courts had forbidden them to keep us in solitary for more than ten days, but they got around that by making you sit ten days at a clip in total darkness, hauling you before a doctor, who'd check you over, mostly your eyes in case you were going blind, and then they'd throw you back in for another ten, and so on. You try it—with only your toilet bucket for company! I can't shake it even now. I dream at night that they've pinioned my arms behind me and I can't move and I start screaming, and then I awake and Clare's shaking me. "You're all right!" she's saying. "You're here . . . you're with me."

Delancey has now routinized the tour of Alcatraz that the residents first took that day. All through the summer months when school is out they take parties of ghetto kids in their double-decker bus. It rattles down to the wharf. From there they go by boat to Alcatraz where the children are shown the end of the road. It is all understated since the prison itself speaks so powerfully. The day I joined them we saw the corner cell where Al Capone sat for twenty years. All his power and influence could buy him just a glimpse of the sky, his being the only cell in the entire prison that grants that mercy. The children filed into the dining hall, where the now-empty canisters of nausea gas hang over the long tables. As a climax to the tour, a "guard" threw his weight upon a giant lever on the wall. The door to every cell on every tier closed with a clang that resonated throughout the prison. The children jumped at the sound, but Mo Hodges, who was our guide, stood still, leaned on his stick, and remembered. Every day, six times a day, for more than a decade, he'd heard such sounds.

When Delancey decided that forty-six years in prison was long enough for Bob Wells, they chose Jack Behan to spearhead the campaign to free him. For Jack the campaign became a personal odyssey, and he threw himself into it with an energy that proved his own turning point. His team printed campaign buttons and bumper stickers; they made a forty-five-second tape and talked a score of Bay Area radio stations into running it free, once an hour. They dragged their mobile prison cell through the city and the suburbs, asking the curious to imagine being confined in a space eight by twelve feet for forty-six years. They rallied outside San

Quentin and Vacaville, where Bob was imprisoned. They hired the Goodyear Blimp to float over San Francisco, blinking 46 YEARS IS ENOUGH. They got on television news programs and local talk shows. They deluged the California Adult Authority with four hundred letters. When the nephew of the chairman of the Adult Authority was admitted to Delancey, he and his father accompanied Jack Behan to the chairman's office. The chairman had earlier declined to discuss the case, but faced with his own brother and nephew he relented and they talked for hours. Meanwhile Tommy Grapshi, an Attica alumnus, explained to other members of the Adult Authority that pickets of a dusky hue were being readied for duty around their suburban homes. When the Authority met a few days later, a near-unanimity on Bob's release had developed. Charles Garry, Bob's attorney, called it a miracle. John Maher has a more profane explanation.

Much of John's public irreverence comes from his conviction that you dignify your political enemies by waxing righteous over their errors. You should never ride a person out of town when it is possible to laugh him out. A case in point occurred when local Nazis in full regalia invaded a San Francisco School Board meeting. Yvonne Golden, a high school teacher, rose to denounce their presence as an affront and to ask the chair for their removal. Moments later fighting broke out, and the Board, in a curious misjudgment, charged the lady with incitement to riot. Perhaps they thought it was a good way to get rid of Mrs. Golden, who bothered them more than the freak show. It wasn't. A large coalition of activist groups rushed to oppose a board who appeared to favor fascists. They met in heated session at Glide Memorial Church.

At the meeting John rose to his feet to opine that "Nazis should be spanked." Some press critics saw this as an advocacy of violence, but of course it was metaphorical. John uses a kind of existentialism-in-reverse on his opponents. Whereas he and his followers acknowledge the childlike banality of their earlier lives and have created from these fragments a new social purpose, the "purpose" of Nazis must be reduced to its banal elements and treated to childlike "spankings." Do not confirm evil by taking it seriously. Disintegrate your foes in laughter.

To clinch their victory, the coalition pushed a resolution through the Board of Supervisors banning the wearing in public of uniforms of a foreign power. John had to support his friends, but in a situation reeking of overkill he had no intention of losing his sense of humor. Delancey Street's black residents turned up at the hearing in Ku Klux Klansmen's costumes, John, Mon Singh Sandhu, Bill Toliver came as Keystone Cops, and there were several assorted Mountain Men. Nazis in San Francisco, John was implying, were no less laughable.

Some time later I was inveighing against the practitioners of behavior modification and telling John just what I meant to say to them at the annual meeting of the American Psychological Association. But John was shaking his head.

No good—you could talk at each other indefinitely. What you should do is go along to their social hour, tipping off the press in advance. About twenty of you arrive with those little electric buzzers in the palms of your hands. Go through the crowd tapping each of them lightly on the fanny, and when it buzzes and they jump with surprise, you shout "Modify! Modify!"

But even beneath Delancey's more frivolous capers there is often serious wheeling and dealing going on. The double-decker bus and several residents were featured among the I.R.A. contingent in the St. Patrick's Day parade in 1975. I had assumed it was merriment or part of John's private indulgence in the Easter Rebellion (he plays Irish revolutionary songs on his phonograph in the small hours of the morning). But, in fact, a number of local unions are headed by Irish-Americans, and John got several union jobs for his black and Latino residents as a result of his participation in the parade. His politics are Byzantine in their complexity, but the end result is that several hands scratch his back.

Delancey's buildings and businesses have been chosen and created with the same calculated mixture of motives found in much of their other sociopolitical activity. The old Mein mansion, for a time the Russian consulate, stands above the city at the corner of Broadway and Divisidero and commands a magnificent view of the entire Bay Area. John occupies part of the top floor suite as befits the man-of-vision. The immaculate appearance of the mansion with its gardens, sculptures, and flowering shrubs belies at a single glance the popular prejudices against convicts and addicts.

The location of this building and that of the Estonia Hotel, just a block away, are eminently strategic. The wealthy and fashionable area has the effect of insulating Delancey's newer residents from the temptations that abound downtown. It is not that John wishes to escape the poor and their troubles, but he does wish to engage them on *his* terms in *his* time, wherever and whenever he feels strong enough, and with his seasoned troops, not his patients. On most days some group or groups from Delancey sally forth from their strongholds on the hill to confront the oppressors. In the meantime their home base is as free of drug dealers and like predators as can reasonably be achieved within the bounds of the city.

The Ebbtide apartments across the Golden Gate Bridge in Sausalito reveal other elements of calculation. Four buildings, each with two tiers of balcony apartments, overlook a swimming pool decorated with palms and wooden icons. The pool attracts other members of the Foundation who do not live there but are free to use the facilities. It is mostly married and trial married residents of long standing who get to live at the Ebbtide, but all residents can see the rewards of hard work and mutual affection evident there. They have only to hop on one of the constantly circling Delancey buses which link all the buildings and most of the businesses.

Had the intention been to maintain community and facilitate social control, the Sausalito complex could hardly have been better designed. The doors are of glass; the balconies adjoin. The pool and the sun pull residents toward each other. Nearly everyone is visible to everyone else, and the whole is perched atop a very steep hill that insulates would-be sinners from the sink-holes of Sausalito. (John plans to take over Sausalito as soon as he can find the time!)

Delancey's "family style" sidewalk café and restaurant on Union Street had the same mind at work on its design. John conceived it as a trap for chic flies. It spills flamboyantly out onto the sidewalk in splashes of colored umbrellas, flowers, and checkered tablecloths. Funnel-shaped, it draws you down into its interior where large copper pots bubble with hot soup on an old-fashioned stove, and Wild Black Hickok of the Haight grins his welcome. The waiters have a fine line of sotto repartee with each other. Herb Caen of the *San Francisco Chronicle* has reported a sample:

"You'd better take Women's Liberation seriously—like I do, man—because one of these mornings you are gonna wake up and find a broad is President."

Most of Delancey's businesses represent the spontaneous ideas of its residents translated into reality through sustained effort and sheer hard work. John invites written proposals in which concrete plans and sequential steps are spelled out and in which peers have critiqued the idea and/or joined in the sponsorship. This is how the flower business, the moving company, and the construction company all began. The businesses are designed to survive recession. Auto repairs increase in recessions, and people must move to cheaper lodgings. John is so proud of this design that he became quite apocalyptic during the recent recession, a veritable Noah looking for rain clouds, with visions of a doomed humanity beating on his ark.

Several key persons at Delancey invented their jobs and grew with the Foundation. Joe Sierra had a friendship with musicians Mongo Santamaria and Tito Puente and grew from handling this liason to negotiating with thirty national newspapers and journals and dealing with the Paramount Pictures invasion.

Paramount made a fictionalized feature film called *Delancey Street,* using genuine locales and generally stopping all business with miles of cable, blinding lights, and the recruitment of residents to play bit parts and extras.

Joe has a message for those who thought the film was bad. It would have been a lot worse but for him. Early versions of the script had John pushing a female reporter out of his moving car, giving Kung Fu chops to all and sundry, and being wafted from the roof of the Russian consulate by a police helicopter that conveyed him on the end of a rope ladder to rescue one of his residents holed up at the top of Coit Tower! Early rushes contained no women and presented Joe as some kind of Robin to John's Batman.

But the film had its moments: Bill Toliver playing his Old Self in a flop hat and shiny black coat and Walter McGinn playing John singing "Oh What a Beautiful Morning"—a sentiment that John—who can't sing anyway and who sleeps late in the morning—has never yet been known to utter.

Sylvester Herring, a black West Indian, grew with Delancey's political office, known as Tammany Hall. He explains the issues to hundreds of volunteers who rush hither and yon for the candidates of their choice while Delancey's formidable fleet of cars and buses make sure the old folk, veterans, and handicapped get to the polls. Meanwhile John sits by a huge map of the precincts, juggles two telephones, and sticks pins into key parts of a huge map. There is a gleam in his eye. John's heaven-on-earth is a smoke-filled room with St. Peter as a power broker, surrounded by horse-trading cherubs.

Delancey could never have succeeded as it has without its squares. Lawyers Danny Weinstein and Mike Berger not only cope with hundreds of details on behalf of residents, but also use the law aggressively against opponents of the Foundation.

"Look!" says John. "We're not likely to *win* this action, but we can keep the sale tied up. We just need a legal stiff in a back room to keep our suit active."

"You have one," says Mike with the ghost of a smile.

Dugald Stermer, another square, acts as a one-man advertising agency and artist-writer extraordinary. Widely regarded as a hopeless case of compulsive niceness and irredeemable goodwill, he reserves his rage for those he imagines are ripping the Foundation off and for the copy of his political announcements.

"If you are aware of the English government's concentration camps in Long Kesh and its policies of economic retaliation against women and children who are related to concentration camp victims and still you don't help, then GOD DAMN YOU TO HELL!"

An unforeseen dividend of Delancey's dramatic style is a home-grown crop of delightful eccentrics. Patrick O. McGillycuddy III is a director and the foremost discoverer of the fact that the Foundation's moral structure is paradoxical. As we have seen, depending on whether you are in Games or elsewhere, you behave rudely or politely, you subvert by impulse or you defer gratification. Pat is the only person capable of expressing *both* moods simultaneously. "Everything is *wonderful, it's fine!"* he'll shout, his face suffused with fury. It is possible to enjoy with Pat a conversation out of Harold Pinter. The twists and turns of Pat's life have been visited on his syntax and facial expression. Abandoned by his parents at the age of eighteen months, he grew with a speech impediment. He has since learned to shift this disadvantage and perplexity to his listeners. He was last heard of in Chapter 5 hustling stolen stereos from the back of his car with the aid of a police informer. This evening he is sitting at the bar nursing a cup of tea and staring ruminatively into its depths.

"Hi Pat—what are you thinking about?"

"Aswam," he says with a finality that suggests that only a fool could fail to understand exactly what he means. My mind is racing, trying to remember earlier conversations which might help to decode this one. Pat has trouble with his *n*'s and *m*'s so what he probably means is Aswa*n*. Pat rephrases entire thoughts and sentences to avoid these deadly letters.

"You're thinking of Egypt then—the dam?"

"Extracts of cactus in the water supply—see?"

"No, I'm sorry I don't."

Pat sighs, eyeing me with resignation. Lifting the veil of ignorance from the eyes of the multitude is full-time work. He decides to give me another chance.

"Stops the evaporation. Water expands." He's spelling it out slowly for me. "Boom!" He slaps his hand on the counter, eyes shining at the prospect of some distant cataclysm.

"The whole of Egypt swept into the Mediterranean by a tidal wave sixty-feet high. *And all because they laughed at him!"*

He shakes his head, his sympathy clearly with some risible Moses rather than the Egyptians. He appears to be reenacting the scene in his teacup. He swishes the dregs around the cup as the tea leaves float helplessly in his Deluge. He smiles down at them. (Pat's serious facial expressions are reserved for his jokes.) Then he turns to me with the punch line: *"Worked its way through the sewer system."*

I shake my head.

If you persevere with Pat, there is always a perfectly logical explanation, even if the premises are suspect. He has been reading a novel about the Aswan Dam. The tragic hero has refined a substance extracted from cactus plants that can be sprayed upon drought-threatened crops to prevent evaporation. This genius attends an international food conference in an Egyptian town close to the Aswan Dam. He explains his discovery and is laughed off the stage. Returning to his lodgings, he flushes five gallons of his world-saving substance down the toilet before committing suicide. The substance enters the reservoir, prevents the usual evaporation, and so overloads the dam that it bursts, flushing the conferees, the town, and most of Egypt into the Mediterranean. The moral—and this accounts for Pat's obvious relish—is that those who fail to heed the divergent thoughts of mavericks are liable to be swept away in short order.

It would be entirely false, however, to leave the impression that Pat is the house clown. On the contrary, he is closer to its hero, and the Foundation might never have made it without him. In the days when its survival was touch-and-go, Pat worked first as a car-wash attendant, then as a messenger boy at an automobile showroom on Van Ness Avenue, where he rose by leaps and bounds to manage the entire dealership. Every penny he earned he gave to the Foundation, asking only for a few dollars to be sent to his foster parents who were old and ailing. Then he began the process of setting up Delancey's businesses one by one.

The very same tricks of language that once caused Pat to be locked up lent him an impressive air of mystery as soon as he was promoted to high position. The difference, as John would probably point out, is one of power. When the impotent mystify authorities, they get screwed. When the powerful mystify a client, they make sales and get commissions.

The clearest case of using your past to feather your future is Delancey's one and only Albanian booster, Tommy Grapshi. He claims a sinister relationship on his mother's side to the late King Zog. One of his aliases is Bonaparte. He dropped it to avoid derision, but picks it up again, on occasion, as a conversation piece. Standing five feet seven inches he feels the occasional need for a tall hat and a Corsican connection.

Grapshi's "thing" at Delancey is his Thieves' Theatre—variously known as Bonaparte's Boosters, the Rip-off Seminar, The Theatre of the Abhorred, and The General Thievery Make-out Show. It consists of a four-person group of ex-shoplifters who tour department stores to reveal in dramatic form their various techniques. On these occasions Tommy enjoys himself immensely. It is his Magnificent Confession. For years he melted into crowds to pick pockets, living not only in obscurity, but *through* it, and grateful that the attention of his victims was turned toward sundry important persons, while he slipped the inside out.

Now that he has "turned around," as residents put it, he gets two hundred fifty dollars per performance *and* the attention, too—a far superior m.o. After years of hiding his artistry, he now can display it, and he does so with an irrepressible bounce and impish grin. Watching Tommy perform reminds me of a childhood visit to a pantomime to see Max Miller, The Cheekie Chappie.

Not that Tommy plays the Rip-off Seminar for laughs. Much of the time he resonates with security-mindedness, elaborates on the world's social malaise, and makes incisive analyses of "your average bored housewife." But there is always his grin—as if he'd swallowed the canary and was on the verge of a dramatic regurgitation. You cannot take him entirely seriously, because he refuses to take himself seriously. The Albanian Conjurer has something up his sleeve and it's tickling him.

The son of a professional family, Tommy came to America as a toddler in 1934, in the company of his mother, to join his father. The language barrier proved insuperable, and his father was obliged to work as a cook. As the Depression deepened he became unemployed. Tommy's mother suffered a mental breakdown when they moved away from the small Albanian community on New York's Lower East Side and settled in East Harlem. His younger brothers were sent to a foster home while Tommy remained with his parents. His mother retreated first to girlhood and then to childhood, lisping only in Albanian. Tommy's memories of that time are obliterated by an oppressive sense of shame. His parents were destitute, foreign, and mad. He invited no one home and became street-wise, picking pockets, boosting, and dealing a bit on the side. His favorite game was to don his best blue suit and slip into important public functions by tagging along at the tail of some group of prominent persons, most of whom were too dignified to challenge him and so surrounded by deference as to protect him. ("Who *was* that little man at our table?")

On one particular December evening I accompany Tommy, Mo, Vivian, and Nancy to a performance before the sales staff of a Palo Alto department store. The staff is young and female, barely out of high school, and we are in cramped quarters, the conference room at a motel.

Tommy rises before his audience and introduces himself and his colleagues. Behind him are the props: an electric cash register, a row of dresses and suits hanging on a rack, and a large oblong box, gift-wrapped with a blue ribbon.

He is forty-four years old Tommy tells us. Seventeen of those years—more than half his adult life—have been spent behind bars. He has more than fifty arrests on his record, mostly for petty thievery, shoplifting, shortchanging, and picking pockets. His life has been a revolving door—six months inside, then rarely more than two or three months before rearrest and reconviction.

Strategically the whole thing was stupid and self-destructive. He does not, he assures us, stand here as a mastermind to be respected much less emulated, but we should understand that shoplifters can be *tactically* cunning and that their techniques, where successful, will be repeated time and again. What makes shoplifting so hard to combat is this very combination of recklessness with ingenuity.

Parenthetically we might note that the crazy lifestyle allied to a tactical intelligence is typical not just of Tommy, Pat, and most shoplifters, but of Delancey Streeters generally. They operated at such high levels of risk that even the Keystone Cops would have caught them eventually. In the short run, however, people like Tommy could live in relative comfort and support sizable drug habits. As the years passed, he found himself totally unqualified for any other work. "Before you know what's happening, that's *all* you know."

Driven to keep up appearances before his friends, among whom ready cash and generosity were marks of status, Tommy lived in short affluent bursts of ripping and running, wedged between lengthening prison sentences. The twenty dollars he received each time he was released was just enough to transport him back to his old haunts and habits. Besides, his months of enforced boredom and austerity made him yearn for the weeks of excitement and high living. He oscillated perpetually between maximum security and maximum danger, and each phase contained its own secret craving for the other.

The pattern broke when he turned forty, as he suddenly became obsessed with a single thought: he would die in jail. He wrote innumerable letters to his brother begging that his body be burned on the outside. When he heard of Delancey on the prison grapevine, he became convinced that it could reprieve him.

"There's a common mistake you make in sizing up shoplifters," Tommy explains. "You underestimate his sheer recklessness. I once pulled out a whole drawer of Parker 51 pens, hoisted it on my head, and made straight for the main door exit. There was a doorman and for a second I saw his fisheyes upon me, but I knew that I mustn't even break step. I marched straight up to him, gave him a cheerful grin, shouted 'Carpenter! Excuse me!' *and he opened the door for me.* People are *embarrassed* to upset the confident expectations of others. It makes them anxious. An experienced booster will always make it tense and awkward for you to question his purpose.

"It is especially easy to rattle young women," Tommy sounds sympathetic, almost paternal. "I'd never play the same tricks on some old battle-axe that I try on an impressionable youngster. I used to sense social awkwardness and go straight for the jugular. It could be a little thing—like pretending to recognize the young woman behind the counter. Odds are she'll feel so embarrassed trying to remember who I am and guilty for not remembering that I or my partner can clean out the store around her while she blushes.

"A black booster, like Mo here, can easily embarrass a white person. . . ."

Mo Hodges, the back of whose head joins his neck at some uncertain point on a single bulge and who looks like an African version of Oddjob, suddenly thrusts his face toward the audience.

"Do you object to my color?" he snarls. "You don't *like* black folks?"

Most of the front row turns scarlet, and one girl gives a shrill nervous laugh. There is a general exhalation of breath as they realize it is a joke.

"While you're stammering out your denials, his partner—that's me—has walked out with the cash register. . . ."

Tommy's voice has come from close to the side door. Sure
enough he has the cash register in his arms. The audience
half-turns, gasps to see him there, then breaks into applause.

"The booster strikes the moment he sees you under some
psychological disadvantage," Tommy goes on. "In this case
you wouldn't expect a nice looking white fellah like me," he
grins broadly, "to be working with the likes of him."

"Or you wouldn't expect a *man* like me"—Mo expands
his massive chest—"to have a colorless little sidekick."

There is to be a demonstration; Vivian and Nancy move
to center stage. Vivian, a black woman, is behaving "shiftily," holding up one dress as a screen and fiddling con-
spicuously with another. She gives many a sidelong glance
like a stage villain about to confide her dark deeds to the
audience. Nancy—sweet, demure, and lily-white—approaches a salesman, played by Tommy.

"That woman—over there!" she whispers. "She's behaving strangely . . . I'd keep an eye on her."

Tommy thanks her excitedly, hunches his shoulders like
an amateur detective, and goes stalking. In the meantime,
sweet Nancy helps herself.

This scene dissolves into another. Nancy is at the cash
desk, when Mo, leaning heavily on his stick, hobbles up to
her with a small purchase. As the cash drawer opens, he
leans forward and tries to reach for a pack of cigarettes; but
the cane slips, and he crashes to the floor. There is pan-
demonium for he has fallen into the laps of the front row of
the audience, which is sitting on the floor. He was actually
supposed to fall on the *other* side of the register, but that
row of pink thighs was too tempting for him.

His last-minute change of tactic has thrown everything
into chaos. Tommy was ready to leap for the open drawer of
the cash register, but with Mo in the way, he has to ap-

proach from the other side. The spring holding down the money catches half of it. The rest flies from Tommy's hand as he tries to pull it free and scatters like confetti over the fallen Mo and the squeaking row of young women pinioned beneath him.

Grapshi grins and cracks the joints of his fingers. "Out of practice," he admits. "That play money has the wrong texture." The audience, which is now understandably confused about where humor ends and accident starts, is on the verge of collective hysteria.

"Now you realize how we all got caught!" says Mo, who is taking an unnecessarily long time getting to his feet.

The incident reminds me of a remark John once made to a general assembly of residents.

"Ain't nobody more stupid than a cop or store detective—'cept possibly a prison guard. They're probably the stupidest there is. . . . Now we people here got *caught* by cops and caged by guards, so what's that make *us?"*

Certainly, Tommy and Mo would have gone back to jail for that particular performance. But I don't get to feel superior for long. Tommy is doing his shortchanging routine with Nancy at the cash register. He buys a small item, gives her a ten, finds a dollar, asks for his ten back and while she is counting it out, gives her another ten and asks for twenty back. At the end of it all he is nine dollars and fifty cents ahead, she is confused, and so am I. Then the audience begins to see the point. "Oh! Oh!" cries a girl in the second row. "Brilliant!" shouts another a few seconds later, and for the next minute amid "oohs" and "ahhs" everybody tells everyone the point. Except me. Even worse, I still don't see it after Tommy has demonstrated it *twice* back at the Club for my sole benefit. All I do see is less money than I began with. John may have to add another category of fools.

But Mo is back to the subject of unconscious racism

among store employees, and his youthful audience is looking punch-drunk.

"Employees rarely consider that black and white customers might team up to rob the store, and they tend to be more
suspicious of black customers in general. After my white
partner had spent more than six months telling store detec-
tives to look out for me, we tried it in reverse. I said, 'Look
out for that shifty white man!' And what d'you know, that
detective never took his eyes off *me* until we left the store!
'Course if the detective's black. . . . Nor should you think
that boosters are all black and white brothers. The most I
ever got from my falling trick was three hundred bucks, one
half of the six hundred which my white 'brother' pulled from
the cash register. Only the next day it said in the local paper
that over a thousand had been stolen."

"The easiest booster to spot," Tommy is back at center
stage, "is your average bored housewife out for a thrill.
She'll be self-conscious and nervous. I used to spot 'em very
easily when I was boosting myself. A couple of times I was
forced to speak to the woman concerned. 'Look lady!' I
said. 'You're drawin' the heat. Why don't you operate at
this end of the store and I'll work *that* end—that way you
may draw the heat away from me!'

"Another simple one is the man with his jacket over his
arm, especially on a warm day when jackets aren't
necessary. Look especially for jackets with their sleeves
tucked into each pocket—that arrangement can hold a
dozen silk scarves or ties."

A teen-age employee wants to know what she should *do*.
Suppose she suspects someone, what then?

"There's two methods. What really stopped me were il-
legal threats. Some bouncer, probably hired from the Actor's Studio, would sidle up to me and whisper, 'We know
you're ripping us off, punk! Next time you show your weasel
face in this store, you'll get caught with three ninety-dollar

suits, if I have to wrap 'em round your neck personally, understand?' I can't advise that course of action . . . and it wouldn't be appropriate for you ladies." There's a nervous titter in response to this. "Nevertheless you can follow the principle of fighting ambivalence with ambivalence. Just as the boosters are giving out mixed signals to confuse you, you must give out mixed signals to confuse them.

"A good way is to pursue a suspect relentlessly across the floor with 'let-me-help-you' requests. Make sure a colleague knows what you're doing and is watching for partners. If your suspect tries to dismiss you, exude charm and say, 'But you come here often and seem to have trouble finding what you want.' That's an innocent remark *if* the suspect's innocent. Otherwise it's very pointed. Or you can ask for his name and address, saying sweetly that '*regular* customers like you are informed by mail of our periodic sales; then they can start buying.' Never accuse directly unless it's an arrest. Keep the initiative in a conversation, constantly heightening the tension by being as enigmatic as possible, while smiling.

"A store's entire policy should have this dual purpose of polite service and careful scrutiny. I've shown several dress shops how they can serve demitasse coffee directly outside their fitting rooms; that way a woman can ostensibly serve coffee while actually watching for those ladies who emerge with two new dresses underneath their old one."

In fact, the advantage is so hugely with the thief that only a store run by misanthropes and paranoid gumshoes could protect itself completely. Grapshi's speciality was to throw a "heart attack" on the main floor. He popped tablets into his mouth to simulate blood-flecked froth. As he fell dramatically to the floor, he would foam and claw at his breast. His partner would shout "heart attack!" to make sure that the performance was correctly identified and then start to gather up merchandise as others rushed to the scene.

I am thankful that Tommy is *not* demonstrating this one, since his audience is still reeling from the full weight of Mo. It is safer, Tommy tells us, to have a third partner who claims to be a doctor; otherwise you can throw a fit yards from a genuine doctor and have the bastard call your bluff while you're frothing on the ground. More than once he had to make a miracle recovery—and run.

As the exposition continues, I begin to feel an unfashionable sympathy for the store. What if someone *really* collapsed and all the employees did during his death rattling was to lock their cash registers and hug their furs? It would exemplify "fascist Amerika" and "rampant materialism," would it not? Or perhaps a wise precaution.

Another teen-ager raises her hand and is recognized.

"What are we supposed to do after the thief has left the store? He or she can't be arrested *until* they leave, but once out they refuse to return. A couple of weeks ago I returned from lunch to find three men in the parking lot stuffing some of our overcoats into their car. I pulled myself up to my full height [she is every bit of five feet] and shouted, 'That is stolen merchandise! Return with me to the store.' They just laughed, climbed into the car, and as they pulled out, one of them leaned from the window and patted me on the head."

"You got their license number?" Mo asks.

"Sure!" She sounds disgusted. "The plate was attached by an elastic band to one underneath."

There is an awkward silence. Tommy wants to say that the store sells cheap produce, hires cheap labor, and attracts cheap boosters, and so loses by theft some part of what it saves in wages; but he decides in favor of tact and turns instead to the "boosting box."

He holds up a tall, oblong parcel gaudily gift-wrapped.

"These are used extensively around Christmas-time and are difficult to distinguish from genuine presents. If your own store gift wraps, try to have something small but distinctive about the wrapping. Boosting boxes are usually large and long. Observe their placement. If the customer sets his parcel upright directly beneath a rack of merchandise, beware."

Nancy and Vivian, working as a pair, set the box down close to the rack. While Nancy holds one dress at arm's length appraising it, Vivian drops a second dress into the box, behind Nancy's screen. There is a soft "phut" as the spring-loaded flap at the top of the box snaps back into place. Within seconds four dresses have been stowed away.

"Always look for signs of soiling on the box. Boosters are careless and often forget to rewrap their box every day. The other giveaway is the end flap. It rarely fits exactly, and you can often hear the snap. Nancy will now model a pair of booster's bloomers."

Nancy raises her skirt a few modest inches and reveals old-fashioned bloomers with elastic legs just above the knees. She opens her blouse to reveal a longline bra, before she dons a loose raincoat. Again she poses as a customer along with Vivian—this time without the box. When Vivian lowers the dress she has held between Nancy and the audience, the rack is once more empty, as both stroll nonchalantly away.

"Anyone notice anything about Nancy's gait?" Tommy asks. "She *walked* in, but she's *waddling* out 'cause her thighs are twice the size." Nancy raises her skirt to reveal elephantine legs. There is laughter.

Someone wants to know what to do about a stickup. There was one on the other side of the shopping center last week, and it's made everyone nervous.

"Well, it's not going to be a professional. With no disrespect to you—professionals aren't going to bother with a medium-price store. If it happens at all—it's gonna be scared kids playing Arrogant Brotherhood or a kid on his own doing a Lone Loser act. Give him what he wants 'cause he's as likely to shoot as to pee in his pants. Look hard for distinguishing marks—like scars or tattoos. Most holdup men are remembered as four yards high and twice as ferocious because the victim is so scared, but small telltale marks are harder to mistake.

"We can't end this show without reminding you that a great deal of shoplifting, perhaps most, is done by store employees, so a We versus Them attitude can be dangerous. I've even known cases where an employee pointed the finger at a customer to hide her own shenanigans. Watch this scene especially."

Mo limps up to the register with a necktie, priced at $11.98. Vivian is at the register. "Hi, good looking!" she says. "I like your face—why don't we say an even ten?" Mo exits happily and quickly before she changes her mind. His ten goes straight into Vivian's purse, without benefit of bell.

"A tie or scarf can be thrown casually over the top of the register while the wrong price is rung," Tommy warns.

"What about suits for false arrest?" the personnel manager wants to know.

"I'd threaten them sometimes, but it was an empty threat. Whose gonna believe someone with a record like mine? Occasionally we'd lure a particularly obnoxious detective into arresting us—and then when we proved to be clean, threaten the store, but it was never particularly successful. I'd advise that you stick to your guns."

The evening is drawing to an end as Tommy confides his favorite story.

"Where I really made the best money was not in stores at all, but in movie houses—or to be exact during one movie, *Ben Hur.* I'd sit next to a lady, wait for the chariot race, and get into her purse while she gawked at Charlton Heston galloping around the circus. I must have made ten thousand dollars—and, God, was I bored with that film!"

Much as Tommy loves this story, and broadly as he grins,

there is always a trace of enmity in his voice. It is as if those women deserved everything they lost, leering at charioteers while a very personable young fellow, a chip off the old Zog, was sitting beside them in the dark.

The personnel manager has risen to give thanks to the players. I tense myself in readiness. This is where Grapshi grabs the manager's wallet, but not tonight. Tommy keeps away.

"I was waiting for your climactic steal," I complain in the car on the way back to San Francisco.

"Wasn't right," says Tommy. "Not enough room and that manager was real sharp. You never know what he might do to you by instinctive reaction."

Someone laughs from the back seat. "We don't want to do a Kenny Hepper."

The reference is to Delancey's first official graduate, now a director of the Foundation. On his final caper he tried an assault-with-intent-to-rob and chose as his intended victim none other than the judo instructor to the San Francisco Police Department. His last memory before he awoke in the hospital was flying through the air. . . .

Dissipating the Author:
The Early Hours

I HAD NOT INTENDED to volunteer for "Dissipation," but it's Wednesday night and the Game is "on" me.

"The Lord Observer spends all his fucking time interviewing individuals. He seriously expects to hear the truth from them! Can't you shed your role for a few hours, Your Lordship—go help the moving company. . . ."

"Last week," I say.

"Or wash dishes at the restaurant."

"Tomorrow."

"What's that?"

"I helped the moving company last week, and I'll work at the restaurant tomorrow."

They try another tack.

"Well, if you *really* want to know what it feels like to be a resident—if you're really capable of coming down from that great height above us all—you'd volunteer to be dissipated."

"I thought you compelled people . . ."

"Some residents are compelled. Others volunteer. *You* volunteer."

"Okay, I 'volunteer!' "

They seem surprised.

"You sure?"

"Well, it's a spurious distinction, isn't it? I'm an Englishman and a social-psychologist, two categories of person of which you seem infinitely suspicious. So if I'm to write this book, I must scotch this notion of my distance and disdain as soon as possible."

"That's Friday week."

"Fine!"

After the game, Jesse Senora is hovering over me, a gleam of expectancy in his eye.

"You *really* going to sign up for the Dissipation?" he asks, looking like a pintsized vampire obsessed by a smooth, white throat.

"Of course."

"Now," he says, proffering me a form with a dozen scrawled names, of which at least half are crossed out again with such force that the pens have ripped the paper. I shrug and sign.

"You mean I shan't see you for forty-five hours!" My wife is furious. "You let yourself be operated on by those mad surgeons—and there isn't even anything *wrong* with you . . . well not *seriously* wrong." She picks crossly at the loose hairs on my collar. "And you'll be blotto for days afterward!"

The more I think about my approaching ordeal, the worse I feel. I seek out "Kirchperson," a fellow square and Delancey's real-estate developer, a man much teased about his bachelorhood and his singular affection for his dog. It is one of his gloomy days.

"Couldn't stop crying," he recalls, eyes downcast like Eeyore contemplating his burst balloon. "Ever been awake —I mean *wide* awake—for sixty hours with everyone screaming at you and at one another?" He shakes his head. I decide to seek no more comfort.

A number of things are worrying me. First, I have nothing
buried "deeply in my gut" that is "fucking with me," and
yet this is an operating assumption of the Dissipation. Second, I really *do* think I am special and creative, but so does
every superannuated flower child for whom the needle fills
the vacuum of an ersatz originality. Delancey rightly ridi-
cules such pretension. I could do my man-alone-against-the-
multitude number, but that could subvert their policies.
Besides, why demand special treatment, when I'm writing
about the Dissipation in general? Finally, it is also a part of
their doctrine that each individual should embrace his ethnicity, "clean it up" with his parents, and be reconciled with
his roots. Yet Hal Fenton is one of those Americans with a
nostalgia for an England replete with David Nivens and Sir
Aubrey Smiths understating the restlessness of the natives. I
doubt my ability to sob convincingly over this vanished
"heritage."

The appointed evening comes. It is to be unusual. John is
away in Indiana. Hal has barely recovered from a cancer
operation and is looking distinctly sepulchral, an *éminence
grise* amid the failing light in the conference room at the
Russian consulate. Indeed he looks *so* ill that I wonder if we
won't get a message at the witching hour to say that he died
last week in the hospital and has been haunting us since.
  The floor is covered with wires, and men with earphones
and mouthpieces mutter to themselves in the gloom or
whisper to each other in conspiratorial clusters. About
twelve chairs and four sofas are arranged in an oval to make
room for about twenty "dissipants" and eight "whips," who
urge the dissipants to confess. The latter are easily recog-
nizable by their headgear.
  I sit down in a chair of medium comfort in the hope I'll be
allowed to keep it. I am not.
  "That's the whip's chair!" says Jesse, showing his teeth in

a broad smile. As I rise, he demands my watch, my wallet, and my keys, caressing each as he drops them into a large brown envelope. All this takes me by surprise.

"May I call my wife? I promised to . . . she wants to know the setup."

"No calls of any kind to outside persons during the Dissipation," he replies, as if the prohibition were his purest pleasure.

I am obliged to squeeze into a fourth place on one of the sofas next to a Junoesque black woman called Loreen, who takes an exceedingly dim view of my intrusion. "Do we have to sit this close for forty-five hours?" she asks, glaring balefully at me and further averting her nostrils. We do, with the broken spring of the sofa challenging my coccyx and Loreen's formidable hips hemming me in.

Hal begins the introduction. There are no tricks, he tells us. Everything is above board. I feel paranoia welling up inside me. As if the man were capable of speaking two consecutive sentences without an ulterior motive! All my positive feelings about Delancey have evaporated, and I'm looking at the whole environment with a savage eye. What about the time Mo Hodges pretended to be shot and writhed on the floor with tomato ketchup spurting from his side— wasn't *that* a trick? And what about the shadow of the hanging woman which they projected onto the wall? What kind of an idiot do they think I am, these "reformed" con men?

I begin to mutter epithets to myself, devastating put-downs with which to lash them if they try to mess with me. To Hal I will say, "There are more things in heaven and earth than are dreamt of in the philosophy of an unlicensed real-estate salesman." Ha! *That* will get him! I don't say it, of course; it sounds too snobbish but, God, do I feel it!

Hal's short introduction over, the whips engage in repartee among themselves, with the dissipants as targets of the jest. In my mood of growing antagonism, they are ex-

ceedingly unfunny, and with the dissipants being too scared
for anything but a nervous giggle, each ensuing remark falls
flatter than the last. The whips sound to me like a bunch of
cronies snickering over the great unwashed.

"Why," one of the whips is asking, "would a person put
his name on a list, cross it off, write it up again—and then
come in here and sit silently for twenty minutes."

The answer is obvious: because they are scared silly,
which is exactly the intention of these inquisitors. But one of
the dissipants, Linda, breaks the silence. Haltingly she asks
to speak about herself.

"Sit back for a moment," Hal replies, "and listen to our
theme song." He mutters into the intercom and then tells us
to follow the words of the song on the mimeographed pieces
of paper which have been distributed. Moments later the
voice of Nina Simone wails forth.

I wish I knew how it would feel to be free
I wish I could break all the chains holding me
I wish I could say all the things I should say
Say them loud, say them clear for the whole round world to hear
I wish I could share all the love that's in my heart
Remove all the bars that keep us apart . . .

There is more of the same, and although the song proves
exceedingly effective—a few hours from now few will be able
to read it without breaking—it only succeeds in souring me
still further. I have never responded to the blues idiom, and
this is exactly the kind of thing one hears on the radio as a
prelude to advertisements for underarm spray deodorants
and tidi-flush sanitary bowl cleansers. Now there is every
prospect of being tidi-flushed thrice in every goddamned
hour until late Sunday afternoon. Someone should pull the
plug on the lot of them!

Linda starts to "run her story," a farmer's daughter saga

of interminable length and tedium. It reminds me of a pictorial satire on *Christina's World* in a soft-core pornographic magazine. The whips are impatient and persistently interrupt her story with smart asides, which only mires her deeper in the farmyard and slows her account of her loss of innocence. So that her bloomers, first tugged at 10:20 P.M. (by Hal's watch), do not reach her knees till 11:30!

Later I will be ashamed of my foul mood. Linda is one of the kindest women in the Foundation and has always made it her special mission to welcome me. I notice that the eyes of one of the whips, Abe Irizarry, are moist. He will tell me later that he saw in Linda's awkward exposition his own struggles to express himself.

Perhaps I can't sympathize because I'm expecting an attack, and sure enough it comes, as they leave poor Linda compromised behind the combine harvester. Hal is perched beside and above me, a great horned owl with a hearing aid. He murmers instructions to an unseen tape technician and announces that the next tune is dedicated to Charles Hampden-Turner and provides an exploration of the contradictions in his life.

First comes the sound of hoofbeats, then a cry, "The British are Coming!" Then the march of the Grenadier Guards, intermingled with musket fire, and then—the whole thing escalating to a fearful cacophony—comes a fife and drum rendering of "The Spirit of '76." While the fifes and drums are clearly "winning" over the British Grenadiers, the real losers are the audience. I suspect the influence of Walt Disney. There is a lot of good-natured laughter in which I join. But Hal is making his point.

"Tell me, Charles, with that Great Mind of yours, do you see any connection between the British coming over to *observe* the colonists and getting their asses kicked, and you coming here to Delancey to observe us?"

"Even a tiny mind would tell you that the connection is tenuous. I doubt any empires are maintained by observation."

Dugald comes to Hal's rescue. "No, but they looked down at the natives with the same sort of *contempt* that you do—staying above and staying apart."

He is coming close to my mood of the moment, and yet I am riled to be blamed for feeling hostility while he and his cronies actually exhibit it.

"I confess to feeling angry and apart," I say. "But don't *you* at this moment occupy a station above me? Even in the heyday of imperialism—for which I am no apologist—I doubt the British referred to themselves as 'whips' and imposed sleeplessness and sensory deprivation."

"Fucking Christ, you're an arrogant bastard!" One of the dissipants is hastening to identify with the aggressors. "Sensory-fucking-bullshit! Why don't you speak plain English!"

As I try to defend myself, Loreen, squeezed into the sofa beside me, has started to whisper furiously in the proximity of my left ear.

"*Wot* a mothafucker! Bullshitter! Running off at his fuckin' mouth! *Wot* a mothafucker!"

I form the impression that she is talking less to me than complaining about me to herself, but going on as she does for most of the time I'm speaking, it is exceedingly disconcerting.

But Hal has another musical melange for me. It begins with fascist band music, Nuremberg noises, Hitler shouting, bombs whistling, air raid sirens, and explosions. It ends with Churchill's voice resonating from the debris, invocations of the Empire and its finest hour, and so deafening a rendition of "Land of Hope and Glory" that even Loreen's fierce whispering about my carnal knowledge of my mother becomes inaudible.

Before this latest musical presentation has ended Hal is haranguing me about the British introducing opium to the Chinese. *"I* was taught," I say, "that we introduced trousers, syphilis, and the Bible." But Hal is off on opium and other shameful policies.

"Is it *still* the land of hope and glory?" someone wants to know.

"And where is the Empire *now?"* Do I not perceive the same lamentable decline in my own character, the same pomp disguising wretched circumstances?

I take the opportunity to explain that I have never identified in the least with Britain's imperial destiny. I applaud the revolt of nearly all colonies and people under subjection, especially in Vietnam. I am too young to have thrilled to Churchill's words. There are nonmilitaristic elements in British culture that move me deeply, and I will gladly supply the whips with these. In the meantime, a minor conflict has been brought to mind by the preceding noises. I was once very close to my Austrian nanny, who largely took the place of my mother after she died. Much of my most intimate childhood environment—the storybooks, the nursery, and my nanny—were German or Austrian. I was deeply disturbed by the execration of all things German that lasted from my fifth year to my eleventh. It was as if the symbols of my childhood were being uprooted, and the visible reduction in my nanny's status as I grew up did not help. In 1945, I found her crying over pictures of Belsen and Auschwitz. "To think that he [Hitler] was Austrian!" she sobbed. I cried, too, for both of us.

The whips seem more irritated than pleased by this story. It is as if I'd thrown them a curve, although one of them, as we shall see, has taken careful note, and my nanny will reappear in the next chapter beside a lighted coffin! For the moment they are on to another subject.

Why, they want to know, did I say in a Game the Friday

before last that I had no experience of ex-cons and ex-addicts? This could *only* mean that I saw them as a race apart and failed to comprehend that Delancey's real mission was the curing of general stupidity, of which I myself was a prime example.

There follows a general discussion of the sheer depth of my loneliness, the wreckage of my emotional life so clearly written on my face in the drooping of the corners of my mouth and in the elongation of my upper lip. Will I nominate the friends, if any, that I have made in the Foundation since I came? I name half a dozen. Someone claims to have read my books. They are technical manuals, he reveals, incorrigibly complex, a shelter from the emotional demands of real people. When will I get involved? When will I try to grow into a warm and responsive being?

So I tell the story of the taxi driver with which this book opens. It is greeted with derisive laughter. "Bet you passed yourself off as a resident to get a free ride!" Only a 100 per cent bigot would judge another man by the back of his neck, they agree. Why must I always *categorize* people, and *label* them, instead of treating them as the individual human beings they really are? How *typical* I am of social scientists and the whole pack of bullshit, bleeding heart, peace-marching, punk liberals! "Fuckin' unreal!" Loreen is hissing in my left ear.

I try to answer the accusations that shower down on me. Yes, my writing probably is an attempt to work out, on paper, some real problems in my life, but this is true of many writers. I would like to be warmer and more responsive, but the atmosphere in this room is not helping any. I did not mean to imply that ex-convicts and ex-addicts were a race apart, only that life in Cambridge, England, and Cambridge, Massachusetts, is very different from this place and that I felt strange.

This last confession has got Hal talking to the control

room, and a song bursts forth: "I Have a Tiger by the Tail." Several persons applaud this instant vocalization of my feelings, and attention is turned to Dexter, whose troubles will occupy the next chapter.

But we are not far into this tale of love and death, when John pops through the door and starts soliloquizing.

He has returned from harassment at the Indianapolis airport, caused by remarks of his that were reported in the local paper, to find his black, fifty-seven-year-old baby sitter in a personal crisis because someone called him a house nigger, his children in tears because they miss the baby sitter, his personal assistant in a rage because he found John's shoes in the hallway and (mistakenly) assumed that he was expected to shine them, and Mimi upset over baby sitting and a critically ill father. For two-and-a-half hours he "dumps" his rage, his frustration, his exhaustion. By the time he disappears again through the door, gone as suddenly as he came, the thread of the earlier tale is lost.

So we turn to the abject confession of a resident, working as a waiter at the Delancey Street Restaurant, who pocketed a seventy-five-cent tip from one of the tables and, slipping unseen into the dusk, purchased for himself a small bottle of Woolite! Now the Foundation's official doctrine is that petty theft is but the thin end of the wedge and that for coveting Woolite the cause can be lost and all betrayed. Despite this, we are having the greatest difficulty—at 4:30 in the morning—in getting serious about the case of the furtive socks washer. People no sooner get to the word "Woolite" in any particular sentence than they dissolve in laughter. For some foolish reason my mind keeps playing with Sir Thomas More's admonition to his betrayer in *A Man for All Seasons*. It is written, "What shall it profit a man if he gain the *whole world* and lose his soul," but for Woolite, my friend, for Woolite!

But we are saved from our predawn senility by John's

sudden reappearance. He talks at random about the personal failings of several persons present before turning to me.

"Your Lordship!" This, as if my presence among the dissipants were a pleasant surprise. "Tell me, do you cheat on your wife?"

"If I cheated on *her,* I would think nothing of lying about it to *you,* would I?"

"They rarely answer you straightforwardly," John muses. "They always shoot off at the tangent. It is part of the inability to face life squarely. For example, if I were to ask him," he turns to me, "What's the time, Your Lordship?"

"I'd answer that you've confiscated my watch."

Across the room I see Jesse pat the brown envelope that holds my possessions and leer at me.

"Or if I were to ask him whether it's a nice day . . ."

"I would answer that by your design I am losing track of day or night."

John smiles. He is enjoying this.

"Tell me, Your Lordship, you construct theories in which even we may have a place?"

"Yes."

"You make connections between distantly related events?"

"When I can."

"And from this activity you get pleasure—even a few highs?"

"Why, yes I do!" It feels so good to be understood that I'm almost gushing.

"See!" he turns to the others in triumph. "Mad! *Absolutely* mad. Answers tangentially, shuts himself away and theorizes, makes connections, gets high: a theory addict! He's one of us. Welcome to the club!"

It strikes me as a fascinating comparison. The only remaining question being whether the bulk of social science theory is worth more than a hot flush of heroin and a lacerated arm. But the subject of my alleged distance and cold objectivity has returned. I decide to appeal to John against these incessant accusations.

"Will someone explain why, if I'm such an alienated person and so detached an observer on *this* side of the Bay, I have a reputation on the Berkeley side as an incurable sentimentalist and a romanticist of human growth?"

But I have played into John's hands again.

"Simple, Your Lordship. It's all a part of the same syndrome. Alienated people are inveterate romanticists. The one makes necessary the other."

I consider explaining that I regard both accusations as mutually canceling but decide it's all too complicated. Besides John has exited on this Parthian shot, and Hal has decided to launch an investigation into my sex life. I am invited to express my precise degree of sexual yearning for every woman in the circle.

I assure them it is zero, absolutely zero, for one and all. It is about 5:00 A.M. in the grey light of dawn, after a sleepless night. I have an acid stomach full of coffee, an anguished ass, and a hip bruised by the proximity of Loreen. The last thing I desire, I say, is further intimacy in a chilly room reeking of stale smoke. This statement is greeted by speculations that I am a faggot or possibly impotent.

So I tell of a homosexual incident at my public school in England. I tell it not because it "messes with me" but because the Delancey residents have attitudes toward homosexuality strongly shaped by their prison experiences. In prison the *victims,* not the perpetrators, of homosexual rape become "faggots," and the whole topic is undifferentiated from "male" domination and "feminine" submission.

In my story I gain considerable equality with a seventeen-year-old prefect by the mere expedient of allowing him trifling liberties. Whenever he crosses me on subsequent occasions, I feign a "crisis of conscience" and suggest to him a joint confession to our tutor. I go on to explain that many members of the English ruling class were privy to each other's pubescence.

But the whips sense that I'm all too comfortable with this subject and demand details of my early encounters with women.

"I bet you're a rotten lay!" one of the female whips cries belligerently. I look her up and down.

"You're in no danger of finding out."

"How did it *smell?*" someone wants to know, and because I hesitate, the clamor arises around me.

"You accuse *me* of alienation," I complain, "yet it's you who separate sex from love and now smell from sex."

"Cut the bullshit—tell us!" and they suggest every odor of the scullery.

"Well, I really don't know. Certainly there was nothing unpleasant. . . ."

I expect them to accuse me of implying that they do not bathe, but instead Abe asks, "What do you think of this line of questioning?"

"I'm embarrassed but perhaps not for the reasons you think. I feel you are trying to embarrass *me,* and it's not working. You will cling to this picture-postcard view of the English, that they are sexually repressed, wave their Wilkinson swords over battles long ago, and make like bulldogs at the sound of Churchill. I am sorry to disappoint you."

John intervenes to opine that we are wasting time, and on purpose, because we don't want to get to the powerful issues that are crippling the emotions of several people in the room. I agree.

So we turn to a fifty-six-year-old woman, Celeste, with over twenty-five years in jail for attempted murder. In 1948, as a hopeless alcoholic, she followed an old woman home from a bar and gained access to her bed-sitting room. There she beat and nearly killed the woman, robbed her of money and a bottle of brandy, swigged the brandy, and passed out atop her victim.

Hal asks her to read the verse by Nina Simone. She gets to the word "free" and breaks down, reads two more lines and cracks on the same word. Her whole body begins to heave and shake with sobs so rasping that I fear she will choke and collapse.

Gently someone asks her, "After all your years in prison, Celeste, the last dozen as 'Queen of the Pen,' have you anything to say to the young women in this room?"

"Look at me," she whispers. "Look at my wasted life. Don't let it happen to you. For me—it's too late. . . ." Her face breaks into sharp broken lines, like a Picasso abstract of grief. They have recently allowed her to use lipstick and a crimson O writhes against her ashen face as if self-animated. She is mouthing syllables that will not form. Then her head drops into her hands, and she abandons herself to convulsive weeping.

Two days after the Dissipation she will be gone. She will attempt to buy dope—a habit acquired in prison—have her money stolen instead, and flee at the prospect of the group's censure. Watching her now with her last few drops of vitality squeezing themselves from her eyes, we seem to share the premonition of a hopeless end.

No one will attack her, because Delancey's preferred method of challenging the individual's residual strength will not work in the absence of even a residue.

"It's not too late, Celeste," a voice says. "You're with friends. This is your family now." But there is an awkwardness in the room. It's too early to patch people up. There is a sense that she has slipped beyond us.

Seeing it all I am angry, angry that I have to fence with clumsy attacks when psychic wounds are suppurating around me. "Pity for others begins with self-pity" I have heard them say. Well it isn't true for me! What I could feel and do for people in this room, if they only left me the hell alone! That I should scrape the barrel of my past to find tawdry episodes when people like Celeste are dying seems obscene.

But they are not done with me yet. Josh suddenly comes into the room and sits heavily in a whip's chair. I am uneasy.

"Charles, I just want to tell you what an asshole you are. You erect the same pathetic rationalizations that I used to. Seeing and hearing you, I now realize what a fucking idiot I must have seemed, what a ridiculous, cerebral scumbag . . ."

"What the *hell* are you doing here—you fat fraud?" I am furious. "You haven't even *heard* what I said because you weren't here."

"I heard enough. . . ."

"You heard *nothing*—only that I nominated you as one of my friends—one of the people I felt warm towards; so they trundled you up here, you catspaw, and sat you down to betray me! It's because of *you* that any genuinely creative person in this place is not believed. It's because *you* have counterfeited every goddamn trait of intellectual sophistication that I have to wade through treacle to get anyone to believe me. And you have the effrontery to compare your posturings . . ."

"That's a strong word, 'betray.' Anyone in your family betray you, Charles?" one of the whips is asking.

"No, I don't think so."

Then they all get into my family closet, and we rattle a few skeletons. I speak of my estrangement from my grandfather, who raised me and died only recently. It is Lillian, Hal's wife, who finally slips through my defenses by the simple expedient of disarming me.

"How come you used to travel three thousand miles to see this man who is such a stranger to you? How come you cry when your aunt tells stories about his mental breakdown? Why is it so difficult for you to say I LOVED MY GRANDFATHER?"

"Because one does not love by invoking the word. Because my reaction to him was far more complex than that—a mixture of tenderness, pity, anger, shame, puzzlement. He was a man utterly strange to me, a hand reaching out of history, and yet he adored me, and I found I could make his day, no his year, by raising my little finger."

"How did you *feel* when you were told he'd been found in a field running naked?"

"Well, by *that* time, I'd heard so much . . ." But this is taken as equivocation, and nearly everyone shouts and clamors to hear me express feelings. I feel like Alice in Wonderland standing in a shower of playing cards. Finally the snobbery I've been feeling—and repressing—comes pouring out.

"What the blazes do you *think* I felt? My aunt tells me that my grandfather was found running around a field naked and waving a cutlass. I laughed merrily with the rest of my mother's side of the family, with that whole regiment of women, then I went away and cried. I've 'betrayed' him, if you want to be dramatic. DO I HAVE TO DRAW PICTURES FOR YOU? Do you want me to come across like some Victorian melodrama—'Dead! Dead! Dead! and never called me Sonny!' I expect people who are training themselves for sensitivity to *use their fucking imaginations,* to *discern* that there is passion in my reserve, not to wallow in the obviousness of pop sentiment."

Now I've really torn it, I think. The roof is going to fall in. But there is silence for several seconds. Then someone speaks quietly.

"Ah—but you see we're stupid—or rather stuporous. It takes strong words and vivid feelings to get through to people who've been locked away or drugged themselves. Are you gonna help us remove all the bars that keep us apart or practice your own restrained literary expression?"

"I'll try," I say. "That's the first time I really let myself go, and you were right, I'm learning."

The angry clouds are lifting now. I'm even beginning to enjoy the attention, and that's exactly when they leave me for more important quarry.

Deprograming a Heavy

FRIDAY AND MOST OF SATURDAY are gone. We are getting into the serious part of the Dissipation now. It is close to twenty-four hours since we began, thirty-six hours since we slept. The younger people, the squares like myself, and assorted small fry are mainly disposed of, or rather we have been placed on "simmer," while the toughest have been put into the pressure cooker.

Attention is beginning to center on Dexter. Dexter is a program freak, who has moved from Synanon to Daytop, through sundry forms of halfway houses to an organization we shall here call "Program." There he worked directly under the founders, a committee of faceless men known as the Fathers. Dexter's organizational skills are legendary. He is also a veteran of Program's "pyres," ten-day, nonstop inquisitions into which fresh penitents are thrown every few hours. In Games he has already exhibited a well-marshaled threat system. He is looked upon much as an untreated cube steak—something that must be pounded to make it tender and palatable.

Organizational life at Program has had its highs and lows,

and Dexter, who has tended to merge himself with its machinery, has long exemplified this roller coaster existence. Perhaps ex-addicts want such a lifestyle to substitute for what drugs once produced—or perhaps they have not really changed but are now addicted to a hierarchy that periodically writhes to shake them to the bottom. Dexter has reached the pinnacle several times, only to be cast down.

Less than three months before this Dissipation, he was rash enough to argue with his superior at Program. (He'd been busted again.) Forbidden even to say good-bye to his wife, he was driven to the nearby bus terminal in his work clothes, with a quarter in his pocket. He was thus banished in less than an hour from the only place of work and habitation he had known for years. He left unmourning and unmourned.

From the terminal he called Delancey Street and contacted his former wife Beth, who had split from Program to join Delancey a year earlier. She drove to San Novato and brought him back. There was a hurried evening conference with John. Yes, he could be admitted, and since he was "clean," he could have the standing of a one-year member.

Such arrangements are rarely popular. Residents who remember their own bald-headed days of drudgery feel that everyone should go through it. Added to this resentment there is fear of Dexter's business acumen. Will he change familiar patterns in the name of efficiency? Lastly—and most seriously—Dexter has held high office in the hierarchy of several of Delancey's forerunners and rivals. Many a resident is a refugee from one or the other of these organizations, which haunts him still like the sound of a different drummer. What follows is in part a ritual exorcism of the Ghost of Programs Past. There is a maelstrom of ambivalence, of love and hate, of attraction and repulsion, swirling around this issue. Dexter is both its symbol and in part its substance, for the residents want him, but not *all* of him. That is why he sits tonight, morose and hunched-up, awaiting psychic surgery.

Almost from the beginning of the Dissipation there have been jokes and asides about Dexter and mouthwash. One of his falls from grace at Program was precipitated by his drinking a bottle of Aramis (a men's cologne), presumably for its alcoholic base. Yet Delancey's house humorists insist he drank mouthwash, whether to counteract his perfumed breath or for some imagined lift found in Listerine itself. In any event, the story has a life of its own, with but nodding acquaintance to the facts. Part of Hal's original introduction touched upon the legend.

"You'll find soaps, towels, razors, toothpaste in the bathroom. We even have mouthwash cocktails for the connoisseur. There's Lavoris-on-the-rocks, Scope frappé, Listerine gimlets, and Micrin sours. . . ."

When Dexter explains that his Jewish father ran a bar in an Irish neighborhood, there is much good-natured speculation on what was served. But well into Saturday night the mood changes. I can see Beth and a platoon of "special whips" assembling beyond the door. They include several of Delancey's ex-Program people. John is actually in midsentence when Stew Slade walks into the room, draws a footstool into a position exactly in front of Dexter, sits down, and launches his attack.

"Dexter, there's something I and the others who were in Program want to tell you, something we've wanted to say for years and years, except we were afraid to say it. You're a cocksucking, sneaking bastard, Dexter! We tell you this so you'll have a *feeling*. You haven't expressed a feeling in ten years! You're nothing but TALK and canned data, you phony! You know all the official answers; you're the Chief Twister of philosophy. You know all the law—*but you've lost the human subject*—you lost it years ago!

"What are your *feelings* about the people you ran out of

the door? Because you had the fuckin' *record* for busting people *and* for just fucking them up because they saw what you were—and *gave up in disgust!* I swear you've got 'em lined up in cemeteries from here to New Jersey. Remember Bill Tallich? *Dead!* Hal and I buried him last month. O.D.'d. You told him he'd die if he left Program; then you made his life so miserable, he ran. So he died. *Are you satisfied?* Remember Ann? Dead! Cancer of the breast. She told me last year—I'll see Dexter in hell! And you've got nerve enough to talk your way in here—and try and spread your poison."

John interrupts, miffed, perhaps, at having his own exposition cut short. "Look, I invited him in. He didn't talk his way in. We're swinging wildly. Let's get down to cases and be specific."

James Mulloy takes over the assault. "There's nothing *to* you, you cocksucker. You bring nothing but destruction with you wherever you go—your wife, your baby, the people under you—*for years you built machines while wrecking every human being you touched!*

"If the Fathers had said the moon was orange with green and purple stripes, you'd have nodded your fuckin' head. You evoke as much human sympathy as Boris Karloff! Talk about party line, it exuded from your guts like a spider's web. *You* knew what was going on, but you never stuck out your bull neck for *anyone.* Why don't you tell us about your child?"

Dexter is sitting hunched over, muttering replies into his own midriff. He seems to have opted for a policy of "riding the punches" and offering token resistance.

"My child is dead," he replies dully. "You know he's dead. . . ." There is a hint of reproach.

But James won't let go. His cloud of free-floating hostility has found an object.

"You know the indictment. I'm talking of *you* and the ice water in your veins. You haven't a feeling *in* you. When you die, they'll flip one of your own index cards, like that! Dexter! Gone!"

Stew has darted back into the fray. "You always knew what to say at the right time to catch the Fathers off balance! They were in charge, but *you* had the information on which they decided, and you let them know what you wanted them to know! You stood at attention without flinching and let flies walk over your face, and you did it while *your own child was dying!* You'll have a graveyard named after you, you evil S.O.B.!

"You know where Jed Crasco is now—the man you ran out of Program because you were scared shitless he was after your status and power? You didn't know he was dead, did you? How *could* you when you're so busy covering your own ass. Jed cut his wrists three times, and the third time he was out on the street where *you* put him—all alone—so he bled to death. The man worked for you for *three years*. Was he ever more than an instrument to you—an extension of your system? Did you ever *look* at him? I tell you, Dexter, you're a rotten bastard—a cipher, not a human. I *hope you die of cancer*—fuck you in the ass!"

Stew storms out of the room and subsides in a chair in the hall outside. "Sorry," he says to Beth, who is sitting there, "I overdid that a bit—thought I was talking to the Fathers for a moment."

But a strange couple has pushed into the room. The man is pointing his finger at Dexter.

"How do you think my wife and I felt when we were given *five hours' notice* to leave Program? We had to pack and leave and get out of our house before dark. And all the other tenants were so fucking scared they'd be evicted, too, they shut their doors on us and wouldn't even say good-bye! And

it was all because we refused to put our kid in a Program
school. Were we supposed to *donate* our child to the
Fatherhood?"

It is the wife's turn. "You did absolutely *nothing* to help
us. You never did anything for anyone that might *remotely*
jeopardize your own position."

Dexter makes an impatient gesture. "I wasn't involved in
that. I didn't know. The Fathers didn't even know. It was
an unauthorized action. The people who ordered you out
lacked authority to do so. I felt very bitter about it when I
found out."

"Bitter? Ha! You filed your feelings away with the
memos!" The wife is not to be mollified. "Did you know
that we were all laughing at you in those days. We watched
you scuttle when you got your orders. 'There he goes,' we
said. 'His master's voice.' And what is sad is that you didn't
have to make out your three-by-five cards and create a computer system—you *only* had to be a man and take a position
and hold it, and you'd have been respected. In Delancey we
want people of principle."

Hal Fenton is developing the same point. "It's interesting
that you never played a game with the old man at Synanon
[Chuck Dederich]. You never risked annoying him. John
here started his own Foundation, and the old man talks to
him. I could go to the old man any time still and say, 'I'm
sick. Will you help?' And he would, you know, despite my
big mouth. But you, who were closer to him physically than
anyone else, who discharged his every whim and never
bucked a trend—he wouldn't *spit* at you!"

At this moment someone comes in and presents Dexter
with a giant bottle of Scope and a cocktail glass. There is
laughter. "This record is for you, Dexter," Hal announces.

We hear the sound of boots, goose-stepping, the Horst
Wessell song, gunfire, and Hitler screeching, followed by a
deep roar of applause. Then comes the voice of Ed Murrow

reporting on the Nuremberg trials. Goering, Hess, Ribbentrop, and others plead not guilty. Later, guilty verdicts are read with a news report of Goering's suicide in his cell.

"This man," says Hal by way of explanation, "put his own wife in a Program Pyre although she was nine-months pregnant, scared to hell, and complained to him of feeling ill. A few days later she was rushed to the hospital where her child—*your* child, Dexter—was born deformed and died within a few hours. Only he wasn't there, *were you,* Dexter? He was kissing spiritual ass at El Golgotha!"

"I was there. I buried the kid. . . ." Dexter is almost inaudible.

"How could you *do* it?" someone shouts. "She begged you to let her off—your *own wife,* you bastard!"

"I was ordered . . . I had no choice. The Fathers wanted wives especially in that Pyre. Can you imagine my position if I'd made a special exception of my *own* wife? When Beth said she was ill, I asked our resident doctor. He said she could stand it, that there was no reason . . ."

"But *you* were in charge of the facility—it was *your* decision . . ."

Beth later told me a fuller version of the story. Program as an organization had made two major decisions that were to "mess" with its members. It had abolished its graduation program, so that now its residents were there for life; and it had applied for federal funds which required the employment of professionals. The problem of having its upper echelons blocked by ex-addicts was met by purges in a classic confusion of means with ends.

Beth was caught in a purge aimed at the wives of prominent superiors. Wives had not been promoted as far or as fast as their husbands, while Program-run nurseries and schools gave mothers a diminished role in rearing their children. Not surprisingly, several wives of superiors had begun to maneuver behind their husbands' positions to gain personal objectives, which in turn divided the loyalties of the directors and gave the Fathers less than total control over their lieutenants.

Rumors spread through the organization that superiors' wives had been denounced upon high as "albatrosses" around the necks of their husbands. The recently opened facility at El Golgotha had been turned into a boot camp for the training of an elite cadre—a sort of youthful Red Guard that would purge the rest of the organization to restore its discipline and élan. Recruits were needed who would perform "exercises of the iron spirit." In the meantime they all wore cassocks and had their heads shaved.

The instrument of the purge was to be a week-long Pyre. Dexter was in it from the start. Beth was scheduled for "remartyring" after a few hours. She soon learned that a "penitents' place" for superiors' wives had been placed in the center of the circle as a target for all other participants. While waiting for her appointed hour, she called a long-time friend in Program, a woman who had recently returned to the facility after a spell of reeducation at El Golgotha. More than anything Beth wanted to hear a friendly voice.

"How *are* you!" Beth enthused. "*Do* let's get together. . . ." There was silence. "Sally! Are you there?" More silence. Then a coldly venomous voice answered.

"See *you* in the Pyre, bitch!" and the line went dead.

When Beth entered the Pyre, she was directed to a seat in "penitents' place". "Siddown! We're gonna traumatize your kid!" Besides the twenty or so "bitch martyrs" and the seated circle of other participants, there was a "jeering section" of new residents—many of them withered flower children—standing around the walls. Beth was soon experiencing a more articulate level of abuse than usual.

One young man with wild eyes suffered a psychotic break. Rushing into the center of the room, his thin arms flailing, he began a crazed denunciation of the chief whip, calling on those assembled to shave the man's head and depose him from his position. Beth was sitting next to the whip's wife in "penitents' place." The wife suddenly sprang to her feet, her face distorted beyond recognition by hatred for her husband.

"Yah! Shave the bastard's head! *Bust* him! *Break* him!" she screamed.

Seconds later Beth felt violently ill and ran to the bathroom, where she vomited for several minutes. She was also dimly conscious of leaking from the other end and believes her bag of waters broke that night. But she was not left alone to leak. The door burst open, and she was ordered back into the Pyre. "I was on the street as an addict for eleven years," she told me. "I have slept with guns and knives beneath my pillow. I have had companions who I thought might kill me. But I've never in my whole life been as terrified as I was in that Pyre."

The week eventually came to an end. The investigators moved on. Dexter remained in charge of a house full of residents who were exhausted but still tense. One evening, desperate to escape from the suffocating atmosphere if only for an hour, Dexter and Beth went down the road for a sandwich. In their absence, a retired superior called and wanted to speak to Dexter. He was told that Dexter had stepped out for a moment. The caller complained directly to headquarters. Early the next morning Dexter was busted and sent to the kitchens.

The next turn of events was curious. Under normal procedures Dexter would have remained "sequestered," or in disgrace, for a period of months or longer. Perhaps the Fathers relented, or perhaps they needed Dexter at that moment as an instrument of their purpose. In any event, Dexter was offered, and accepted, immediate overnight transfer to El Golgotha to manage that avant-garde facility. He left San

Novato and Beth—and shortly afterwards a worried doctor rushed her to the hospital.

With this in mind let us return to Delancey's Dissipation. It is near midnight now. Hal has announced another record, "Money, Money, Money," a reference, if one was needed, to Dexter's preference for corporate objectives over human relationships.

During the record Beth comes in and sits on the footstool opposite Dexter. She looks pale and frail in the gloom—like the spirit of Innocence Lost haunting her despoiler. By now, twenty-eight hours into the Dissipation, the hallucinations are starting. Persons will tell me they saw black clouds gathering over their shoulders and the heads of various participants climbing up the walls to hang there like carved African masks. They felt that the room was changing shape as if it were a shoebox twisted in the hands of an unseen force.

Sitting there I continue to be amazed by the ease with which Delancey's residents fall into archetypal roles and positions. Dexter looks every bit the villain. Central casting could have sent him down if he hadn't spent a lifetime volunteering for the role. A short-legged man, with a barrel chest that brings him up to medium height and a thick silky thatch of black hair, he speaks as if gravel were being churned perpetually within him. Either he has not shaved or the moustache that will be in evidence a few days later has made a scraggly start. Add to this the ravines that divide his face from nose to mouth, the collapsed bridge on his upper jaw which causes his nose to protrude, and he looks like some debauched dragon trailing soot from burned-out nostrils.

Meanwhile the whips are throwing a rag doll from one to the other, exclaiming, "I don't want the kid!" *"You* want it?" "Naw!" "Is it deductible?" "Can we write it off?"

"Here you take it!" The doll finally falls at Dexter's feet, as Hal speaks, indicating Beth.

"Look at her, Dexter! Goddamn it. *Raise your head and look at her.* For the first time in your life behave like a man! Now you told us yesterday that your father ran an Irish bar. Was that for the benefit of John Maher, you creep? When you were working for Chuck was your father a friend of Gulf Oil? And did he turn into a hot gospeller when you were working for the Fathers? The truth is that you're a *Jew*—only you've never owned to that—just like you disowned your wife and child. You know what next Thursday is? Yom Kippur, The Day of Atonement, when the old guys open up the doors of the synagogues for pricks like you. Now is the time to clean it up with Beth. . . ."

In slow, ritual motion Hal rises and places a yarmulke on Dexter's head and drapes a tallith around his shoulders, as the voice of a cantor singing Kol Nidrei fills the room. The chandelier on the ceiling glows faintly, before flaring into a pale orange ball, waxing and waning continually like a mad moon in a time machine. A mournful cry of *Eili Eili* emanates from the speakers. (My God, my God, why hast thou forsaken me?) Then Beth leans forward and begins to speak.

"Why did you make me go to that Pyre, Dexter? You knew I was scared. You knew I'd been sick with that pregnancy. You knew I was worried about our baby . . . and the pains I'd had. *Why couldn't you stop them, Dexter?*

"I never told you what happened later because you never asked and didn't seem to want to know. I was rushed to the hospital shortly after you were transferred to Golgotha. I was in labor for hours, and the doctors kept poking me and saying to each other, 'something's wrong.' It was late at night, and I kept crying for you. . . . And they said, 'We may have to give you an IV in case you go into shock, but we can't find a vein.' And they were cutting and cutting at my arms . . . looking for a vein . . . and I was crying and saying stop! . . . please stop! It's no good—they've all collapsed . . . I've been using for ten years . . . and it was like a flashback on all the fixes I've ever had, when the guy with me is jabbing for the vein—like it's a real *macho* thing with him that he can still find one—until I'm so crazy I take it under the tongue. And I begged them, '*Stop* it—my arms are all bleeding!' 'Okay,' they said, 'but you gotta sign this form—so the hospital isn't responsible if you die.' And I said, 'I'll sign anything, only stop cutting me and help the baby.' "

Dexter is muttering something into his chest. I can catch the words. "Waiting room . . . wouldn't let me see you during surgery. . . ." But Beth is off again, her voice climbing to a shrill crescendo just this side of hysteria.

". . . and they gave me some anaesthetic so I couldn't feel anything below the waist, but I could hear them cutting and see their faces. And they cut the baby out, and I heard the slap . . . and there was silence . . . and another slap . . . and still silence. Then there was a third slap and I heard my baby cry and I thought thank God! Oh, thank God! Then I asked them, 'Is it a boy or a girl?' and there was silence again, and they turned their faces away. And I shouted, 'Tell me! What sex is it?' and a voice answered, 'WE CAN'T TELL,' and another voice said, 'It's not normal.' But I could see it all swaddled up with just its face peeping out, and I said, 'He's beautiful! Show me the rest. I want to see my baby!' And they said 'no' and took him away, and I was crying.

"Then the doctor leaned over me and said, '*Stop* crying. *Please* stop crying, or we can't sew you up.' And so I stopped myself . . . but life's *always* been like that, with Program, with you, with the doctors. 'Stop crying!' You all say, 'Stop it. . . .' "

Beth's voice has reached its highest pitch and cracked.

Now she is crying so forlornly that I think of banshees wailing to warn others of approaching death. Dexter is speaking again, but still is not looking at her although they are only a yard apart. I can hear the words. "Arranged to have the kid cremated . . . talked to you the next day." But his words have brought a shriek of recrimination.

"You saw me for *five minutes,* you creep! You said, 'The baby died. I'm sorry. Now I must get back to El Golgotha. You'll be all right! You'll be all right!' Then you left, just like that! I *know* why you went. I know why the Fathers did it. They had to show me and the other wives who had the *real* power over their husbands, who you *really* belonged to. Well you chose, Dexter, you chose."

Beth chokes up again, as another female voice, older and more somber, speaks. It is Lillian.

"Your present wife in Program didn't even want to say good-bye to you, much less follow you. You'll never have another child now. You blew it, Dexter. In seven years, if your child had lived, you could have had a bar mitzvah for him, but not now. And to think you've never known how Beth felt and how she suffered, because you couldn't bring yourself to *ask!* There's never been a more lonely and desperate man. Ten years in programs and no one anywhere gives a fuck for him. Rejected by two wives, friendless, jobless, forty-six years old, drinks hair tonic."

"Cologne," Dexter corrects her, tidying up details to assuage his misery. It was after he had taken the genderless body of his child to the crematorium and returned to El Golgotha that he had seized the bottle of Aramis from his dresser and downed it. Seconds later he was retching in the alleyway behind the building, his job, status, and ambitions gone with the contents of his stomach.

"He's not a bad fellow. . . ." This opening could only be John's. "He's not personally spiteful. Few cruelties originate with him, but he will believe *any* kind of unscrupulous bullshit, and he will go along with *any* program, so long as this helps him to evade taking a personal stand or showing any character or any dignity. You see killing Jews or shooting hostages requires great *self*-sacrifice. Dexter responds to pressure. It wasn't a question of standing for good or evil. It was a matter of not standing *at all,* of total *self*-abasement . . ."

There is a long silence. The room has grown darker. Silhouettes cluster around Dexter, black chess pieces gathered for regicide. Then Beth's voice rises anew.

"When I eventually got to El Golgotha, you were fucking well out of your *mind!* You had a bald head and brown cassock and you looked like a CLOWN! There was no job for you to do—no real reason for you to be there. . . . No, I've *never* got over it . . . never."

"I'm a Jew, and I'm ashamed of you." Lillian is speaking. "We're supposed to be learned, compassionate, feeling people. But you'd do *anything* to keep your rank—out of your loneliness, your desperation, at the cost of your dead child and of nearly killing your wife."

"Did you ever *really* want that kid, Dexter?" Beth wants to know.

"Yes, I wanted him badly. I really did. And although I *was* at the hospital most of the time . . . I never knew how bad it was. But I knew . . . or I think I guessed . . . how deeply you felt. . . ."

"How *could* you know? I never had *time to tell you!* You were always too busy. When I went to Golgotha after the hospital . . . it was *you* who fell apart! *I* was the one who had to carry you around for months. I was the one who had to patch *you* up! *You never once asked me how I felt about it.* You were worried about whether you could be a superior again or a mentor or something else. And you were worried whether the Fathers were still mad at you. Do you know I *dreamed* about it? After I split from Program and got a job, I

used to dream about that scene in the hospital . . . and they
opened up the kid's robe . . . and you were there . . . and the
Fathers were standing around me . . . I couldn't sleep
dreaming all that . . . and then I began using again. . . ."

"What did *you* dream about, Dexter, you rotten bastard?" someone asks. "Climbing to the top of a fuckin' dung
heap?"

"What's scary about this," John is speaking, "is even at
this moment we haven't heard it all. After being married to
Dexter for eight years, this woman has a deformed child.
The child dies. She is smashed. Her husband can do so little
to sustain her that she leaves him and Program, goes back
on the street, goes back to her drug habit, and when she's
reached the bottom of everything, O.D.'s in a suicide pact
with another man. He dies. She survives—just—and is returned to Program. Now tell us, Beth, has he ever asked you
about *that?*"

"No . . . he never asked."

"I pulled strings to get her back into Program. I arranged
things with Flo [the bondswoman]." Dexter is morose now,
and almost inaudible.

John shakes his head. "He has the mentality of a German
border guard who let one Jew go. . . ."

But Beth is remembering. "The only time we had any contact was when I was serving you dinner as a waitress in the
dining room. And you wouldn't even look up at me. When I
started Inquisitions again, they would always say, 'What
have you done to Dexter? He's never been the same since his
baby died. It's *your* fault.'"

"Did you know *that,* you scumbag?" Stew is shouting.
"Did you know they were blaming her? What the fuck *do*
you know? You know the mechanics of getting her back
from New York, but when she arrives you can't even *look* at
her!"

Later Beth will recount to me her long plane ride from

New York back to Reno and Program. She chose a window seat, turned away from the passengers to stare out at the sky, and cried for five hours. "I knew they wouldn't let me cry at Program. No one ever talked about the suicide attempt or the man who died. I wrote a letter to Dexter during the flight, saying I knew he'd helped me and 1 was grateful. But at Program they took it from me and tore it up."

Back at San Novato she was put to scrubbing floors in the main hall where the residents signed in and out, a labor as perpetual as the feet that came and went. She remembers Dexter's shoes. She would scrub next to them, but she dared not look up and he did not speak down to her. Often during those early days she sensed his presence, as if he was watching over her. "I was a splitee—you understand? We weren't supposed to fraternize. In one sense I've always known he cared, but it's not the same as being held and told."

Now they are trying to get Dexter to speak to Beth, but he can manage only deep rumbles of regret addressed to his own midriff.

Stew is shouting again. "YOU STILL CAN'T RESPOND TO THIS WOMAN WITH FEELING! You know she's *never* seen you cry! Oh, you've whined about losing status, but have you ever wept for *a human being?* And you can't do it now, can you? Well fuck you! Sit there! We've other people to talk to."

Hal is pulling the yarmulke and tallith away from Dexter.

"Take those robes off. You're not fit to wear them! All you can say to your stricken wife is 'I'm sorry' while looking like a sullen child."

I cannot imagine that the whips have more in store for us—but they do. Attention has moved to Licia, a thirty-five-year-old Latino woman. The huddle around Dexter dissolves, leaving him to sit alone, and a new one forms around Licia. It works with the precision of a football game. I am so traumatized by Beth's story that for several minutes I cannot concentrate on this new phase. They are talking to Licia with a quiet urgency, while she covers her face and shakes her head as if she was trying to rid it of the import of their words. I can see Mike Berger, one of Delancey's lawyers, and Willie Harper, a senior black resident. I can catch only a few of Willie's words.

"You were really wrapped up in that dope shit when I used to visit your apartment, and that kid of yours was running around hearing it all, seeing you fix. Now you have to consider, lady, what it was about you as a mother and a role model that could have turned this kid into a killer. Well, it was double murder, wasn't it?"

One can depend on Hal to spell out the lurid details.

"Double murder, armed robbery, sodomy, and burglary. ... Killed a married couple in front of their eight-year-old daughter. Sexually assaulted the woman as she was dying. . . ."

"So you have to ask yourself," Willie continues, "what *you* did to raise a fuckin' MONSTER like this. . . . Let's talk about *your* position and *your* responsibility."

But she is still not "hearing," and John's voice breaks in angrily.

"We're telling you, Licia, *the death penalty is back in California.* Nixon changed the complexion of the Supreme Court. The state legislature has written it back into the law."

Then Willie tries again. "You weren't with your son when he needed you, when he was breaking into his first drugstore. You were doing something *else,* weren't you? Why don't you tell the people here what *I* know about you. Clean it up, and you might have a future."

But Licia is still shaking them off, and John is losing his patience. He asks Mike to explain to her the legal situation of her son. I can see Mike's lips moving and Licia screwing up her eyes, but the words are inaudible. On my immediate right there has been a "fall in," the name given to an impromptu confession by a member of the audience. He is shouting that he cut his father's arm off with a machete. His father was beating his mother. Several people are comforting him. Over this clamor John's voice rises again.

"Is *this* the time you want a fix, Licia? You want to run an' help your kid and perhaps *fortify* yourself on the way! Or are you gonna be a woman and *fuckin' face reality?* When he comes up for trial, it'll be murder one! They got the evidence cold, the weapon, the money, the fingerprints, the blood, the informer he blabbed to, and an eight-year-old kid. When the jury hears that kid get up in court and say, 'That man killed my mommy and daddy ... I was there,' they're goin' through the roof! You can't even *cross-examine* the kid in that situation. Your son's gonna be sentenced *to the gas,* lady, he's *gonna get the pellet!* An' I'm surprised they didn't gun him down the day they brought him in, considering that repulsive crime!"

A long, shrill scream breaks from Licia. John pauses —and speaks more gently.

"Yeah, I know it's hard. But you people *will* give each other false hope." He breaks into mimicry: 'Ah know a cousin in Alabama caught with the axe in his hand, an' he walked!' *Then* you get disappointed and *use it as a fuckin' excuse to shoot dope.* Listen! I'm telling you, WE CAN BEAT THE PELLET. We got the best lawyers in town. Chances are he'll get gas from the jury; *then* we'll knock it down to a five-to-life on appeal. The *real* question is whether he'll ever see the street again in his lifetime, and *that* depends on you. Ten years from now, *if* you're clean and got your life together, we can say to a parole board, 'Here's his mama. She's someone he can look up to. She's held responsible positions for years.' And we can get your kid paroled into our custody.

"You *really* want to help that kid? Well, it's gonna be a TEN-TO-FIFTEEN-YEAR JOB, with a LOT OF HARD WORK, no fixes and no fantasies, and a capacity for courage you ain't shown so far! Because right now you couldn't help your kid if you wanted to! You go down to court and do your weepy-whiney dope-fiend act, and they'll put him away forever!"

There is another scream from Licia. She hides her face in a breast close to her and sobs, "I wanta die! I wanta die! I'll kill myself!"

"YOU AIN'T GOT NO RIGHT TO DIE! Not until you get the man *you* brought into this world *out* of that mother-fuckin' jail!" John is implacable. "You have to do what your ma and grandma did for you—though it meant scrubbing floors for a lifetime. I *know* what you're thinking, Licia. I've seen it a thousand times. You're babbling to yourself, 'He's gonna get out! He's gonna get out! It's a special case . . . a special case . . . a special case.' You mothers want to buy your kids back with one bad check and a quick fix! You wanna work a month and pray for miracles. You don't *like* work, sister? TOO BAD! 'Cause when you make a baby that's A LIFE'S WORK!"

John has reached the end of the room in his walking disquisition. Now he comes up to Licia, places a hand on her shoulder, and speaks with measured intensity.

"So get it into your mind that you and your son can come out of this only with great nerve and great realism and great dignity—and no weaseling out on a cheapo catharsis like this one and false hope. To get this boy out we *first* have to get his mama well—only mama keeps fantasying. . . . You'll kill yourself? What happens to him *then?* Ain't difficult for you to die, lady. You been dying for years. It's difficult to *live*."

There is a commotion in the room. They are bringing in a

lighted coffin. It is the symbol of a general catharsis. Soon there are knots of people around it crying and comforting each other. While John continues to shout about hard work, Max, who wrestled his grandmother over a television set he'd stolen and finally knocked her senseless, is crying, "Forgive me, Grandma, forgive me!" over the coffin. Geordie, who has described a dying father with cancer in his spine and curses for his addict son, is crying in the candlelight, "I'm clean now, Dad, I'm clean. It's what you always wanted."

Beth is up by the coffin, too, and three or four people are wrapped around her in a composite embrace. Suddenly a lone figure makes his way through the group. It is Dexter.

"Siddown, Dexter!" Stew and James shout. He is led back to his seat and made to sit down, but moments later he has popped up and is on the move again. After several attempts he gets through to Beth. He is repeating the same words over and over again. "Beth, I'm so sorry! Beth, I'm so sorry! Beth, I'm so . . ."

I continue to marvel at how perfectly Dexter is playing the part intended for him. Accused of being a detail man, he has, under stress, disputed only details. Accused of a machinelike deference to programs imposed upon him, he is now mechano-morphosed before our eyes, walking and talking with the stiffness and repetition of a clockwork soldier. In the surreal atmosphere of flickering lights and hallucinogenic exhaustion, I imagine an enormous key protruding from between his shoulders.

Nearly everyone is around the coffin now. Dugald touches my arm.

"Want to go up to the coffin?"

By now I am so suggestible that I'd stick my head up the chimney. He leads me forward, and I put my hands on the casket. But it is Beth I am thinking of—her and her dead children. (The first drowned in the bath while Beth fixed and

lost consciousness.) The picture in my mind's eye has fused
with the mandated drowning of my puppy when I was a
child. A little creature spread-eagled in water clouded with
regurgitated milk, the limbs still waving, slowing, and then
still. The tears are running down my cheeks on to my chin. It
is at this moment that Dugald has an inspiration.

"All right, Charles, it's your nanny isn't it? Want to talk
about it?" In my pliant condition, grief is attachable to any
memory.

"They froze her out," I say.

"*You* froze her out, Charles, *you* did it!"

Some residual spark of anger and resistance flickers to life
within me. It's their fucking doctrine again. Accept responsibility, for *everything!* But I'd returned from boarding
school to find my nanny dismissed.

"It's *not* my nurse, damn it! It's Beth!"

He leads me to Beth, and suddenly we are hugging each
other. I am amazed at how thin she is—so that each of my
arms almost encircles her—as she trembles with sobs. I try
to tell her of my day and night in the Boston Lying-in
hospital. How I held Shelley's hand through eleven hours of
labor, only to hear that she must have surgery. The head was
stuck. And how, at the end of it all, there was a son,
beautiful and perfect. And for Beth it had been so hideously
different . . . so lonely . . . with this ultimate nightmare at
the end. It is *so* unfair, so incredibly cruel. I want to strike
out in fury at some vengeful God, leering from the clouds to
exact this penalty. All this I *try* to say, but heaven knows
what came out.

Beth is crying that it is too late for her. "I'm too old to
have another child. It's too late for me . . . if only one could
have one's time again. I've wrecked everything I've touched
. . . two men O.D.'d . . . two babies dead. . . ." She becomes
incoherent.

"Siddown, Dexter!" but he comes on. I can hear his ap-

proaching rhythm. "Beth, I'm so sorry. Beth, . . ." This time
they let him through. They want him to see me consoling
her. They let him stand there, while my arms are still around
her.

"Speak to Dexter, Charles! What do you have to say to
him?" I know what they want—furious denunciation—but
my tenderness for Beth and my anger at her Fates are
somehow completely separated from any hostility toward
Dexter. I believe in human pain, in circumstances that con-
spire, but I don't believe in devils. Dexter is no more a
Himmler than I am George III. Threaten either of us
sufficiently, and defensive, unlovable traits appear. But the
threat system is chiefly responsible for that. Still I am expected to say something.

"I can't judge you . . . I've never been where you've been.
I'm not God. All I know is . . . she's hurt, and I'm holding
her because you couldn't . . . or didn't."

At last Dexter breaks the rhythm. "I cared," he whispers
hoarsely. "I really did care."

I am suddenly conscious of being in the way. It's not over
between these two—and Beth has her arms full of English
Surplus. I say fatuously, "The love you had leaked away
slowly. Perhaps it has to come back slowly, too."

A few days later Beth will confirm my impression. She
wanted to contradict me, to say that she still loved Dexter
and always had. But this is his time of purgatory. The patch-
up is still twelve hours away. Someone orders Dexter back
to his seat, and I hear a fierce whisper in my ear.

"Still won't judge people eh? *Still* a fuckin' observer!"

I shrug it off, and Beth and I go to a corner of the room. I
explain how the story she told me about her first child, on
the occasion of my exploratory visit to Delancey the previous year, had literally "moved" me from Massachusetts to
California to write this book. She talks about the baby and

the few wonderful times before the tragedy . . . I am struggling to recall Wordsworth's *Intimations* but it won't come.
Three days later I found it and sent it to her.

> What though the radiance which was once so bright
> Be now forever taken from my sight,
> Though nothing can bring back the hour
> Of splendor in the grass, of glory in the flower;
> We will grieve not, rather find
> Strength in what remains behind. . . .

10

Mopping Up and Patching Up

THE COFFINS, THE CANDLES, and Beth are gone. The dissipants have returned to their chairs. Sunday's dawn shows dimly through the curtains, altering all the shapes and shadows and giving me the feeling that we are in a different room on quite a different occasion. Yet there is an oppressive sense of weariness and anticlimax. It is forty-six hours since most of us have slept. Someone brings us flannels soaked in cold water, and we press these to our necks and faces. There are at least eight hours still to go.

John begins to speak quite softly, and I have to shake my head and squeeze the water from the flannel down my back before I can concentrate.

Okay—you've had your cheapo! You've had a good cry. Pentecostal churches do it easier and quicker. Ain't difficult to get people screaming and sobbing. It's difficult to get them sorry for more than themselves and to instill an understanding that survives the candlelight. The person I'm *really* worried about is you, Hal. There have to be some real feelings behind what's happened to you lately.

How many people here know that Hal has just survived an operation for cancer? They took his kidney out. He promised us

210

he wouldn't work on this Dissipation for more than a few hours, and he's been here more than twenty-four hours without a break. Did you know that he's supporting wife, mother, children, grand-children, while paying off debts and fighting suits for civil fraud that stem from his old days as a con man? Did you know that his son-in-law recently beat up his daughter and kidnapped his grandchild? Did you know his daughter was in a car with friends that went over a cliff and rolled down three hundred feet—and all six kids walked away from the wreck?

I mean we have to keep things in proportion. There's people in this room with the mentalities of adolescents, sniveling about acne spoiling their sex lives, and this man who sits up all night holding the little pricks while they holler, he's got problems and tensions inside of him could blow a volcano.

You will adopt these mock-heroic postures, Hal. It's a jail-house habit. You do it all the time. So let *me* say that when those cancer tests proved positive, just seven weeks ago, and you came to see me in my room, you were fuckin' scared to death! As we talked, I could feel it; you were writing your will. We weren't *really* talking about Delancey Street; we were deciding that your mother, wife, daughter, child were going to survive if you folded; so why don't you let it all come out? The cancer's out—but the feelings aren't.

Hal begins to talk about his earlier years as a con man and a kidnapper. He had started to visit Synanon as a square and play Games. After one late-night session with the "old man" he returned home with a resolution. The next day he closed his business, sold his house, and began the process of returning all his money to those from whom he had im-properly obtained it. He had begun something yet to be completed—the cleaning up of the first thirty-eight years of his life.

Prompted by John, because we are all fighting sleep, Hal comes straight to the latest of the long series of crises that have been his life.

I was very, very frightened. I had never been in a hospital before for so much as a day. Lillian said, "You'll see—it's only a cyst," but I said, "No, I think it's going to be horrible." So when they'd run the tests, which were far worse than the operation, I went to see the doctor. "You want it straight?" he asked. "Yes," I said, and he told me it was cancer and gave me the percentages.

We had this friend, a rabbi, and he said prayers with us, and then he told me, "You make a deal with God. You may have messed up over and over, but God will make a deal with you."

I was still awake after I'd been wheeled into the operating room. The doctors had their masks on. The anaesthetist was about to put me out . . . and that's when I knew . . . I knew that whatever happened to me—my wife, daughter, grandchild, and mother would be okay, because John and Delancey Street had promised to look after them, not just with money, but with everything else a family means. I have to have something like this family to stop me going crazy, and John can spot it in a minute when I'm going crazy.

And when I hear *punks,* like some of the people here, whining and saying they've lost their family or never had a proper family . . . and they don't seem to realize that they *have* a family, the best, with John and Dugald, Mike and Abe . . . friends with whom I could face any fucking horror in this world and *know* they'd stand behind me. This *is* my family, which I can trust completely, and I'm an untrusting guy who's cheated and been cheated by those I trusted.

Those were my thoughts as they put me out—those along with the vision of the people in the beds around me in the ward, who'd been bleeding on the floor and dying like flies around me. When I came to, it was all hazy. There were these curtains around my bed. Then I saw Lillian coming toward me, and she grabbed my hand and squeezed it and said, "It's all over." And, man, was I happy, 'cause I thought I was dead. I could handle it if some guy blasted me with a gun, but lying there helpless—that's tough! And if you [Lillian] hadn't been with me every hour and held up, I don't think I could've come through.

Hal's voice is choking and he is about to break down and sob openly, when rage comes to his rescue and he veers into attack.

And when I hear puking whiners like *this* one [he jerks his thumb at a dissipant] saying, "I don't trust Delancey," well *fuck them* and throw them the hell out! I'm not so kindhearted as you,

John. Someone like this, whom we put through college, people busting their backs in the moving company to educate his ass, and he shoots dope, 'cause he doesn't trust us! I could take him out and blow his brains out. It wouldn't bother me at all! I'm forty-eight years old. I never went to college. I can't start again. This is it for me. And he kicks our family in the face, just as he kicked his own parents.

Hal draws his breath for another assault, then lets it out in a long, weary sigh, his shoulders drooping, eyes hollowed. He looks closer to sixty-eight than forty-eight. For a moment he sags forward in the tall chair in which he perches and glares at the miscreant who does not trust Delancey. In the dusk of dawn Hal resembles a gargoyle come to life and poised to swoop upon a sinner in the cathedral square.

There is silence for several seconds. Incredibly, nearly all of us are alert and tense. There are no fewer than eleven cases of parental cancer in this room. Hal is Delancey's patriarch, its primitive conscience, its relentless superego. Now he stands for every parent abused by an ungrateful child and left to grope a lonely path into oblivion.

Our silence is suddenly punctuated by a loud snore, a second, and then a hoglike snort as a sleeper is awakened by a spray of water in the face. Peering through the gloom I can recognize Kurt struggling to wake up. Hours earlier by the coffin he had confessed that he had robbed a café with four companions, then cooperated with the police to save his own neck. All his companions were imprisoned. He was sent to Delancey as a condition of probation.

John has risen from his chair and is circling Kurt, his eyes narrowed in anger.

Now get this, you punk! 'Cause this is a symbol of what you are and why you blabbed and blabbed down at that police station. For a few hours we do show business, and you weep and we forgive you. "I'm sorry!" you wail. "Oh my mommy—I love my mommy!" But you can't sit up with a man who nearly *died* a few weeks ago and who's got feelings and troubles that dwarf your own!

That's why you're a rat—'cause you know what's wrong with you creep addicts? Deep down you only give a fuck for number one. It's always *you* first. I, me, mine, want, now! You'll listen so long as the attention is centered on you. You'll listen so long as we're talking about rape or tricks or blowjobs. But when we're trying to help a man who's barely recovered from major surgery, who's taking a real risk with his health in being here at all. . . . Know why he does it? To help you! To substitute for the parents you've already kicked to the edge of their graves. Know what your response is to all Hal's troubles? Fuck all that shit—it isn't me! I'll go to sleep!

I got a problem here. This lady [Lillian], who's spent several hours trying *to save your life,* is likely to blow her stack over how to raise a grandchild and a daughter while caring for a sick husband. She's had to build up all her own defenses in order to concentrate on helping other people. It's hard to get her and Hal to talk about themselves. And it's hard to listen, sometimes, 'cause we're all tired. We do it to thank these people for helping *us.* We do it to become a community and learn something about each other, and most of all we do it to get outside the little prisons that so many of us are, and have been, in. That's what happened to you at the police station, wasn't it? The cops caught all five of you—but you thought, "Me first! Fuck the rest of them! *I* don't wanna go to jail!"

John wheels around upon another dissipant, who slept during the saga of Dexter and Beth.

Any man who can remain indifferent to that woman's pain has at least one ingredient of a psychopathic killer—a total absence of human empathy. If you people haven't learned in the last two days that you have to make it for yourself in this world, and that you make it by *showing concern* for other people, if you have not grasped that love is something strong and tough-minded, *not* soft and pitiable, something that endures the night and sleeplessness and can look every fuckin' horror in the face, if you've not grasped *that*—all weekends in the world ain't gonna help you!

The first rays of sunrise are filtering between the drawn curtains. Someone tugs them half open. It is a glorious morning. The sun is just lighting the hills of Marin County across the Bay. The upper reaches of the Golden Gate Bridge shimmer in the sun, but mist and shadow obscure the lower part of the bridge and the entire surface of the water. The vision resembles a causeway in the clouds leading from a dark foreground to a bright horizon.

> *And I saw a new heaven and a new earth:*
> *for the first heaven and the first earth*
> *are passed away; and the sea is no more.*

I turn around to inform St. John the Divine that all is revealed, but he has gone out to breakfast. By now we can smell our own breakfast. Soon it is brought in on trays with steaming coffee. Our spirits soar as we devour eggs and bacon. This is the home stretch. We've survived the final night. Even Hal is back in his usual humor, laughing about his trip to the hospital.

"Know what I went to the hospital in? This was after days of notes and memos, in color and in triplicate, sent to our vehicle department. Well, a *tow truck* pulls up outside my door! They've come to get the old wreck. 'What are you doing here?' I asked the driver. 'Dunno,' he says. 'Charlie B. says someone needed a ride.' So I climb into the funky seat, pushing the oil rags and the toolbox to one side . . . and we get half a mile down the freeway, and there's a police siren right behind us! We pull over and it's a sergeant on the truck detail. 'You know you've no lights at the back?' he says. *Somehow* we convince him that I have to get to the hospital."

"How about the night they came to pick me up at the hospital," Lillian prompts him. "Or was it *you* they came to pick up?"

"I'd just come out of the anaesthetic—I was really groggy—when Doug Wyatt comes in, dressed in mechanic's overalls. 'Where's Lillian?' he says. 'We were sent to take her home from the hospital. What bed is she in?' I peeped under my covers. 'She's not in here. . . . Look, why don't you hop into *this* bed, put these tubes into your nose and vein, and *I'll* drive her home. Might be safer . . .' He just stared at me!"

After the dishes are cleared away, we begin to work on the "holdouts"—those who have sat through much of the Dissipation in silent, rigid postures. It is a general supposition that they must have something of major proportions that they want to hide. Attention begins to center on Casey, a burly black, the backbone of the construction crew. A day earlier the whips had tried to get him to model a shiny black coat to "show His Lordship how you used to look when you hung out in Oakland—he has lived above and beyond you!" Now Casey has curled up at his end of the sofa, shaking his head. He won't discuss his father, dying of skin cancer in the next county, nor will he say why he hasn't visited his father in weeks.

As the whips try to coax him into talking, Casey risks only one platitude after another, an awkward apologia on stilts.

"Gotta get ma shit together. . . . like . . . you know . . . be a man. . . . respect maself . . . an' get off ma ass . . . to demonstrate concern . . . for . . . well . . . ma brothers an' sisters. . . ."

"Very commendable!" Hal's impatience is acrid. There is a lot of muttering into headsets. Black whips are replacing white whips in several of the swivel seats. More black faces are clustered beyond the door. Hal begins.

"Tell me, Casey, you remember your good friend Rudi—who split two months ago?"

"Yeah."

"You two were really close?"

"Yeah."

"Rudi wouldn't have any reason to want to hurt you, would he?"

Casey is silent.

"*Would* he?"

"Can't think of none."

"What happened when you and Rudi went on that special construction job in Sacramento?"

"Nothin'. . . . We stayed at a hotel . . . couple of nights."

"We received a telephone message from your good friend Rudi. He called John's office on Friday night. He asked after you, and we mentioned you were in a Dissipation. Then he said, 'You must get Casey to tell you how we both got dirty together in Sacramento. Tell him not to be an asshole like me and split in sheer fucking guilt. Tell him it's too late for me; I'm in [parole] violation, and I'm going back to jail. Get him to clean it up, so he won't follow me.' Now why would Rudi say that if it wasn't true? Why don't you tell us what happened in Sacramento?"

Casey is frozen immobile, several beads of sweat glistening on his brow, his eyes fixed upon his own extended feet.

"Is *this* why you've been so verbal these last two days?" Lillian asks.

Another whip begins to muse. "Sacramento . . . two months ago . . . just about the time you stopped talking to people and started to work like some manic nut . . . almost ruptured yourself. . . . Don't you have anything to say?"

But Casey sits "hugging his gut" in a classic pose of retention.

"It'll kill you . . . that's all," Lillian murmurs. "It'll only eat your guts out . . . until you tell us. It's already sent *one* man back to jail, probably caused your brother to split, . . . that's two lives. Why don't you ask Bryant here what it's like to lie and lie for more than a year . . . lose your friends one by one . . . until even his old lady can't stand the stench of lies about him. . . . It'll choke you to death, that's all . . . *fuckin' choke you to death."*

Someone brings a mirror and holds it up in front of Casey's face. Lillian goes on.

"Look at yourself. That's a sad, sad face. Look at the line of your jaw, clenched tight . . . that's how you'll be hour after hour, day after day, until you clean this up. Now! Is it true or is it not that you got dirty with Rudi in Sacramento last July?"

The question is really rhetorical, for Casey has withered and sickened before our eyes—like the Jackdaw of Rheims, cursed by the cardinal. Left and right he turns his head to evade his reflection in the mirror; then he covers his face with his hands.

"It's true!" he mutters.

"Tell us about it."

"We were staying at the hotel. We got the manager to pour us two whiskeys and add it to the price of the room on our bill."

"How much money was involved?"

"Two dollars—a dollar a drink for each of us."

"Crazy!" Hal exclaims. "This man has *two* five-to-life's back to back. If we threw him out of here, he could rot in jail till 1990, and he risks it all for one drink. . . . Madness!"

"What *else* have you done?" Bill Toliver, Delancey's leading black resident, wants to know. "You've had a job in Richmond. What happened there?"

"Look, it's no use giving up *half* the shit," Willie explains. "The rest will kill you. *We* told *you* about Sacramento, so that doesn't count in your favor. It's time for you to start talking—and fast."

"You want a *parade of witnesses?"* Hal shouts, "or are *you* gonna tell us first? GET IT ALL OUT! We've had close on a dozen cancers in this room—and that's not counting me. Your own father has it. It spreads and spreads across his skin—they can't stop it! If you have just a little left and you don't cut that out, it will grow until it destroys you. It's the same with that fuckin' poison in your soul, Casey. *Give it all up!"*

There is silence. Then Casey whispers, "I shot dope in Richmond—two bags."

"Where'd you get the money?"

"Two five-dollar tips from customers. I handed over all my tips . . . except those."

"This is the man," Hal says grimly, "who advised us to throw Bryant out the door. When Bryant told us last night, up by the coffin, that he was dirty and had been lying about it for more than a year, we pulled in Casey here. 'What would *you* do with him, Casey?' we asked. 'You're a brother; what would you do with Bryant?' 'Throw him the fuck out!' says Casey. Now we have to decide what to do with Casey for the same offense. Tell us, Casey, are you willing to be judged as you judged Bryant? SPEAK UP! You think we should throw you out, too?"

Casey remains paralyzed.

"Why don't we ask Bryant what he'd do with him. Bryant! This black brother of yours told us last night to flush you away. You reminded him of his *own* guilt. What would you have us do with *him?*

"Give him another chance," says Bryant, himself in tears. "That's what this place is all about, another chance."

Hal seems unimpressed by this generous sentiment and murmurs, half to himself, "They either forgive too readily or not at all."

"Perhaps Casey *wants* to go back to jail," Lillian speculates. "Charlie, why don't you tell him what years in prison are like?"

She has turned to Charlie Mack, a black veteran of

southern jails. His face is creased with lines. It's as if the shadows cast by every cage had etched themselves into his skin.

"When I got *my* sentence . . . there wasn't no Delancey Street . . . an' black men weren't paroled. I had a five-to-life, too. I served eighteen years of it." Charlie's face is quite composed, only the tears trickle down his cheeks as he remembers. "Have you ever tried to sleep with one eye always open and your back to the wall, 'cause your crazy cellmate has a blade? You *try* that for a year or two. This place is paradise, man. . . . When I think where I've been . . ."

It is back to Lillian. "Why don't you open your dumb mouth, Casey, and start talking? Maybe he doesn't like a roof over his head—or meals served to him in the dining room—or living around a swimming pool in Sausalito . . ."

Next, Bill Toliver goes through the list of people who've helped Casey and worked hard to encourage him. What will this do to Mon Singh, to John, to Mo, to Willie? Bill repeats all the sentiments of admiration he has heard them express for Casey. What will they say now?

"You know the trouble with you motherfuckers?" It is one of the new black whips who is speaking. "You always say to yourselves, 'I'm gonna hold my mud! *They're* not gonna break *me!' Look into our eyes, punk!* And ask yourself, how many of us are crying? You 'broke' *us* some time ago! Now you explain to us why the people in this room care more for you than you care for yourself? When are you gonna learn that a *real* man shows feeling for his brothers?"

All this time people have been filtering into the room, and at intervals Hal has jerked his thumb at Casey and repeated . . .

"Know what this punk did? Stole our money, falsified a bill, drank booze, shot dope . . ."

Soon John is standing there, shaking his head resignedly.

"They must *want* to destroy themselves. It isn't as if he gets roaring drunk or buys enough dope for a real high. I got seven kids sucking on a reefer that's too damp to draw . . . I got one fellow who wrung out the lemon in a martini glass . . . symbolic disobedience at its most infantile . . . yet it starts a process that can kill them."

Hal tells Casey to read the verse by Nina Simone. He does so, mechanically, only his trembling hands revealing his agony. The words I despised a few hours ago move me now. I look out the window and down over the rooftops to the Bay. The sun has burned off the mist, leaving an expanse of wrinkled water.

> *I wish I could do all the things that I can do*
> *Tho' I'm way overdue, I'd be starting anew*
> *I wish I could be like a bird in the sky*
> *How sweet it would be if I found I could fly*
> *I'd soar to the sun and look down at the sea*
> *Then I'd sing 'cause I'd know how it feels to be free.*

As Casey concludes the verse, Geraldine enters. She is Casey's old lady, although her blonde hair and youthful bloom belie the term. I rub my eyes in disbelief. They *have* to be putting us on! In the length and breadth of the Foundation, *no one* could be better cast as Anguished Sweetheart. Geraldine habitually talks with a catch in her voice, as if she were about to cry. Surely she was conceived for this moment!

And yet it is all genuine. Hal has broken the news to her just outside the door. She immediately bursts into tears, pauses on the threshold to locate her lover, and then rushes into his arms.

"How *could* you!" she wimpers, clasping him around the chest. "I *knew* there was something wrong! I knew it every time we were together and couldn't get close. I was so *proud* of you . . . getting all those tips . . . and all the time . . ."

"It was only once . . . ten dollars. . . ." Casey is crying now.

"But if you did it once, why wouldn't you do it again? How do you know you'll stop? I don't want to lose you! Clean it up, please, clean it all up!"

"This is unbelievable!" Abe is beside himself with rage.

"Everyone in this fuckin' room is crying over your worthless black ass! It's time *you* showed some sorrow. It's time you asked *us* whether you can stay."

Abe is not feigning his anger. One of Delancey's success stories, he still pines for the fair-haired girl who left him behind when she split from Delancey . . . and here is this "punk," his face washed by the tears of Geraldine.

"You want to stay?" Hal shouts. "I'd throw you out! But *if* you want to stay, here is your jury!" He indicates a solid phalanx of black residents. "You convince your own people. Go on! Ask them one by one if they'll let you stay. You drove Rudi out of the door. You've left your father alone to die. You jab needles into the bloodstream of your community . . . and spread your fear and sickness!"

Casey starts along the row of accusing faces. "Bill! Please! Can I stay? Licia, I'm so sorry, can I stay?"

The litany is interrupted by the appearance of Alfred, who at eleven is Delancey's youngest resident. Hal is briefing him . . . "Know what he did? . . . ," etc. Alfred is ushered into the circle of black heads that now surrounds Casey. I can no longer see who speaks, but I can hear the injunctions.

"Look Alfred in the eye! This is the kid who looked up to you. Aren't many adults in Alfred's life who haven't betrayed him! We older black men and women are the only parents he has. How's he gonna grow up with models like *you,* you yellow creep, who sell your brothers and sisters for a five-dollar bag!"

Then I hear Alfred's voice, shrill and plaintive above the others. "If you were gonna shoot dope, why didn't you *stay* out there?"

"Help me!" screams Casey. "Please help me. I'm sorry, Willie, please let me stay! I'm sorry, Milt, please, I wanta stay. I'm sorry, Charlie . . . please . . ."

But Charlie, who has him by the shoulders, is hissing, "This is my *home,* Casey, and you fouled it, man, you fouled it. What *is* there outside this place for you an' me. We're *niggers* without this place, steppin' and fetchin', steppin' and fetchin'—that's all there *is* without Delancey. You fucked over our *dream,* man, you fucked it over!

"Ask Alfred if you can stay!" a voice cries.

"Please, Alfred—I'm sorry. I turned my back on you and all the brothers and the whole Foundation. Can I stay?"

"I want you to stay," says Alfred. "If you can't make it—there's not much chance for any of us."

Casey is still making his rounds. I can hear his repeated requests, although he has now sunk into a muttering of plea and response. It is like a religious service. I can hear one voice stronger than the rest.

"Okay, Casey, but no more! We gotta be stronger than that, we just *have* to be!"

Finally Casey faces Bill Toliver, his tribal elder, who gives the last rebuke.

"You're the kind that keeps us cripples. It isn't always the man who messes us about—it's you and your kind that keep us slaves. You better start helping Alfred and the others—that's the only way *you* gonna change. You show me in the next few weeks that you're a new man—Okay, brother?"

He grips him on the forearm for emphasis, then relaxes. They embrace. It is the signal for a general forgiveness. The brothers and sisters are embracing him now; then Geraldine lays her wet cheek against his.

John is standing back from the ceremony, pronouncing judgment. He is always a bit uncomfortable with these scenes. They are necessary but are not his style.

"All right! This has been a shock for him and it's taught him some humility. Let him keep his job, his apartment, and his relationship. He copped on his own accord to the more important offense, and he's an excellent worker; so we take the position that he has demeaned himself, and we'll just shave his head. No additional punishment."

John, in the opinion of several of the ex-Synanon people, is a softie on the issue of punishment. Just then he catches sight of me and the tears streaming down my face. He smiles and approaches.

"Your Lordship is moved?"

There is a hint of satisfaction in his voice. The English are undone. The blessed Irish martyrs rest more comfortably.

"Tell me, how would your friends in Berkeley *measure* the emotion in this room? Could small plastic funnels be taped to our cheeks?"

But Hal has encountered poor Dexter, in a state of shock, wandering among the soup and sandwiches in the anteroom. Hal guides him back to his seat. "Dexter wants to express some real feelings," he announces.

"I just want to say," Dexter is glassy-eyed, "that I don't feel that I fit here . . . in this Foundation. I really feel in a bind . . . that I'm stuck now with this label and reputation as a professional loser, which I'll never shake after today. I'm embarrassed, and I feel I *am* an embarrassment to all of you so long as I stay here. . . . I love Beth . . . very much, but since I seem to bring her nothing but pain and disgust . . . I'd just rather leave . . . since it's what *you* obviously prefer, . . . and you are not going to be able to trust me after this."

John shrugs. "You're a grown man. You can leave any time you want to."

But Mike Berger is indignant. "Stop the *blackmail,* Dexter! We're not that programmed. Do you really imagine that we did this to *get rid of you?* You think we sit up two nights with you to destroy you? You confuse us with yourself! That was *your* game! *We* talk to people out of concern, not to look good or to come out on top, but so that we can *live* with them back in the house.

"You want to leave? Okay! But where else in the whole world are you gonna find people who'd stay up even *one* night to save your miserable life? On the day John decides he doesn't want you here, you'll know! We only lose sleep helping people. Getting rid of them's easy. No shouting, no crying—just the door!"

Dexter sits there dimly comprehending. At a signal from Hal, Beth comes forward. She stoops to embrace Dexter. There is a moment of awkwardness. He is still sitting, she standing. He seems too weak to rise. He is helped to his feet. Suddenly he comes to life and clasps her. The tears are running down his face, at last. The only time in their entire, tragic life together that she has seen him cry.

"I feel such a fool," he whispers to her. "Such a damned fool."

The whole room begins to stir—the patch-up has begun. From the speakers against the wall comes the voice of Martin Luther King.

With this faith! We shall be able to hew from the mountain of despair a new soul!

With this faith! We will be able to transform the jangling discourse of our nation into a beautiful symphony of brotherhood.

With this faith! We will be able to work together, to pray together, to struggle together, to go to jail together, to stand up for freedom together. . . .

The room looks like a checkerboard. The blacks, the Latinos, and the whites are all huddled separately. Those who have had the hardest time are in the center, patted and consoled from all sides, hugging and breaking, hugging and breaking with each participant.

Then the ethnic huddles dissolve, and each turns outward, black and white, Latino and black, men and women.

I say to you today, my friends, Let Freedom ring!
From the hilltops of New Hampshire, from mighty mountains of New York . . . from every hill and molehill in Mississippi . . . Let Freedom ring from every house and hamlet, from every street in every city . . . When Freedom rings we shall be able to speed that day, when all God's children, black men and white men, Jews and Gentiles, Protestants and Catholics, will be able to join hands and sing in the words of the old Negro Spiritual. Free at last! Free at last! Great God Almighty, we are free at last!

Now the whips and the dissipants are embracing each other. I clasp Dugald. "I hope I didn't make you too angry," he says, with such simplicity and charm that I can only shake my head. Others are clustered around Hal. "Thank you," one whispers. "I know now how my father felt . . . all these years," says a second. "Look after yourself . . . please," says a third. Dexter and Beth, John and Lillian, Stew and James are having a special patch-up of their own with the other ex-Program people. It is almost like a minuet as they kiss Beth one by one. I feel a pang of jealousy. Finally they restore her to Dexter. Across the room three black participants have led Casey back to Geraldine. Her arms and his entwine, and they rock gently to and fro. "It's all right, now," she murmurs. "It's all right!"

We got some difficult days ahead. Some people are concerned as to what would happen to me from some of our sick white brothers.
Well I don't know what will happen to me now . . .
But it really doesn't matter to me now . . . because I've been to the Mountain Top . . .
Like everybody I would like to live a long life . . .
Longevity has its place . . .
But I'm not concerned with that now . . .

*He's allowed me to go to the Mountain Top—and I've looked over
and I've SEEN the Promised Land*
*I may not get there with you . . . but I want you to know, tonight,
that we, as a people, will get to the Promised Land.*
So I'm happy now, I'm not worried about ANYTHING
Mine eyes have seen the Glory of the coming of the Lord!

There is a "phut!" Someone was supposed to fire a cap
pistol to signal King's assassination, but the gun has mis-
fired. All things do not work perfectly, even here. . . . I look
around and realize it is over.

11

Backlash and Exploration

So it's over ... and I can barely stand. Shelley and three-year-old Michael have come to take me home. Actually Michael has been peeking through the open door for an hour or so trying to locate me. Just as John was holding forth on the depth of my alienation, "not sick mind you—but *utterly* estranged," Michael spotted me, and I had a terrible foreboding that he would confound John's words by rushing into the room to hug me. I am rarely that solicitous toward the image of authorities. They must have done something to me.

I wobble down the stairs into blinding sunlight, which assaults my senses after days of twilight. It is 3:30 P.M. on a cloudless Sunday. I almost sit down beside my car instead of in it. Shelley is driving. Michael is bouncing on the back seat. "I couldn't *see* you!" he shouts. "You were in San-ran-fisco—too far away!" He hugs me so unexpectedly around the throat that I gag and think of throttling scenes from Mafia movies.

We start to drive down Broadway. The speedometer reads twenty-five miles an hour, but everything is rushing toward

228

me twice as fast as it ought to be. We shoot into the tunnel
and out again into the honky-tonk strip. SEX AND THE
SINGLE VAMPIRE, THE KINGDOM OF KINK, I
BOYNAPPED MY BROTHER. What it is to be back to
normal! I feel like a mole that has surfaced in Times Square
and seen the light—in acid day-glow green.

"Well tell me about it!" says Shelley, as we halt at the
traffic light beside the naked lady wrestlers in the mud bath.
Without thinking or considering that she herself is pregnant
again, I tell her about Beth and her night in the hospital. We
are moving off Broadway onto the freeway that leads to the
Bay Bridge and my story is reaching its grim climax when
Shelley sideswipes another car, her only accident in fifteen
years of driving. We stop. I jump from the car but fall back
as I am almost hit by a truck. "Don't stop here!" a patrolman is shouting as I sit there stupidly. "There's a turnout
two hundred yards up." The other car and we drive on to
the turnout. I try to rise again, but the bridge and the Ferry
Building clock are spinning in slow circles. "We crashed!
We crashed!" shouts Michael, beating a tattoo on my head
with his small fists.

The driver of the other car has ignored my wife and come
to talk to me. It is not a successful conversation. The
patrolman joins us. "Never stop on the ramp," he insists,
but only Michael is listening. *"Never* stop the ramp, Daddy.
It's naughty!" The patrolman and the other driver go and
inspect the damage to his car. I can hear a hissed conversation.

"But he's *zapped,* I tell you! Loaded—*spaced out!"*

"Well, you both stopped on the ramp . . ."

"I was driving . . ." Shelley has assumed her deep, not-to-
be-ignored voice, and I can hear nothing more because
Michael is making ecstatic crashing noises inches behind my
head.

Somehow addresses are exchanged and the other driver

gives me a last suspicious look and we drive on. I wince every yard of the way, convinced that the bridge is sagging, that we are in the wrong lane, that Shelley had better get a grip on herself since her face is blurring, and that I have an incubus on my neck. "Leave Daddy alone, Michael," she says. "He's feeling sick."

It was *not* the right thing to say. Michael has his doctor's kit in the back seat, and moments later he has scrambled over the seat and is kneeling firmly in my groin. He presses his toy stethoscope to my chest and furrows his brow. "Tell me now, what's your address?"

As I stagger into our house in Berkeley, I hear myself promise Michael that I will watch him bounce on his trampoline before I go to bed. But the trampoline and my bed turn out to be one and the same, and the last thing I remember is a stern lecture on *sharing* things. I can sleep on *my* part of the bed, while he bounces on *his* part. It's bad to be shellfish.

When I awake at six the following morning, the room still seems distorted, but I feel better. Michael is asleep, and as I look down at him, he suddenly appears to be of such incredible beauty and perfection, and I am so happy and grateful, that I begin to cry.

I have always known intellectually—I have even taught—that one must face death with people to appreciate life, encounter deformity to really marvel at perfection, and comfort the despairing to rejoice fully in one's own good fortune. I have known it but not experienced it with the force I now feel. I pick up Michael and squeeze him with such intensity that he awakens . . . and promptly continues with a dialogue he's been having with himself.

"Trouble *is,* you see, my Big Wheel doesn't have a brake, and I could *crash*. We'll *have* to buy another. But it's a waste of your time driving all the way to the toy shop and only buying *one* thing, . . . so I have a plan. . . ."

For the next week or so, moods of extreme tenderness will suddenly overwhelm me. I will see Shelley or Michael at some routine activity and become unaccountably affectionate. Shelley is only moderately rapturous about it all.

"Are you sure this has anything to do with *me?*" she asks suspiciously.

The Dissipation certainly has a permanent effect on those who went through it together. We embrace whenever we meet. To some twenty residents I will never be a stranger nor they to me.

And yet . . . my critical faculties were only dormant, and like teeth ravaged under Novocain, they come slowly, angrily, and painfully to life in the weeks that follow. Have I been the victim of flimflam men? If it's true that a statue was never erected to a critic—at least pigeons have not crapped on his head. John will get the statues, if any; I must look to my lucidity.

What troubles me most is that I distrust moral absolutes and dramatic stereotypes, and still I have let them seduce me. I have seen Dexter as music hall villain, needing only to twirl his black mustache, and Beth as the not-so-young Innocent Betrayed. It is much too close to the lives of illusion in which many residents indulged before coming to Delancey. Taking Superfly to the point of superfluity was precisely the original disease. Are we much better off with Supershrinks and Superdramas? A month later I watch a second Dissipation, and from the gallery it seems far more contrived than I remembered my own.

Nor do I see how Dexter, especially, is supposed to have been improved by the exercise. His failing, according to the group's indictment, was that he went along with group and institutional pressures. The Cure, apparently, is for another group and institution to place him under enormous pressure, *in the name* of independence. But since the process of teaching him is by psychic gang-bang, it is difficult to see where the "independence" is going to be learned, or whether it can exist in his mind apart from the group's definition.

Moreover it seems absurd to blame Dexter entirely for a train of events set in motion by others. What about the institution that placed him in the moral dilemma, that polarized his loyalty to Beth with his loyalty to the cause? To make Dexter the villain of the piece is to lose sight of what organizations do to contribute to villainy. To the extent that Delancey stigmatizes him, does it not let *itself* off the hook for failing to help such a "loser"?

I begin to ask people these questions, and I get the general impression that Dissipations move in mysterious ways and what happens by candlelight is not meant for discussion in daylight. "Listen to the feelings!" says Hal. "They do not lie." Perhaps, but their feelings have betrayed the residents of Delancey in the past. I invite Stew Slade, who led the attack on Dexter, to have lunch with me at the Delancey Street Restaurant.

"You should not isolate the Dissipation from its wider context," he tells me. "Look at what's been done for Dexter since! He's been promoted in record time to a position where he coordinates the activity of all the businesses. The house wouldn't have tolerated that if he hadn't been put through the mill."

"But isn't that how he's *always* been used," I say. "He's been publicly promoted and privately humiliated, and that gap between public and private estimates of yourselves is what so many of you suffer from."

"It may have seemed humiliating to you, but remember he's a tough old bird—a Program inquisitor from way back."

"But that's my point!" I am getting excited. "To prove to Dexter that he's not in 'bad old Program' any longer but in 'young new Delancey' we have to go after him harder than even Program did. I've talked to him. That was the worst night of his life. A doubtful victory, don't you think?"

Stew says he has a stomachache and leaves the table.

I fare even worse with Dexter and Beth. I am trying to clarify the actual sequence of events, but I only succeed in annoying them both. They pull me into a Game, and with Hal they hammer at me. I am intruding. I am trying to get one to call the other a liar. Dexter does not want any contradictions of Beth's viewpoint. I must tell it straight or not at all.

"I refuse to continue our dispute in print. It's over. She had her say. She was entitled to it. I'll grudge her nothing. As for Program, it saved my life and Beth's, too. I will take the responsibility."

"But it doesn't follow," I protest, "that a second or a third perspective on what happened belies the first. Different perspectives can enlarge your viewpoint. I really do believe that you and Beth are going to have to choose—to go on playing moral charades or to try to establish genuine intimacy, which involves fusing the way you see things."

"Are you trying to write a book or therapize us?" Beth demands.

"I'm trying to steer between the rock and the whirlpool. Look, what I have to say is a bit heavy. Please bear with me. All moral absolutes like Innocence (positive) and Guilt (negative) come in pairs, and the pairs attract, positive to negative, like magnets. But moral absolutes also come in reversed pairs, for example, Naiveté (negative) and Man-of-the-World (positive). You two put on a magnificent and sincere performance of Innocence Comforted and Guilt Cast Out. But Dexter has an escape, and he's taken it. To the extent that the story was true he is the Guilty Outcast, but to the extent that the story was exaggerated he is Man-of-the-World Martyred. I talked to Dexter, here, less than a week after the Dissipation, and already he had made the transition from the negative image in which the group cast him to a positive one. His attitude to you, Beth, was surely-I-have-borne-her-griefs-and-carried-her-sorrows, and the exaggeration *entitles* him to that. It's not illogical!

"Moral absolutes in black and white only *seem* to give us certainty. With simple sleight of mind they are reversible. The truth is that both of you now think of yourselves positively, but the positives are incompatible; they repel. Beth's Innocence Comforted *has no need* of Dexter's Man-of-the-World Martyr. Beth's positive can only communicate with Dexter's negative, the Guilty Outcast. In short, *the absolutes you cling to repel the intimacy you need.* You are both dependent on Dissipations and Delancey to mediate these games you play and to sanction their exaggeration. What you achieve is a candlelit, cathartic intimacy that cannot survive the daylight. What made Dexter so angry with me was my attempt to qualify and moderate the group's indictment of him, for in its exaggeration was his own salvation. And that's why you two are both so volatile, Dexter especially, who casts himself down periodically. The positive and negative images live together inside you, black and white, unintegrated; so you swoop from high to low and back again, depending upon which gains the upper hand."

My audience has become understandably restless during this harangue. There are the usual suggestions about where on my person I might lodge my lecture notes. There is general consensus that someone with so big a mouth is obviously not getting laid on a regular basis. Now if my wife would only play Games . . .

Three months later Dexter, the Master Builder, tumbles again from the pinnacle of his own edifice. He is found dead drunk on the floor of the Club and is busted to the kitchen.

Having failed to find support for my dissent, and still reluctant, on the other hand, to deny the validity of that surge of feeling in the Dissipation, I seek out Mimi Silbert. For a long time she was in an anomalous position at Delancey, a qualified criminologist among amateurs, a certified success amid certified failures, a square *and* a resident. All of her Ph.D.s had been earned, but her status *inside* the Foundation came to her suddenly and by attribution. John chose her as Queen Consort and such preferences were private.

But the year 1975 had seen a totally new departure. The Board of Directors had appointed Mimi executive officer of the entire Foundation. John would henceforth deal with the politics of Delancey's relationship to outside forces. In the interval of three years Mimi had earned the status given to her. She had done it the hard way—not by lecturing—but by sitting up more nights with Delancey's walking wounded than anyone dared to count. They would even forget, sometimes, that she was a square.

So I lay my thesis on Mimi, and she listens carefully to my complaints.

"You're perfectly right about polarities impeding the later stages of growth and recovery. Our problem is that the earlier stages of recovery are different, and I'm presently trying to create a transition from the earlier to the later, and that involves major reorganization. Let me explain.

"Most of the people we get here are character disorders when they first come. That means that their feelings and their impulses betray them. They are too greedy, too angry, too impulsive, too scared, too lazy, too aggressive, too submissive, or whatever. They are *so* compulsive in their pursuit of narrow objectives that they crash. So two things have to be done when they first arrive. They must be taught new behaviors, and their mostly hostile, inappropriate feelings must be severed from those new behaviors. So we have Games where the feelings are literally dumped, got rid of, and we have work where they do as they are told, 'unfeelingly.' Now that's not your ideal or my ideal, but it's a necessary stage in the process. At this stage most residents conceive of virtue as external to themselves in the form of role models or the organization's objectives.

"After people have been here about six months and the beginnings of a positive image have emerged around their work, then we put them in a Dissipation. The purpose is to dissipate the self-hatred and the guilt which has already been severed from behavior and values. Experience suggests that the old, despised parts of themselves cannot be let go until there's an alternative. That's why we wait six months. In the Dissipation we attack, very strongly, to get through the defenses to the self-loathing which is underneath, and we clean it out."

"But what I'm saying," I interject, "is that this attack is just the opposite extreme of the behavior being objected to. We go from Dexter's Organization Man syndrome to an absolutism of Individual Responsibility. They are equally unviable, and moreover they foster each other, because a person *held* individually responsible by an organization and blamed for its machinations *becomes* its victim and its servant."

"I agree," says Mimi. "But first things first. Most people who come here cannot acknowledge the force of values opposite to those they want for themselves. You *have* to dramatize that opposite. If someone has been blaming the system all their lives, you have to say to that person, 'No—it's *your* fault.' Whether or not that is empirically correct, it is the correct *antidote* for his chronic dependence. It is by going to the 'extreme' of self-determination that he breaks the chain."

I check on my comprehension. "So what you're saying is that one extreme must, at least initially, be checked by its opposite extreme—a stigma will do to beat a dogma."

"Exactly! But you are right about the situation being

volatile and unstable. I think of Dexter's situation in different terms from you, but our views are probably compatible. As I see it, he's caught in a vicious circle. He feels unloved; so he gets into a position of power that forces people to relate to him. But these relationships are never sufficiently satisfying; so he abuses power, feels secretly guilty, hates himself, and destroys his own position. Once in disgrace, he feels unloved, seeks power, and the cycle begins again.

"So what I've done is ask people to show affection for him when he's down. Instead of ostracizing him among the pots and pans, we've shown him small kindnesses. If there are free movie or theatre tickets, I've asked people to take him along. The idea is to break up the connection he has made between love and power and show him he is 'basically' likable. For the same reason we're putting him in charge of the warehouses when he comes off contract. That's a place he can use his skills, and it's very valuable to us, but it's not a power center."

"But I don't see how you are going to stop this constant oscillation between extremes by making a quiet exception of Dexter. The system has to be changed . . ."

"The system *has* been changed," Mimi says. "Let me bring you up to date on the changes I've instituted. After a resident has been here and clean for around eighteen months, and after he or she has acquired a specific set of values by enacting them, we introduce a totally new stage called 'The Explorers.'

"There are now nearly a hundred explorers in five groups of twenty, each headed not by a barber who gives haircuts, but by an advocate for their personal growth. In this stage we concentrate on bringing the values previously polarized together. In that way they become more ambiguous, less black and white. You learn that in real life there are fewer 'pure' situations. You rarely have an opportunity to scream out your feelings, and you try to avoid jobs where you just 'go through the motions.' You have to do something in between, neither shout 'motherfucker' at your boss nor obey him to the letter. It isn't that the values they've been taught are wrong; it's that the explorers must now learn for themselves what particular combinations of values suit their particular situations. The individual becomes responsible for that balance, moment by moment, day by day, in situations that are never quite that way again.

"Whereas in the earlier stages we concentrate on behavioral objectives, *'do it*—and never mind how,' we will now concentrate on the *process* of making decisions—how to reach decisions by awareness of the values involved. You discover that even with the best will in the world it may not turn out right, or that what is right for you is wrong for your wife. But it's important to see that the later stage *builds on the earlier ones.* Your ethics cannot be permissive or situational unless you understand the elements you are combining and can make use of the entire range. That's why the Dissipation you experienced is still useful. It exercises the very extremities of feeling—anger, strength, responsibility—and once you *have* these in your repertoire, you can use them, but that's *not* the same as always using them at full force.

"We need the explorers urgently for at least two reasons. First, we can't graduate people who alternately abuse their supervisors and obey them. Second, anyone in a major position at Delancey has to be able to think multidimensionally and see the point of view of other departments and resolve the disputes that break out between different functions. If you present a one-year member with an ambiguous situation, he can still go crazy because he doesn't know which of the moral absolutes that he's learned applies to a situation in between.

"The garage began losing money last month, and the

restaurant was down. Know why? Some therapist had sent the mechanics to the restaurant and the cooks to the garage! Now that's a good tactic in moderation. We don't want someone who used to support his habit by working on automobiles to just go on working on automobiles. We change his situation—make him stretch. But there is a limit! The garage *has* to give service to our customers as well. You cannot apply the therapeutic principle to the exclusion of the service principle or vice versa.

"Again, if we want people to achieve independence of judgment, we have to take them out of contexts which tell them exactly what to do. Our advocates do not tell their people the answer. They act as sounding boards and stimulate the process of exploring alternatives. Unless our people learn this, they'll make mistakes en masse instead of individually.

"For instance, I had Jim Stokes in my office last week. He wanted a job change. 'Why?' I asked. Because the construction crew of which he's a member had taken the roof off one side of the Sausalito apartments and left it on the ground for a week. 'That's not the way it's done,' he told me. He'd tried to protest, but the others had called him a prima donna. 'It doesn't rain in Marin County in July!' they said. Well, I looked out the window and it was raining! We hightailed it over to Sausalito. Too late! Two thousand dollars' worth of damage! They'd worked on the interiors for a month, and now they were flooded. And the occupants were all shrieking and lamenting, 'my water colors, my clothes!' Jim's the hero of the crew now. They've flipped over from admiring consensus to admiring his judgment—but it's too late. Unless you teach the *process* of independent judgment, you'll never stop the kind of 'group think' that Dexter bowed to and our construction crew represents."

"I've a story that matches that one," I say. "My wife knows a landscape architect who was working at a site downtown. A truck with three tons of earth dumped it in the wrong spot and blocked the intersection. The police were threatening this woman with all kinds of penalties if she didn't get the earth moved at once. She called Delancey, and they sent a crew down quickly, but then they leaned on their shovels and asked her, 'Do you know the Delancey Street story?' and they began to tell her, shoveling a symbolic spadeful every now and then, while the police began writing citations. So *she* seized the shovel and began to work frantically, while they stood around her . . . running their story."

"That's just my point," says Mimi. "They know they must tell the Delancey Street story and they know they must work hard, but they have trouble deciding which is more appropriate at a particular time, and one moral imperative tends to block out alternatives. Also, having been shouted at in Games, they are often unable to pick up softer signals, like Shelley's friend shoveling the dirt herself, a reproach obvious to us but lost on them.

"I've now embodied within the Foundation this notion of balancing and orchestrating different values. Every week or so we hold Summit Meetings, where the heads of the three main divisions of the Foundation meet. The War Department—that's the money-making businesses; the State Department—that's the legal, finance, maintenance, etc.; and the Vatican—that's the therapeutic side, the barbers and the advocates.

"Let's suppose the issue is a job change. The moving company wants a particular person who's working somewhere else. He'll be present at the meeting along with his barber or advocate. The barber will say something like 'We'd rather not move this fellow. He's working well with the old people north of Mission. He used to mug 'em; now he escorts them to the park and stops them being mugged, and it's important that he restores his self-respect.' And the head of the War Room, that's Mon Singh Sandhu, will say, 'We need the money the moving company brings in, and if we can't get him, we'll have to turn down new business. Since when can't an ex-mugger redeem himself by carrying things?' Then Mary Ayres of the State Department will say, 'If the revenues from the businesses stop rising, we're in a real crunch.'

"It's up to the personnel manager, Abe Irizarry, with some help from me, to resolve the values involved. He'll ask the individual who, let us suppose, is prepared to go to moving but would prefer not to. So then Abe asks, 'Doesn't the moving company do free jobs for the old people,' and Mon says, 'yes.' 'Okay,' says Abe. 'You can have him if you agree to put him on the truck that does all the free work, especially the free work for the old people,' and it's agreed.

"Apart from giving us practice at resolving different claims, it is very good for the residents involved. They can see that we are concerned for them, for the Foundation as a whole, and for its outside customers. We had Sylvia in here last week. She'd been working in a spot where six people gave her work to do, and it had reduced her to tears. When we wanted to shift her, she went into a bag and said no one loved her. So we called her in with her advocate and the Finance Department. She discovered that we *did* care for her and that her suffering in a job she couldn't handle was bad for everyone concerned. When she left that meeting, she was walking on air.

"You make a good point that we're in danger of being seduced by our own dramatics. As you know we had a whole rash of weddings a year or so ago. We had Greek Orthodox services, weddings on Alcatraz, weddings-over-swimming-pools. We had ethnic parents weeping for joy! 'My boy! Back in the fold of his ancestors!'—and all in all it was great fun. But it didn't last. You can count the stable marriages in this house on the fingers of one hand.

"We had Joanie and Barney in here last Saturday. At 6:00

P.M. they decided on an immediate divorce. By 8:00 P.M. it
had changed into a separation. By 10:00 P.M. they were
reconciled. At midnight they woke the block by screeching
at each other, and at 6:00 A.M. when someone came to wake
Barney for his early driver's shift, they were in bed together.
Then Joanie told me last week that only an immediate
pregnancy could save her marriage! They are like high
school students.

"Our rush into marriages is not unconnected with the
residents' idea that values exist outside themselves. If a couple can have a fun ceremony, like the fun ceremony we gave
another couple, and if *we* tell them they're married,
everything will be roses. Or they tell me that if they were
really married instead of *trial* married and had a honey-
moon in Mexico, then they'd relate better to each other.
That's another reason why the explorers were overdue,
because, as I've tried to explain to them, commitment to
each other is something they do for *themselves*. If a couple
doesn't love each other *before* the aqua-lung wedding at five
fathoms, they aren't going to make it afterwards.

"We're discouraging weddings until after the people involved have explored for several months, at least, and we're
telling couples who want children that they should consider
graduating.

"I'm also concerned that we've been buffering our people
from the consequences of bad choices. From now on they
pay for their divorces, and they do not get automatic
bachelor quarters on the basis of seniority as soon as they
break up.

"Explorers' meetings are quite different from Games.
Instead of telling people off, we listen. We provide a non-
critical atmosphere where the choice is theirs. Games put
you in a jacket, and often you must wear it for a year or
more, because it's hard to break out. But explorers can lose
their jackets and change their images. 'Okay,' we say,

'you're no longer an asshole. Question is, who *are* you and what do you want to become?'

"There won't be any more Dissipations for explorers unless they are in it to help someone else. There will be Explorations instead. Less stagecraft, less emphasis on one or two strong whips who 'dissipate' everyone else, and much more mutualism and journeying together by people facing similar problems in their future."

"But there's something in *my* Dissipation," I say, "that I don't want to lose. All the things I've been writing about, intellectually, I *felt* as I've never felt before. My mind greeted my body like a long lost brother. It isn't just character disorders—it's all of us. We try to be a success by extending one 'thing.'"

I look at Mimi for agreement, but she only smiles ambiguously.

"You'll have to explore that," she says.

12

The Directors Meet

THE DELANCEY STREET FOUNDATION is run by a board of directors and associate directors—residents, squares, and experts who are especially invited. People become directors who have worked hard for the Foundation—and if John feels he can safely turn his back in their presence. There is a notable absence of financial sponsors on the board. Money is more than welcome, but it will never be the primary reason for including a person among the directors. In fact, all of the squares donate their skills and services rather than their capital.

The directors meet in the same large conference room at the Russian consulate that accommodates the Dissipations. At first I thought that some hallucinogenic effects had lingered in the room as a residue of my Dissipation. The inscriptions on the ball-point pens are in gibberish, the printed lines on the paper pads run in alarming directions, and the cloth-covered tables are of random heights. But these are only the effects of living in a world of factory rejects and donated merchandise.

Delancey's directors meet around a T-shaped table. John

sits in the center of the short arm. No other seats are reserved, but members do distribute themselves roughly in order of influence, with proximity to John as the indicator. Today, Mimi is on the left arm of the T and Hal on the right, which is politically symbolic even if accidental.

At the moment, John's seat is vacant. He is late arriving—which is usual. Meanwhile, the directors are chatting about the ruckus of that morning.

"There was this terrific crash—followed by John roaring 'unconscious sabotage!' That's when he kicked his bedroom door in."

"Well, it was at least partly *your* fault, Pat." Pat smiles enigmatically at the mention of his name but holds his peace, transcending the gossip of lesser mortals. "Instead of telling John right out that our three-ton truck caught fire and is a write-off, Pat delivered one of his celebrated sideswipes—something about Delancey lighting a torch on Route 101. By the time John had deciphered Pat's code, frustration was piled on the shock of the news itself."

"What happened?"

"Bryant was out with our new three-ton truck. It ran out of gas, or so he thought. In fact, he'd failed to switch over to the second tank. He got some gas from a station and tried to pour it in. You can't do that with those trucks. The whole thing exploded—blew him onto the sidewalk and burned the truck to a crisp."

"Should have been the other way around!"

"Our insurance will be canceled—you can count on it. There was no fire extinguisher."

It is Hal Fenton, the resident Jeremiah speaking. Hal is a walking, talking clearinghouse for disaster information and predictions. It is almost as if crises bide their time until he stalks upon the scene. A week earlier one of the cooks had been burned in the kitchen just as Hal entered. I greeted Hal a day later only to be regaled with graphic descriptions of the burn ward at San Francisco General Hospital and to be told that Jimmy T.'s brother had been found dead at San Quentin Prison's farm "beneath a pile of garbage." Such charming detail, absent from all other discussions of the incident, is the Essential Fenton. (You can imagine my horror when I pulled up outside the Club a few weeks after this meeting to see Hal *running* toward my car! Sure enough my wife had gone into labor and been rushed to the hospital.)

But John has now entered the room, and the meeting comes to order. He has just heard, he tells us, that our insurance has been canceled (even as Hal spoke?). Delancey has been put into the assigned-risk pool—and that could mean a twenty-thousand-dollar hike in premiums. Bryant will be up before the drivers' council in the morning. All high-risk drivers will be moved into other jobs. If we can go a year without further accidents—the rates could come down again. John sighs and shakes his head.

"It is inconceivable to me how a bald head could have been left in sole charge of our most valuable vehicle. . . ." He looks down his agenda. "Let's get the worst over first."

"Bob Wells—our great cause—I've been hearing all manner of strange things . . . what's happening?"

The directors with the relevant information report in turn.

"He was arrested for driving *too slowly* on Van Ness Avenue . . . seems he hadn't driven a car since 1928 and was being careful. When they tried to arrest him, he lay down in the middle of the road and backed up traffic to the Golden Gate Bridge. I don't think they're pressing charges, but they might. Seems that while recumbent, he made insulting gestures to the arresting officers."

"Does he have a license?"

"I don't think so . . ."

"But how did he get a vehicle . . . didn't we refuse . . . ?"

"He has a woman friend—it's hers."

"We got a call from the city controller's office. He's been

calling them repeatedly demanding an electric typewriter . . . says the city owes it to him for all these years in prison. He keeps shouting 'forty-six years!'"

"That tallies with complaints we've received from Cartwright Buick down on Van Ness. Cartwright says Bob's been coming into his showroom, covered in 'Free Bob Wells' buttons, climbing into the cars, and suggesting to any customer who comes in that they buy him a Buick. The dealer's in despair. Says it's costing him thousands. He called us, then the police, then the police called us. *They* say Bob's pretending to be a car salesman—anyway, they are going to take him into custody the next time he shows up there."

John winces.

"Is that all?"

"No, Bob's been claiming to have unlimited credit at Wells Fargo Bank."

"What, blood relations?"

"Dunno, but the bank keeps getting calls from retailers, checking."

"And he's been going up to people sitting on the bench, interviewees, and relieving them of their valuables. He tells them they won't be allowed to keep their watches or rings and then collects them. . . . It's embarrassing because we don't *accept* all applicants, but if a man's already half-naked and Bob's made off with his clothes, we *have* to take him in."

"But he could get those sort of things—even the *same* things—down at the warehouse."

"We've told him, but it's not the way he operates."

"Poor bastard," muses John, "after all these years he has no one left to hate; so he's making himself a few enemies. Who's talked to him *seriously?*"

"I talked to him," Mimi says. "He was virtually in tears. He *has* to have a Buick, he says. This is what all the years of suffering were *for,* his right to drive a Buick. This is the dream that sustained him—this and his trumpet."

"*Trumpet?*"

"Yes—all the way through his imprisonment he nursed his trumpet."

"Are we responsible for him?" John is exasperated.

"Not legally—he was never more than a guest, and he's refused to become a resident or play Games. Then last week he told us to go to hell; he was moving out. I gather he tried to move in with his lawyer. I received an agonized call from the man. He returned from luncheon to find Bob in his garden. Says he's represented Bob for years—at nominal fees—but this is too much! Unfortunately, we didn't clean out Bob's room, because he was back in it again two days later."

"Didn't he break up the AFL-CIO meeting, the one held in our lounge?"

"Yes, they had Albert Shanker as guest speaker. Bob arose from the ranks of the faithful and called him a racist."

"And that's crazy?" asks someone.

"No, but he brought a couple of friends he'd picked up into the dining room. They were both loaded. We had to kick 'em out."

John raises his hands as if to ward off blows.

"That's it! That's all we're gonna take. Next time he walks out on us, clear out his room and lock the door. He can come back in as a proper resident playing Games and accepting discipline, or he can leave, . . . but *this* can't go on. You realize that a few months ago we didn't have a single arrest in three years among our residents? Now we have a dozen—*eleven* for the same man!"

"But that doesn't count—he was a guest . . ."

John pursues his point. "It all comes from treating the wretched man as a social cause, an abstract indictment of the system, instead of a human being. The liberals, the com-

Ed Turnbull
Ed Turnbull

John Maher with Jimmy Carter, former Governor of Georgia, one of Delancey's many political friends.

Mongo Santamaria has given innumerable benefit concerts.

Shelley Hampden-Turner

The Advocates meet to discuss their Explorers: John Wagner, Jo Ann Figueroa, and Mimi Silbert.

Abe Irizarry in full acoustic regalia.

"We have malignancies inside of us, in that quaking protoplasm we call a soul, and you have to cut yourselves open. . . ."

Ed Turnbull

Ed Turnbull

Mon Singh Sandhu (Delancey vice president) playing a spirited Game. "Oh, Reginald, there I *do* differ!"

Ed Turnbull

The Waterhead Hearings. "It says here that Buzz stole a color television set from his next-door neighbor and left it on his doorstep while he tried to steal another."

Four of the Whips: Dugald Stermer, Lillian and Hal Fenton, and Ray Figueroa.

"With this faith! We shall be able to hew from the mountain of despair a new soul!"

Ann Dowie

"... if you want to stay, here is your jury! You convince your own people."

Ann Dowie

The patch-up of a Christmas Dissipation.

"To see that we're scum is to realize that we don't have to be! Recognition clears the way for change."

Kenny Hepper, scuba diver, Delancey director, and its first graduate, once tried to mug the judo instructor of the San Francisco Police Department.

Ed Turnbull

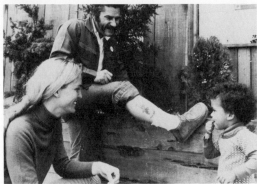

Laurie Hodges, director of education, with her son John and Allen Mikesell, who works outside as a welder and contributes his wages to Delancey.

Shelley Hampden-Turner

Tommy Grapshi, in a typical gesture of humility, draws attention to fellow workers in the Restaurant.

Ann Dowie

Rallying with Italo-Americans. Sylvester Herring in foreground, John Maher pointing.

Dave Silva and Pat Donnelly protecting Cesar Chavez. Delancey practices non-violence but doesn't believe in looking gentle.

George Camarillo, Patty Rodriguez, and other residents marching with the UFW. "Let's educate ourselves — okay? So we're not poor and ignorant and dominated all our lives. . . ."

Ed Turnbull

John speaks to supporters of the
United Farm Workers.

Black residents at a meeting of the
San Francisco Board of Supervisors, in Klansmen's costumes to
protest the wearing of Nazi uniforms by spectators at an earlier
meeting.

Ed Turnbull

A Summit Meeting: Abe Irizarry,
Mon Singh Sandhu, Mary Ayers,
and Mimi Silbert.

Shelley Hampden-Turner

munists, and the literary intelligentsia were all willing to champion the symbol, but no one wants to deal with the real man. He's refused to become a resident here because he's been treated as a hero, and he believes it, and this place is for fuck-ups, and he knows it. Why *shouldn't* a hero blow his own trumpet in the front seat of a Buick while writing his memoirs on an electric typewriter? Maybe *he's* not the crazy one. We do him no favor by letting him get away with all this. So either he lives by our rules or he lives somewhere else. We have to make that clear to him. He's yesterday's headline. The Beautiful People are off to macrobiotic cooking. Idealistically he was useful to them—realistically he's a social embarrassment and always will be, till he cleans up his act. When he's used up his last guilty liberal, he'll be back. We can't deal with people here until they recognize their own desperation.

"While on the subject of embarrassment, I have a note here for JoAnn." The reference is to JoAnn Mancuso, Delancey's first female director and now one of three. "I was passing the blackboard, and I saw that we have a nineteen-year-old gal teaching a seminar on Human Sexuality. How did that happen?"

"I've put a stop to it already," JoAnn assures him. "It began as a class on Nutrition; then it mutated into Human Sexuality by way of Body Awareness. She tells me it all has to do with health, but she had a roomful of men drooling."

"Okay, you handle it, but we gotta watch these adolescent squares who want to minister to our awareness.

"This is not Es-al-on—that sandbox for surplus populations. [John always mispronounces Esalen with relish.] We're not having any fucky-feely or ego massage *here*. I know some of you think we're very intolerant on this subject, but people who've already wasted half their lives have gotta learn to spot fraud and forms of self-indulgence at a great distance, if they don't want to waste the rest of their lives. These open-minded people keep saying to me, 'Don't judge the Maharaj ji until you've walked a mile in his underwear!' That's okay if you're a professional spectator living in Berkeley. But if you've gotta grow up today—in order to survive tomorrow—then you have to ask yourselves, what is the likelihood of an overweight adolescent being a perfect master of *anything?* Besides *we* are not children of the upper middle class; so we haven't time to stand around while some big kid pops his perfect pimples or this girl child lays her wet dreams on us.

"Let's turn to some *good* news. Over a hundred of our people marched to the Gallo home in Modesto, with the United Farm Workers. Twenty of us acted as Chavez's bodyguards, and we had a good sprinkling of clean-cut, short-haired waspy people that looked like their daddy was important, or like they worked for the media. As a result it was nonviolent 'cause the cops and the Teamsters didn't attack us. Cesar Chavez was on the phone a couple of hours ago to thank us personally. Over twenty thousand people made it to Modesto, and a couple of newspapers identified *us* with the lack of violence. That's important. UFW has always come across for us, 100 per cent every time we ask. It was good that we could do something for them.

"Charlie Brown, Willie Harper, and Sylvester worked their asses off and organized with real skill. Let's do something for them—a dinner party at the restaurant perhaps. Meanwhile let's talk up their success around the house.

"We'll be continuing our policy of renting our facilities to our friends at nominal fees. The Coalition Against Racism and the Bay Area Women's Liberation group will be using the dining room area at the Club next Wednesday and Thursday. Bob Wells ain't part of the deal, so will someone *guide* him out? Our people shouldn't be there unless specifically invited. We'll be renting our double-decker bus to some black senior citizens in Oakland who want to share this weekend with the president of Pacific Gas and Electric. Thought they'd chat over the garden gate in his lily-white suburb about how cold it's getting where they live."

"P. G. and E. are sponsors, I think." Mary Ayres is looking through her accounts.

"Too bad! We'll survive without 'em. Are there any objections to our coming out for the Retail Clerks Association? They've been striking Sears over the threatened closure of its branch on Mission Street. Sears may close it just to punish them for getting organized. They claim that prices have been raised to show a loss, to justify closure.

"Anyway, there's a couple of Mexican community groups in the area who are very worried. They say that their people are afraid of downtown and need that store. They helped us with our Spanish-speaking voter registration drive last fall; so we wanta help them and the union. It was the first union in this area to come out against the Vietnam War and for equal hiring; so let's show our support . . . some telephone calls, a few pickets, okay?

"Now, Christmas trees. We've sold ten thousand—that's good. We got a few hundred left. We're sending 'em down to the crippled children, the autistic children, the retarded children, and all the kids' wards in San Francisco hospitals. I assume we can do that?" John looks at Mike Berger, Delancey's lawyer, who nods.

"What about the strike at KQED [the local public television station]? They've been out eight weeks—must be hurting. Can we give 'em trees for their families?"

Mike shakes his head. He rarely wastes words.

"Couldn't we dump 'em in the parking lot and have 'em find them while they're picketing? No? Well, let's talk after the meeting. Has to be a way . . .

"If you look out the window at that big house two doors down, you'll see our friendly neighbors with their movie camera filming everything we do. Luckily they are still making the wrong case against us. They're accusing us of sleeping here, which we don't. We only carry bedding in and out, for their benefit.

"What about the Arabs?" John refers to the Egyptian consulate, recently vacated by Delancey Street when it moved to the edge of Golden Gate Park. Attention turns to Mimi.

"Well, they *might* sue us—it's about fifty-fifty. They're incredibly suspicious. Last person we sent over to talk to them had a .45 flashed at him. They're all armed to the teeth."

"That's ironic! The ex-cons and addicts move out, and the 'normal' folks with their guns move back in."

"What are their complaints specifically?"

"They say we've weakened the attic and unwired the intercoms. They seem to think it's a plot. We want to collapse the roof and stop them talking to each other in the rubble. We offered them a written contract to make some repairs in return for a waiver of all claims. They're hesitating. It's a matter of distrust. They think we could further weaken their building."

"They think you're an Israeli spy?"

"Could be—or just malicious . . ."

"Well, we *did* hold a Jewish Seder in the Pan-Arabian room." Pat is savoring the contradiction.

"And didn't we present Assemblyman Willie Brown with the Aswan Dam Award for nominating George McGovern? It was in the papers with photographs."

In fact, communication with the consulate has never been of a high order. On a television broadcast John had earlier characterized the rental agreement:

"I just went to the Egyptians and said, 'Do you want to

rent me the place?' They're kinda crazy. I offered them fifteen hundred dollars a month. They said they wouldn't take less than a thousand—so we made a deal."

This general level of understanding seems to have continued.

"We can always counterclaim," says Berger. They didn't perform landlord's duties."

"But they have a case, too." Mimi is trying to be fair. "Someone unscrewed their front door. I found it in our warehouse."

"Let's be *very* nice to the Arabs." John is pushing for a conclusion. "Do the repair work. Help in every way we can, while admitting to nothing."

"And if that doesn't work?"

"We take the broad-gauge philosophic view—fuck 'em! While on the subject of buildings, why don't we review the various sites we've been offered for our regional intake centers?"

"The people Pat and Sue saw in Paris have called a couple of times. The French authorities will donate the building. They might do more if they knew we were serious."

"McNulty called from Dallas. He's found a mansion. He can get the down payment if we'll keep up the mortgage."

"Where is it?"

"Not sure . . ."

"Across from the book depository." Hal is blackly humorous.

"If we agree to locate in Eureka, the city will give us a Christmas tree farm. . . . We haven't seen it yet. It's nearly a thousand acres."

"Joann's going down to San Diego next week to look at that house on Pill Hill—it's a medical neighborhood."

"That reminds me," says John. "We saw Mayor Bradley in L.A. last week. He says there's a place in the Cleveland district. We gotta get a systematic evaluation of these different offers. We can't spare enough people for more than one intake center this year. Can the accounting people run some estimates for us?

"Okay, now I've something to say about unconscious racism and sexism. Our moving company is eighty per cent black. There's too many blacks in our culinary departments. Watch those ratios. Too many women are waiting table in the dining room and restaurant. That's not to become women's work. I want to see more blacks and women on our sales team and voter registration drives. Never mind if their initial sales are lower. We gotta help them and push them. This 'capitalist racism' that blames customers and takes the line of least resistance isn't for us. We will *not* compromise our integrity for short-term gain.

"We've talked before about developing leaders among our own minorities. You can't *give* them their rights any more than the government can give us what we want. It has to be claimed. So let's try and work with and through the more assertive people now on their way up. Encourage them to speak out for their own people or sex and to fight prejudice by their own examples.

"It's at *this* point—after the founders have installed themselves—that most self-help organizations get constipated. What we must do now is open up new avenues. We gotta "career" our new people. The expansion in the next two years will be in our business and new intake centers. I want *empire builders* among our rising generation, people who aim to double their sales volume every year. They'll be as essential as directors, only doing different jobs. We must play the role of immigrant parents—be proud that our kids can go beyond us. Help them to be better than we are. We are tribal elders, spotting talent in others and developing it and enjoying vicariously the success of others.

"Up to now we've tolerated craziness in our business. There were never enough of us and there was always some crisis. It will be better for our new people, and let's be *glad* of that, instead of bragging how we slept on the floors and how soft it's getting now. Our younger people will provide the tools to put Delancey people in city hall and the state house.

"The disease of all poor peoples' movements is their lack of indigenous leadership. They panic and try to hold each other down. They mimic the middle class 'cause they've no other models and hire middle class agents until they're absorbed. We have to be different. We must find the courage to let our people grow and not cripple them by our envy and our insecurity. When we started there was no education, no trades, and no business. We created the present opportunities, and now we must see that they are used *to the full*. We can't play favorites or, like some Jewish parents, cast favorite sons in roles that we covet. I've two sons. I'm not *permitted* to love one more than the other.

"I want the people in this room to know that they are SAFE. We're not going to fire or superannuate our senior people. It's because you're safe that I ask you to take *risks,* on your own accord, to help develop our new people and their businesses. Do not be afraid of them. They cannot replace you. We, as elders of the family, give meaning to their work. They provide the dynamism, we the direction. The money they generate is for the family we head.

"On a more concrete level I want the coffee bar at the Club to become the hearth and center of our family. Coffee and tea are very important. They are small, sweet substitutes for what many of us have kicked. They are the only stimulants we allow. I want senior people to work behind the bar, help hold us together, and keep an eye on as many people as possible. It's a relaxed atmosphere where people come to ask for some coffee—and for anything else that they might need. Incidentally, how are the plans for Family Day?"

"They're in hand for the thirtieth."

"Well, let's work to make it a success. People get sentimental around Christmas and our split rate soars. We need to get as many families here as possible, and get *our* family elders behind the bar.

"I think that's all . . ." John looks down his list. "Oh yes! Something I wanted to say to square directors. People like you, Dugald, should please *not* buy your Christmas tree from us. You will get it free—for the same reason we sent your kids to Guatemala. It's important for the family to give things to those who've helped us. Apart from your need to receive it, we need to give it. Okay? We must strive to avoid the dichotomy of dependent insiders and independent outsiders. You help us by depending more, and we become more independent when we help you.

"That's all I have to say. Is there anything else which anyone wants to bring up?"

There is a pause, then Dick Kirchman ("Kirchperson") raises his hand.

"I want us to rethink some aspects of our graduation program. I've been concerned for some time that only a small proportion of our longer-term residents are graduating in the prescribed manner. Most have just upped and left. I've known a number of these people before and after they left—and they're mostly leading constructive lives free of drugs or crime. We have helped and changed these people—by *any* other yardstick than ours they would be adjudged successes. Yet they are not allowed to visit us. We are not allowed to celebrate with them the new directions in their lives nor to claim them publicly as examples of our worth.

"My impression is that these people left because they

didn't want the *burden* of formal graduation, the constant questioning in Games, the live-in-work-out system, and the whole gamut of public discussion and scrutiny of their plans. They just want to go their own way quietly and without fuss. Perhaps that's why they prefer graduation to holding senior office in the Foundation—but then we make it harder to graduate than to stay! It isn't easy to justify to a group of people one's desire to leave them or to go out into the world with their dire predictions ringing in your ears. No wonder they just say, 'The hell with it!'

"I think we have to ask ourselves whether we have not occasionally been wrong about a person's readiness to leave. Don't we sometimes confuse our need for support with the other's need for independence? As individuals we freely admit mistakes, and it's often said that so-and-so ran a person out of the door. But as a collectivity we tend to claim infallibility. Those who split are no good, period. It is not unknown for Professor Higgins to resent the new-found independence of a protégé he pulled from the gutter. But can we *teach* independence and then refuse to recognize the exercise of independence *from us?* If a person has left against our advice, yet after a year or so they are doing well on their own, should we not applaud an independence of judgment vindicated by subsequent events? No one is suggesting that we welcome those who split only recently, but can't we work for rapprochement with those whose independence is fruitful and established?"

There is silence. Dick has touched on a long-simmering policy disagreement. It has been a source of some tension between residents and at least some of the squares. While John takes plenty of advice, he is known to distrust "outside" viewpoints which "insiders" are supposed to implement and live with. John refuels on coffee, draws on his cigarette, and begins his rebuttal.

"I'm not clear as to what more we are expected to do. A

resident coming in here makes a commitment of not less than two years. He breaks it and splits. Is Ron Babcock supposed to bust his hump on the moving company and return to the Club to find some splitee-motherfucker eating the food he works for? Most splitees burn their bridges on the way out. They flaunt their peccadillos like some exhibitionist and run. What are we to do with these compulsive drinkers of half a glass of wine? Forget they thumbed their noses at us? What of those who walked out on relationships and trial marriages? You want them haunting their old loves?

"Why should *anyone* keep their word when they see those who've broken theirs made welcome. Splitees want to come back as visitors 'cause they're lonely, and they're lonely 'cause they don't stick with their human commitments—and never have. If the family is what residents work *for,* why should they work if shirkers can join our celebrations?

"It isn't as if these guys who've split send us any money—or offer to work for us—they rarely do. They want our friendship and our food. There are two periods in the life of a resident. For the first year he mostly gets our attention and concern, and then as he improves we expect him to give it to other newcomers. It's at the beginning of the second period that we lose people. They say, 'Fuck you—I've got mine!' and they run off with a yellow Volkswagen to live in a ticky-tack. We ask our potential graduates to live in and work out for six months, partly to ease their transition, but also so that they can give their earnings to the Foundation that pulled 'em out of the gutter and kept 'em out of jail. I don't think that's too much to ask.

"On the other hand I've heard some pretty clutzy Games played around the subject of graduation. We had a fifty-year-old man with a 90 IQ advised to go to college the other day. You may be right that Games are not helping the graduation process. Mimi will be working with the advocates to develop different kinds of group dynamics for differently situated people. We have yet to give graduation the same kind of respect and encouragement as other paths. We're working on that."

A less-determined man than Kirchman would fall silent, but he tries again.

"You say that those who split after a year have broken their word to the Foundation? But under what circumstances was this word given? In many cases the alternative was jail, and Delancey was at best a vague idea to them, a word on the prison grapevine about how to beat a rap. It is common knowledge among us, and has even been admitted on television, that people come here because they are tired, desperate, and want to escape worse alternatives. Their motives are opportunistic. It is *later* that they change. Can we really take a pledge uttered in extremis and refurbish it into a sacred vow? If we admit that needed changes come later, might not some of those needs be for early independence, 'different strokes for different folks?'" Dick knows he is quoting one of John's favorite slogans. He continues his case.

"I think we should also admit that some long-term residents split as a result of policy disputes. They had dreams for Delancey, too, only different ones. Such disputes may once have threatened our perilous existence, but now we can afford to be tolerant."

John has been humming noisily to himself—a habit he has when ruminating on his next statement. He has figured out Dick's argument some time before its conclusion, and he responds at once.

"It is true that people come here under duress. It is not *our* fault that we are the better, sometimes the only, alternative. Poor people and minorities are habitually confused and coerced. If that excuses them from keeping promises, I don't see how they can turn their lives around, ever. After residents have been here a few weeks, they begin to discern a clear choice—perhaps the *only* clear choice of their lives. They can stay and help those who helped them, or they can leave. If they are no longer desperate, they should for that very reason feel indebted to us.

"I would urge our highly educated squares to consider that while *your* definition of freedom is a freedom *from* the coercive demands of authority, the freedom that most of our residents seek and need is freedom *for* the pursuit of basic necessities. A number of human possibilities emerge if, and only if, lasting social bonds are formed with a group of supporters.

"Those who leave us know perfectly well that we will plead with their probation officers not to violate them, that we will provide references if there is anything nice to say, and that we don't even turn the cops on those who steal from us. Since we try to save from jail even those who run away from us, there has to be *some* mechanism by which we register our opinion of them and our preference for those who stick with us.

"Do you think if I let Red Loftus come back to our parties, he'd *admit* I found him a job after he split, and a *second* job after he fucked up the first? Can't you see him propping up the coffee bar at the Club, spreading enough bullshit to fertilize the Napa Valley? You think he'd tell anyone that we slipped him the money to get to his father's bedside *after* he walked out on us? Privately we've helped half a dozen of those bastards, but if we make it public policy it will kill our people, because they can't see through a shit-kicker like Red. They'll *believe* you can screw your friends, then make it and return to boast in their bar. We *cannot* bless incompetence and share the faint hope of liberals."

There is another pause, then Kenny Hepper, Delancey's first graduate, testifies.

"I gave my word and I managed to keep it, and every day

of my life has been better as a result. I'm glad Delancey didn't compromise, because I needed those two years, every bit of them."

Mon Singh Sandhu nods in agreement.

"I lied to almost everyone for most of my life. This was the first big promise I ever kept, and it turned me around. I'd resent it if others who hadn't stuck with us came to share the fun."

John senses he has carried the meeting and moves to wrap up the discussion.

"Let's keep the rule for the time being. God knows we're liberalizing fast enough. We can discuss exceptional personalities who have donated to the Foundation on a case-by-case basis. This has been a good discussion. Anyone have anything else to add?"

Pat nods sagely and raises a finger. "On the subject of splitees, I would counsel absolute rigidity—on the other hand, I understand and I applaud flexibility."

The meeting breaks up with nervous half-smiles in Pat's direction. They are never quite sure if he's being serious, . . . and Pat, gazing impassively into the middle distance, is not about to tell them. . . .

13

Synthesis and Celebration

FOR YEARS AND YEARS, it seems, experts on penology and rehabilitation have been giving us their ideas on the reformation of the criminal or the addict. What does it take?

Are *jobs* the answer, and are *occupational qualifications* necessary for the job market? After all, ex-convicts and ex-addicts have poorer chances on the conventional job market, and much more financial opportunity, glamour, and excitement in criminal careers. Can we seriously expect the dream of quick riches to give way to the life of a working drudge? It is a matter, as sociologists say, of *differential opportunity structures,* and new legitimate structures of competing attractiveness are obviously required.

Or you could say it is a matter of *making restitution.* People who have done lasting harm to others are rarely given the chance to set something against this which is of equivalent or greater benefit. What "turns you around," surely, is *helping someone worse off than yourself.*

But one should not forget the importance of *group therapy to repair inadequate socialization.* Criminals and addicts are largely devoid of social learning and tend to grab at sensations that socialized people achieve interpersonally. Or is that just a vague language for *systematic rewards and punishments* with appropriate "reinforcements" coming immediately after "behavior"?

How shallow, though, to look merely at surfaces! Cannot the experts understand that *repressed guilt and hatred* must first be brought into consciousness? Not that any can expect to repair the results of broken families and fatherless homes, unless they provide *an alternate family structure* and a *substitute for the failure of the nuclear family.*

One is frankly sorry for those in rehabilitation who do not seem to understand that *prejudice and racism* must first be overcome if its victims are to feel any respect for law and order. Any law that upholds such *gross inequality* must expect that people withdraw allegiance. Or is that just a weak-kneed excuse by liberals for avoiding the need for *firm discipline and close supervision?* It is absurd to think that the system can long survive without *respect for authority.* Have we, in this secular age, forgotten the *reality of sin and the need for atonement?*

Come to think of it, little can be achieved without *decent housing* and *improved physical amenities.* People have very little chance if they must live in crumbling environments. The answer is to get them *out of the slums.* Visits to the countryside with plenty of fresh air and *team sports* and *physical exercise* provide a healthy release of energy.

Fundamentally, is not the problem the *loss of community,* the absence of a *sense of rootedness and cultural continuity?* Has not the *decline of religion* left us adrift without spiritual anchors?

It can all be summed up by the *sociopolitical and economic powerlessness of the individual* in the modern state. Crime represents the fitful grabbing for control by the otherwise impotent. Genuine liberation consists in *moral crusading and*

struggling to change the system that has oppressed you. It requires *proper legal representation* and *enough economic resources* to make the system respond.

But in the end doesn't it all come down to *inadequate
moral values,* normlessness, or *anomie?* People need to be
trained in *cultural and dramatic arts of communication* if
moral values are to be conveyed and fulfilled, although we
should not forget what nearly all convicted and addicted
people lack—*a nonexploitive, deeply intimate love relationship with a significant other.* What is required is *a social
matrix fostering intimacy and mutualism.*

All of which is useless without *gun control,* a commitment
to *nonviolent conflict resolution, the removal of addictive sub-
stances,* and *adequate nutritional diets.*

That makes at least thirty-four "different" approaches to
rehabilitation. Under normal procedures it would require
close to a dozen federal agencies, as many different professions charging their highest fees, and hundreds of
millions of the taxpayers' money siphoned off to those who
don't pay taxes and mug you to boot. It is hardly a promising political prospect.

What has happened is that each approach, joined with
perhaps one or two others, has been touted as *the* Answer
and been made to vie with all the others for limited public
funds. Each approach has failed for lack of the other supporting ingredients.

Delancey, of course, contains *all* these approaches in synthesis. But it is not just a matter of doing everything at once.
There have been Indian reservations with a ratio of one
social worker to three Indians, and multiservice delivery
systems have zeroed in on their luckless targets from all of a
dozen directions, and the despair only deepened. The solution never was *in* the separate ingredients themselves so
much as *among* them, in the combinations and constel-
lations of meanings thus formed. The principle of self-help

must assure that the mix of ingredients in their vital proportions are under the day-to-day control of the people concerned. If growth is a balancing act, no mandate from Washington or advice from experts can tell the tightrope walkers to lean left or to lean right. They *must* respond to a homeostatic sense coming from within themselves.

At Delancey, the clues to psycho-social development lie in the way different approaches have been connected in self-correcting clusters. For example, the businesses are regarded as operating *for* the economic sustenance of family members, yet family members find themselves and develop skills through the increasingly effective operation of these businesses. The spiritual intensity of Dissipations would fade with the morning light were there not a myriad of social, political, economic, and educational ventures to employ the changes of heart, and the ventures would soon become obsessive and manic but for long nights spent searching the soul. There is a social and psychological *ecology* in the patterning of these elements, a "justice" in the sense of balance among them. They are more than the sum of their parts, synergistic in their mutual enhancement.

Delancey maintains this balance and gives an overarching meaning to its synthesis in two principal ways. One is the dialectical processes of bargaining among War Department, State Department, and Vatican, which were described in Chapter 11. The second way is through a series of semicultural, semireligious celebrations, which elaborate myths and metaphors to give meanings to the whole.

Delancey celebrates Thanksgiving, New Year's Day, Christmas, and St. Patrick's Day among others, but we shall concentrate here on three celebrations important to the maintenance of a multiethnic community. These are Mexican Independence Day, Lincoln's Emancipation Proclamation, and the Jewish Passover Seder. Each is run by the ethnic minority concerned. Each minority invites the participation of others and attempts to generalize the meaning of the celebration to include its guests. Universalism and particularism are joined. Each culture tries to bring its own enlightenment to the larger community.

On Mexican Independence Day 1975, I am in the audience when Delancey hosts Cesar Chavez and some leading members and friends of the United Farm Workers. George Camarillo, a resident Mexican in his late forties with more than a decade in various prisons, presides as master of ceremonies. He first introduces the musicians, Joe Cuba, Mongo Santamaria, and Tito Puente, who are due to give a "Spanish Harlem" concert this week for the benefit of the Foundation. Then he announces John Maher. There is a burst of applause that changes to rhythmic clapping. It reaches a climax, then peters out. John begins.

Welcome to our celebration ... [There is a commotion. Someone is moving in an extra table to seat a group of priests.]

Make room for Father Boyle and his friends—'cause we like 'em, and the organization they used to represent! I also see in the audience Mr. Gonzales, who stood with us when no one else dared. He'll be a supervisor again if we know anything about it! *Very* liberal towards convicts these San Francisco politicians have become—ever since our people joined four local Democratic clubs and one Republican club. The difference is, Mr. Gonzales here was with us from the beginning, when we were trying to bring Christianity to Pacific Heights, and *that* we don't forget! Any more than we forget our early supporter, the man I hope to resemble if I lose thirty pounds, Senator George Moscone!

But I'm here today to say that it's essential to us that the United Farm Workers win their strike in Northern California. All prisoners—black, white, and brown—stand united behind them; so do our friends, the senior citizens. We stand with the Farm Workers because their cause represents the most coherent moral issue to which we can attach multiracial, cross-class support in a coalition that can assure the freedom of us all. Do not be misled.

The exploiters have not changed. If they're not shooting at us now, it's because they're shooting at the Spanish people. If we abandon the Spanish people, the exploiters will soon get round to us! It is appropriate that we should welcome the leader of the UFW on the day we celebrate Mexican Independence, because cultural integrity is what much of this struggle is about. The growers are even prepared to offer the Teamsters a little bit extra, if they can buy off the necessity of dealing with a self-conscious cultural, political, and spiritual movement, which is concerned for struggling people everywhere, and whose vision and demands are irreducible to dollars and cents.

In the U.S. today there is one man and one group which stands above all others in integrity and morality. We all look to this man—the last of a heroic line of highly visible leaders who struggled nonviolently for freedom in this country. He has *kept the faith* all through the dark years of violence when it was no longer chic, and the writers were spilling ink to explain how *we* could spill our blood, and some of our own brothers confused revolution with being revolting. This man persevered and will ultimately be victorious, and his victory can help Italians, Irishmen, and our black brothers to get back on to the track. I give you the inspiration of us all—Cesar Chavez!

Chavez comes to the microphone looking small after that buildup. His shoulders slope forward, and he holds his hands in front of him as if grasping an invisible short hoe that he must soon stoop to use. But he has a smile of marvelous serenity, and the thin lines that run from the corners of each eye suggest laughter, not weariness.

Thank you, Brother Maher, Senator Moscone, Supervisor Gonzales, brothers, and sisters. I am glad to be here at your fourth celebration of Mexican Independence Day. We are especially grateful to our Puerto Rican brothers and sisters who prepared this traditional fiesta with all the good food. . . .

I look around here, and I think perhaps this is how it will be, this place is the shape of the future, if there is to be one. We haven't had much success . . . living by ourselves . . . each tiny family the hostage to some business or the state. You don't have to be long in this house to sense that the people here are alive, because they know what it's like to live for each other. In a way I envy you, because we Farm Workers ask for and receive far more help than we can ever return, and sometimes I think how can we ever pay these people back? But you have worked out a way to give even when you have only little for yourselves and that is what gives you a stature and a pride that poor people can gain only with difficulty.

We Farm Workers have been struggling for our lives these last two years, and every time things got bad, your help was there, totally and unconditionally, and one day I do believe—I'll be coming to Sacramento to see Governor Maher! [Cheers]

Cesar gives a description of his recent travels. In New York he has persuaded the legislature to endorse the boycott of lettuce, grapes, and Gallo wines. The Governor of Massachusetts has pledged his support. UFW has brought successful suits against Gallo for dumping unsold grapes and against the Teamsters—only the *New York Times* keeps insisting Chavez is dead. He is embarrassed to appear in this continual state of resurrection.

There was this circus . . . and not enough people were coming to it. So the owners tried a ruse to trick the people. "We'll offer one thousand dollars to any paying customer who can move our biggest elephant." They had trained the elephant not to budge, and thousands came and paid and pulled and pushed, but the elephant held still. But one little man waited until everyone else gave up and the elephant wasn't expecting him. He took a long, long run and came up behind the elephant and booted him in the ass, and the elephant moved one step he was so surprised, and the owners had to pay.

"This won't do!" they said. "We can't have people winning. We'll change the rules. From now on anyone who first gets the elephant to nod his head and then to shake it can have two thousand dollars." And once again many people came and tried and failed. Until the same little man came into the tent. This time he walked right up to the elephant and looked him in the eye. "Remember me?" he asked, and the elephant nodded his head. "You want another kick?" and the elephant shook his head . . .

and that's what we're saying to the growers! Thank you very much and God bless you all.

Amid the storm of applause John remounts the stage, pauses, and then holds up his hands for silence.

"Let's do our usual . . . Are we gonna pay 'em back for Malcom X?"

"Yeah!" roars the crowd.

"Are we gonna pay 'em back for Jack Kennedy?"

"Yeah!"

"Are we gonna pay 'em back for Martin Luther King?"

"Yeah!"

"For the Molly Maguires?"

"Yeah!"

"For the Flannigan Brothers?"

"Yeah!"

"Tell them *how* we're gonna pay 'em. WE'LL WIN WITH CHAVEZ!"

"Yeah!"

"Okay! Now during the rest of the festivities we'll be taking up a collection for the UFW. But I gotta problem. Upstairs we got some real, upstanding family men like Grapshi dandling Vietnamese orphans and changing diapers. Only now the kids are asleep, and we musn't wake 'em. So please, during this collection, *no noisy clinking silver.* Rustle the paper quietly and make sure it's the same color as the lettuce you're *not* gonna buy!"

George Camarillo comes to the microphone. He is an older man, by Delancey's standards, with deep lines nose to mouth, a scar on his chin, and streaks of white in his dark hair.

"I would like to thank the cooks for this wonderful meal, and a special hand please for Patty Rodriguez, who conceived the whole notion of combining this fiesta with our invitation to Cesar Chavez."

A waiflike girl of about fifteen with long black hair, brown eyes, and olive skin half rises to her feet, then sits down quickly as the applause mounts. Her neighbors at the table hug her, and she seems grateful to bury her face among the people she knows. George continues:

I have been asked to say a few words on the life and history of Benito Juárez. He is, as you should know, the great patriot of Mexican history, the leader of Mexican independence in the struggle against the French armies of Napoleon III. He was born poor, an Aztec Indian, and he educated himself to lead his people. I would like to say that for many, many years of my life I have been ignorant of Mexican history and culture. I thought of myself in prison as alone. But it was my ignorance, not only the bars, that had isolated me. Mexican history is rich with people who improved themselves and struggled and died so that people like us could hold up our heads and not be ashamed.

So today I want to pay tribute to Benito Juárez, to Villa, and to Zapata, and all the heroes of Mexican independence. Many, many times Juárez was close to defeat as Chavez has been, and always he came back until he had exhausted his foes.

I have been in several Dissipations here. In one of them John challenged the man next to me. "Name *three men* who have been great in Mexican history!" And the man next to me couldn't and neither could I, and I shrank with the shame. And the next day I went to the library, which is the same room where they hold Dissipations, and there I found a book on the great artist Diego Rivera and I found *Labyrinth of Solitude* by Octavio Paz; and I don't pretend to understand all they show, but I've read and seen enough to know that there is thought and art and philosophy rooted in our experience, which we can share and which makes us brothers not just with each other but across the years. Here are men whose work is known throughout the world—as I believe our work at Delancey will be known and is beginning to be known.

So I'd like to have a big cheer tonight for our guest, for Diego Rivera, and for Benito Juárez. Let's educate ourselves—Okay? So we're not poor and ignorant and dominated all our lives. And let us work knowing that there were people who wrote and painted and struggled and even died to give us a better chance. So I ask you to repeat after me: Viva Juárez! Viva Rivera! Viva Chavez!

The audience echoes each cry. Then we all rise, link arms, and sing as the band plays:

Unidos en la huelga
No nos moveran.

My mood is slightly jarred by a short square Jewish lady beside me who is shrieking "We shall Overcome" in a high flat falsetto. For the rest of the meal she insists on giving me the early union history of the song which the rest of us weren't singing. But then the intermingling of cultures is not without its misunderstandings.

Every June Delancey celebrates the Emancipation Proclamation. This year Ed Marcellus, a black resident, is presiding, and there is a feast of ham hocks, collard greens, cornbread, potatoes, salad, and banana pudding. A children's jazz band from Oakland opens the proceedings with a remarkably able performance. This is followed by Erica Huggins, president of the Black Panther Party, reading her prison poetry. John makes a face. He does not like odes to caged consciousness or Promethean prisoners scribbling their defiance on toilet paper. The Reverend Cecil Williams of Glide Memorial Church, who he was hoping would offset this by his sense of humor, was unable to come today. So when John rises it is with more than a touch of dissent.

New holidays keep being grafted onto the American calendar, and unless we are very careful, they degenerate into meaningless opportunities to have lunch. For most Americans Thanksgiving means very little. They rarely celebrate the incredible endurance and courage that was called forth by the voyage to the New World, and rarely is it asked what journeys of similar peril are required of us today.

The forces in charge of this country have systematically deprived people of the symbols necessary for assertion and cohesiveness. They would rather you cheered madly for Chubby Checkers, deluged yourselves in black-eyed peas, and celebrated the first black man to use a fountain pen. They want Jews to be merchants who eat lox and bagel sandwiches and crack funny jokes. They want Irishmen who get drunk and fight on St. Patrick's Day, and they love for Italians to eat spaghetti and belch and shut up until the *next* Columbus Day. That's the "ethnicity" the ruling class applauds. They'll give you your Day to pacify you and let you make pigs of yourself. So please don't fall into the trap we fell into.

The emancipation of the slaves was not a victory so much as an historical turning point—the first round in a continuing contest for black rights. Celebrate this day without reservation, and you subscribe to the dangerous heresy that white men can "give" freedom to black men. It was a right that should never have been withheld in the first place and in some respects is still withheld today. So please remember that this day on which you have a good meal was built *on the bones* of Americans of all colors, but especially black Americans, who struggled for centuries against the evil and repression inherent in this society. So between mouthfuls of ham, let's remember that, or there'll be another pile of bones before they buy you off with the *next* holiday!

Try not to be tricked off by false forms of cultural nationalism that masquerade as true ones. Culture cannot stand still. You cannot go back and reassemble from the dead husks some self-indulgent concept of what you were. There is nothing your rulers like better than building nuclear reactors while American Indians caper around relearning the Ghost Dance. Killers of living things like to stuff them, and blanket-weavers, bead-threaders, and feather-stickers are stuffed Indians, trophies of the white man's conquest. You play that game whenever you are induced to idolize the slave aspects of your culture. When social workers tell you that "black English" is "groovy" and "authentic," don't let yourself be patronized or your poverty mystified. There is no literature in black English, no medicine, architecture, philosophy, physics, or engineering. When the kings of Italy threw a banquet, they didn't serve spaghetti, nor did the kings of Africa serve grits or pigs' knuckles. The diets of the poor are not fit subjects for worship.

You honor your past and your traditions by using them to inform and confront the future, by making of them a springboard to greater freedom and power. I would suggest that you concentrate on *creating* black culture, rather than researching its remains beneath the heels of Arab slave traders and European adventurers.

Let it be a prophecy that bears fruit in your struggles. Ask each year, what did we do *last year* to advance black culture and strength, and what will we do *next year?* And keep the score without flinching. Thank you very much.

As John steps down from the rostrum, a black man I do not know, a square perhaps, reads from W. E. B. Du Bois.

The bright ideals of the past—physical freedom, political power, the training of brains, the training of hands—all these in turn have waxed and waned, until even the last grows dim and overcast. Are they all wrong, all false? No, not that, but each was oversimple and incomplete—the dreams of a credulous race-childhood, or the fond imaginings of the other world which does not know or does not want to know our power. To be really true, all these ideals must be melted and welded into one.

One should attend, if possible, Delancey's annual Seders. The one I saw was orchestrated by Danny Weinstein, one of Delancey's attorneys and son of the late Rabbi Weinstein. Four hundred of us sit at tables set with matzo, grape juice, something that looks like liver paté, small sprigs of parsley, and salt water. Since it is a less-than-mouth-watering feast, I assume it is all symbolic. It is. Danny starts to explain.

Not *every* moment of Delancey's celebrations are magical, and as Danny launches into a hip rendition of the flight of the Children of Israel, I feel twinges of unease. According to his version "everything grooved for the Israelites" until the new pharaoh "went generally crazy," and Moses spoke unto him saying, "Hey, man, let my people go!" But the pharaoh hardened his heart several times until "Moses got heavy with the dude" and "worked out a deal so's the Angel of Death took care of the first born." All of which caused the pharaoh to exclaim, "Take your curses off my back and split, man!" By now I am inured to the prospect of Moses "getting it all together and motoring for the Red Sea" and "making his connection on Mount Sinai," but Danny's jive-talk comes to a merciful end with the final plague, and we and the Israelites escape together as he continues impressively.

We ask Delancey Street residents and friends to join us in this celebration of the Jewish Passover because so many of you here have made your own personal journeys from slavery into freedom and from darkness into light. It wasn't an easy journey for them or for you, and it involved and involves the loss of close friends and relatives along the way. Since this is a family celebration in which everyone from the oldest to the youngest takes some part and since it is a celebration of freedom, we want you to sit back, relax, and enjoy yourselves.

Zev Putterman, an alumnus of Rikers Island and now a television producer, takes over the microphone to explain the ritual questions to be asked by the four sons: the Wise Son, the Wicked Son, the Simple Son, and the Son-So-Simple-He-Doesn't-Know-How-To-Ask.

Delancey has a way of turning things upside down, so when you hear our choices for the different sons who will ask the questions, remember that it's topsy-turvy. The choice for the wisest, the most philosophic, and visionary is none other than Vernon Anski!

Vernon, who must rate among the world's least successful confidence tricksters, comes up to read the question. In his dastardly career he was finally reduced to working as an insurance salesman on Skid Row, signing up winos who looked to his practiced eye as about to meet their maker. He would pay their insurance premiums himself while he awaited their blessed release. But they *would* linger on for months, even years, while Vernie-the-Vulture inquired, with evident concern, about their health, and flapped around the public morgues. But he went broke on his perch, his neck extended in vain expectancy toward the row of recumbent figures huddled over gratings and in doorways.

The Wicked Son—actually a daughter—turns out to be

Sandy Whittaker, renowned chiefly for a seraphic smile and an unwillingness to hurt anyone except herself.

The next choice was a hard one. We had to find the simplest, the most uncomplicated, the least intellectual—and none of you will be surprised at our choice, Patrick O. McGillycuddy!

Pat, of course, is renowned for the delivery of sentences of amazing circumlocution and complexity, sentences that succeed in embracing every positive value that Delancey stands for, while qualifying each with its negation or contradiction and attributing them all to himself at various levels of abstraction and metameaning. He dazzles in Games, like a species of reversed peacock that spreads out its multicolored mind with the object of saving its tail.

The son who doesn't know how to ask is your basic preverbal situation. And for this tender need we have chosen Ed Walker!

Wild Black Hickok of the Haight, better known as "Blazing Saddles," comes up to read his question. In less than four months at Delancey he has dealt himself a very good hand indeed. He is maitre d' at the restaurant, snapping tablecloths and juggling glasses like a pro, which he is. He has a cheerfulness that does not so much infect as inject you and a handshake that will break and take your fingers without asking.

Danny is at the microphone.

Now most of you will have in front of you a piece of green parsley and a glass of salt water. Passover is more than a celebration of the passing from slavery to freedom; it is a spring festival to celebrate the freshness of a new season after the harshness of winter. So we take the parsley and we dip it in the salt water, and we do this to recall that freedom has grown out of discipline and sacrifice, that many of our brothers and sisters are still in oppression, weeping salt tears in their slavery, and that nothing worth attaining comes to us easily. So we dip the parsley and we take a bite and we say:

Praised art Thou Oh Lord our God—King of the Universe
—Creator of the Fruit of the Earth.
Passover is also a celebration that involves the very youngest in
the family. So we have asked Alfred to come forward and read. . . .

It is a tense moment for Alfred, and a silence falls on the
room. Two years ago when he came to the Foundation at
the age of nine, he could not read—although he had a well-
developed line of epithets. Today he has to read in front of
four hundred people. He is shaking but manages the words,
with a few promptings from Zev, who rests a hand on his
shoulder. The audience breaks into applause.

Rabbi Feinberg, who, although in his seventies, counsels
Delancey residents on the secrets of sexual vigor, reads the
responses to Alfred's questions in Hebrew and then waves
his black and white striped cane, which was personally
presented to him by Ho Chi Minh. Everybody cheers. Danny is back explaining.

"We are going straight to a part of the service that should
mean a lot to all of us here. It is called 'The Dayenu,' which
literally translated means 'It would have been enough.'
Barry Torgove is going to read to us a series of statements,
and we ask you to respond 'Dayenu' at the end of each,
beginning softly and gradually raising your voices."

"Had he brought us out of the land of Egypt and not
divided the sea for us,"

"Dayenu!"

"Had he divided the sea for us and not permitted us to
cross on dry land,"

"Dayenu!"

The dayenus mount slowly in volume and reach a
thunderous climax. Then we turn to the special Delancey
Street Dayenu. It was written by Janet Weinstein, Danny's
mother. At the celebration in 1974 she had read it aloud for
the first time.

"Had the original Bush Street apartments helped but a

handful of ex-convicts and ex-addicts and not grown in three years to be the Delancey Street Foundation, with over three hundred residents of different races and religions,"

"Dayenu!"

"Had we just grown and lived together in harmony and not expanded to the Ebbtide apartments in Sausalito and the El Portal,"

"Dayenu!"

"Had we purchased the Ebbtide and El Portal and not developed successfully the moving, the flower, raffle, auto repair, and construction businesses,"

"Dayenu!"

"Had we run these businesses and not opened a restaurant, endorsed as a training school by the Culinary Workers Union, and been granted a beer and wine license by the city of San Francisco,"

"Dayenu!"

"Had the restaurant been endorsed and the license granted and had we not been the first group of ex-convicts ever to have been approved as a federally chartered and guaranteed credit union,"

"Dayenu!"

"Had we been approved as a credit union and not been accredited as a San Francisco high school,"

"Dayenu!"

"Had we been accredited as a high school and not had eighty members of our family in colleges, vocational schools, and private schools,"

"Dayenu!"

"Had we over eighty in these schools and not had others training as real estate brokers, computer technicians, and secretaries,"

"Dayenu!"

"Had Delancey not freed more than five hundred prisoners from jail and not freed those now in its expanded family from the chains of prejudice, freed us to be honest with ourselves, freed us to help fight the injustices of the system,"

"Dayenu!"

"Had our community family gained these freedoms from working here and not wanted to say 'thank you' to the Delancey Street Foundation,"

"Dayenu!"

"But plentiful are our reasons for gratitude, and so with exaltation, mutual affection, and admiration we give you one more cry of . . ."

"DAYENU!"

Danny goes on to point out that other cultures, especially the black culture, have borrowed from the story of Moses.

When things were really bad, the black people of the South would dream of another world that would soothe their suffering in this one. The song "Swing Low, Sweet Chariot" was inspired by just such feelings. But later, as hope grew, the example of Moses leading his people out of subjection caught the imagination of such black poets as Langston Hughes and Paul Lawrence Dunbar and did much to inspire Martin Luther King. The song "Go Down Moses," which our choir is ready to sing for us, was a symbol of the new emerging mood, the dawning hope of a social as well as spiritual salvation.

Four black residents come up onto the stage and sing in perfect pitch without accompaniment.

Go down Moses
Way down in Egypt land
Tell ole Pharaoh—oh—oh
Let ma people go—oh—oh

The Israelites took forty years in the desert, and that's not surprising. It took that long to learn what freedom meant, to grow the muscles and the discipline necessary to exercise that freedom and turn from a rabble of slaves into a self-determined group. That's what we're learning here at Delancey—that it takes time—and if we do in two or more years what took them forty—we ain't doing too bad! I now turn you over to Hal Fenton, who has an announcement.

Hal is in his yarmulke. The evening sunlight has caught the silver frame on the left edge of his eyeglasses giving him a curious half-halo.

I just wanted to remind you that there is a Dissipation going on this weekend, and those who'll be experiencing it are sitting at those two tables. They'll be making their own individual journeys from darkness to light in the next sixty hours. They'll be turning anguish into the joy of mutual comfort and shedding tears so that parts of them long crippled can begin to grow afresh. The shape of the Dissipation, like the shape of the Seder, is that of a dramatic and miraculous narrative, and for both educative and spiritual reasons, which are never far apart, it is necessary for each one of us to make our own pilgrimage and find our own deliverance. So this is more than a religious celebration; it is a reenactment for all those of us who found, or shall find ourselves, in physical, mental, and spiritual chains.

But no symbolism would suffice were it not for the physical reality of our record in releasing men and women from prisons and jails. Something happened just this afternoon to remind us vividly of that achievement. Everyone who has been here more than a few months knows Jeffrey Cartwright. He was here a short time, split, and got into so much trouble that he was sentenced two days ago to fifteen to thirty years. Well, Charlie Mack and Tommy Grapshi went on our behalf to Martinez and spoke with the judge who had *already* sentenced him. They explained to the judge some things about Jeff he didn't know, and they mentioned casually that they had spent most of *their* lives in prison and a "hopeless" case was not perhaps as hopeless as it seemed, and so early this afternoon the judge reversed himself and gave Jack thirty days in prison and probated him to Delancey Street!

The audience rises as one with a roar of applause and appreciation. This strikes them where they live.

"And *that* is what this place and this Seder is all about, and *this* [Hal waves his arm in an inclusive gesture] is what makes it all worthwhile."

A Theoretical Appendix

OR A HEADLONG ASSAULT UPON THE INEFFABLE

What follows is "heavy," as my friends at Delancey would say. It is included for a small hard core of incorrigible Explainers like myself, who are still arrogant enough to believe that human and moral growth is an explicable phenomenon. Those who are allergic to thickets of impenetrable jargon should stop reading here and be glad that I restrained myself so long. Even so, what follows is surely *less* complex than the kind of moral reasoning that will be necessary for survival in tomorrow's world, for none of us will long survive with our giant modern muscles and our tiny, primitive moralities.

My approach to human development is by way of psycho-social learning. We learn viable social codes when we can employ them in working, loving, and communicating with one another. The following is a common-sense model of this process.

(1) Persons EXIST creatively
(2) through the quality of their PERCEPTION
(3) the strength of their IDENTITIES

(4) and the syntheses of these into their anticipated and experienced COMPETENCES

(5) They COMMIT these with *intensity* and *authenticity* in their human environments

(6) periodically SUSPENDING their cognitive structures and RISKING themselves

(7) in trying to BRIDGE the DISTANCE to others

(8) They seek to make SELF-CONFIRMING SELF-TRANSCENDING IMPACTS upon others

(9) and through *dialectics* achieve higher levels of SYNERGY

(10) All parties attempt to ORDER the FEEDBACK from this process into matrices of developing COMPLEXITY

Two aspects of this cycle require further clarification. By "persons EXIST creatively" I mean that while all of us are bombarded by shaping forces and are confined by finite vocabularies, we retain the capacity to resynthesize such information into new patterns of meaning, to prefer some influences over others, and to stand out, "ex-ist."

The *dialectic* leading to SYNERGY is the key to my entire argument and, I think, to a thorough understanding of Delancey. Synergy comes from the Greek *synergia,* "a working with." Elements are said to be synergistic when their action contributes to the strength of other elements and the whole so formed so that the whole is greater than, and qualitatively different from, the sum of the parts.

The cycle depicted in the diagram contains a number of potential opposites, which in the right proportions work *with* each other and in the wrong proportions work *against* each other. Suppose I am seeking for myself an addition to my feeling of COMPETENCE (4). I therefore ask my associates to CONFIRM (8) as much of my new capacities as they are prepared to acknowledge, but not more, so that I am enabled to ORDER the FEEDBACK (10) from their reaction. In this event, all three parts or elements of the process are in SYNERGY (9).

But suppose, on the other hand, that I EXIST creatively (1) and appear so strange before my friends that a huge DISTANCE opens up between them and me, which we fail to BRIDGE (7). In that case the elements are working *against* each other, and every additional degree of self-differentiation impedes the possibility of my integration with others.

Let us take one more example. My COMMITMENT to a belief and my SUSPENSION of that belief are usually regarded as opposites. In fact, they oppose each other *only* when their proportions are unequal, e.g., when I am *so* strongly COMMITTED that I refuse to consider that I may be mistaken. A COMMITMENT of mine that is temporarily SUSPENDED and survives this reexamination *is all the stronger for it, as is my capacity to entertain my doubts in the future.*

Now any moral code that seeks to guide the processes of social interaction must contain axioms that emphasize and de-emphasize every part of that process, so that human relationships can be nudged back into SYNERGY and balanced in just proportions. Take the idea of "EXISTING creatively." You can *emphasize* this and praise Geniuses and Revolutionaries, or you can *de-emphasize* it and praise Obedience, Loyalty, etc. The first group reorganizes received information beyond recognition. The second group reflects it humbly. What you have, then, is a bipolar construct:

Genius... Obedience
Revolution   Loyalty

According to one view, the further you go to the left, the better you are. According to the other view, the further you go to the right, the better you are. But advocates of Left and Right are rarely content to recognize an opposite virtue. Obedience and Loyalty are really *conformity* and *sterility* says the Revolutionary. Genius and Revolution are really *anarchy* and *chaos* says the Loyalist. So now we have positives and negatives at both ends:

Genius/*anarchy* .... Obedience/*sterility*
Revolution/*chaos*   Loyalty/*conformity*

Our moral codes will guide us in growth, or kill us, *depending on where we conceive the Good to be on such a continuum.* I submit, and Delancey Street exemplifies it, that genuine EXISTENCE and CREATIVITY are not *extensions* of Genius into "way out," "wow," and "mind-blowing" extremes, but an optimal synthesis of change with continuity, of radicalism with traditionalism, of new with old. All great works of creation are reweavings of *old* elements into *new* forms. Creativity gives a "shock of recognition" precisely because the separate elements usually are *not* new, but their particular combination *is.*

People who express new ideas in new words, with new grammar, punctuation, and syntax, are not literary lions; they are lunatics, and their "word salads" are symptoms of their schizophrenia.

Now consider the state of mind of a moral absolutist who tries to push either Genius or Obedience to its "logical" extremity. In the first place, he faces an impossible task, since he cannot originate from nothing, and he *becomes* nothing when perfectly obedient to an external force. Such an idealist is likely, therefore, to fall lamentably beneath his own ideals. Worse, he will become painfully aware that his ideal (or idol) is subject to foul misinterpretations by others. People are actually saying that his Genius is mere *anarchy,* that he is a crazy punk who has lost his marbles! And the *more* of a Genius he tries to be, the louder, the more insulting, and the more intrusive their disparagement becomes.

It must even seem to him that his external enemies, the personifiers of *sterility, conformity,* and "kiss-ass," have made common cause with some *sterile* sediment in his own soul. Why else should all his frantic attempts to be different end up looking so much the same? Why does he keep having these nightmares of slipping backward into some homogeneous mass? Soon the sheer, horrifying contrast between the accelerating height of his pretended goodness and the accelerating depth of his alleged depravity becomes unbearable. He must destroy the Enemy without, or destroy the Enemy within, or even both. The next man who calls him "crazy" is *dead!* Let's settle it one way or the other!

So far we have dealt with just one polar construct that inflated and negated the principle of "EXISTING creatively." In fact all parts of the cycle have their inflations and their negations, and each polarity is expressible in positive or negative terms.

Element of the Cycle	Inflation	Negation
1) CREATIVE EXISTENCE	Genius/*chaos* Revolution/*anarchy*	Obedience/*sterility* Loyalty/*conformity*
2) PERCEPTION	Vigilance/*hypervigilance* Objectivity/*voyeurism*	Gnosticism/*myopia* Intuitions/*illusions*
3) IDENTITY	Individualism/*egotism* Character/*narcissism*	Selflessness/*anonymity* Altruism/*effacement*
4) COMPETENCE	Mastery/*dominance* Strength/*brutality*	Meekness/*weakness* Refinement/*impotence*
5) COMMITMENT	Dedication/*fanaticism* Mission/*extremism*	Restraint/*passivity* Grace/*indecision*
intense	Passion/*infatuation* Caring/*obsession*	Self-control/*apathy* Self-discipline/*coldness*
authentic	Truth/*ingenuousness* Innocence/*artlessness*	Subterfuge/*lies* Tact/*trickery*
6) RISK *and* SUSPENSION	Courage/*recklessness* Heroism/*foolhardiness* Self-sacrifice/*surrender* Martyrdom/*abdication*	Caution/*cowardice* Prudence/*fright* Steadfastness/*rigidity* Unshakeable purpose/*bigotry*
7) BRIDGING THE DISTANCE	The Outsider/*the subverted* Rejected Redeemer/*the traitor*	The Elect/*the cult* The VIP's/*the gang*
8) SELF-CONFIRMATION *and* SELF-TRANSCENDENCE	Success/*exploitation* Glory/*gratification* Mystery/*mystification* Supernatural/*religiosity*	Noble Suffering/*failure* Purgation/*frustration* Secularity/*the mundane* Simplicity/*primitiveness*
9) SYNERGY	Oneness/*coalescence* Perfect Unity/*cooptation*	Authority/*authoritarianism* Hierarchy/*Segregation*
10) ORDERED FEEDBACK AND COMPLEXITY	Inscrutable wisdom/*obscurantism*	Fundamentalism/*know-nothingness*

From the table we can derive some clues as to why man is the most predatory beast in the animal kingdom, one of the very few who will slay conspecifics and do it *en masse*. The heel of Achilles, as Arthur Koestler has called it, lies in the semantic traps of our own moral language. The "best" behaviors and the "worst" lie at the ends of the same constructs, and this ambiguity makes us murderous in our guilt and anxiety. Seeing no rational way of distinguishing Strength from *brutality,* or Courage from *recklessness,* we turn upon those who disparage us and try to close their mouths forever.

With the aid of this table we can create profiles of some of the major characters at Delancey Street. Consider Stephanie in Chapter 4. She pushed to polar limits her Genius as a painter, her Gnosticism about the eternal nature of the pyramid, and the riot of her Individualism across her canvases. Furiously she strove for Mastery, Dedication, Passion, Truth, and Courage in her work. She was swept up into a small Elect that glorified her every step up the abstraction ladder until she was engulfed in Mystery, seeking a Perfect Unity with her own canvases.

Yet such unsynthesized extremities must be paid for, and the price was exacted from her private life, which was in direct counterpoint to her art. She was *conforming, self-effacing, impotent* to improve her relationships, *passive, apathetic, ingenuous,* and *frightened.* She *surrendered* to her men friends, permitting them to *subvert* and *frustrate* her. Her social life was a failure, and her style of existence *mundane* and *primitive.*

More terrifying yet was another reality that emerged from beneath her art. Was she a Genius or was her mind in *chaos,* was she Gnostic or *deluded,* the member of a brilliant Elect or of a self-congratulating *cult,* in Unity with her own art or lost to it? Or was she in a *coalescence* that obliterated all boundaries between her self and her environment?

Josh, whom we encountered in the same chapter, pushed the ideas of himself as Hero, Genius, and great Character to their outermost limits. He was the Intuitive reader of women's hearts, the Passionate seeker for Truth in the heart of love who would Sacrifice himself to bring a moment's Glory to a dying maiden and touch her *mundane* life with the Mystery of his presence.

There is nothing wrong with such values provided that their function is not to repress and disguise an opposite reality. The reality was that our Hero had run from almost every major challenge in his life, that the Genius was a dropout, the Character a nonentity at the age of forty, that the Intuiter was a heartless *voyeur* of others' emotions whose Passion was, in fact, a *coldly* calculated rendition of learned lines.

In Josh we saw the tendency to self-destruction most clearly. Exhausted by the hiatus between pretension and reality, he pushed and pushed the limits of credulity, even baiting his audience until they cracked his facade and called his bluff. Disgrace brought temporary relief, but it also brought the obscurity he dreaded; so he had to ham it up again.

There is considerable overlap between my viewpoint and Freudian notions of the repression of unacceptable impulses and ideas until they fester in the unconscious. Those who think in linear terms and pride themselves on their rationalism would find themselves obliged to repress that which is in seeming contradiction to their major self-ideals. For example, the man of Courage would repress his Caution, and when the latter clawed at his guts in the middle of some daredevil feat, he would naturally think of it as *cowardice* and despise the craven creature that lurked within him. Such notions as reaction-formation, compensation, projection, and defense mechanism are all quite consistent with this construct theory.

Yet repression is not the only available device. Stephanie isolated her private from her professional life. Josh repressed to some extent but managed the contradiction, chiefly by a schizoid break between his manifest self and his latent self. The first was an actor. The second a drama critic. The critic commented acidly on the lines the actor fluffed. He was, by turns, an actor fooling an audience, and an audience unmasking an actor.

But the point and counterpoint does not only operate intrapsychically or within the value system of one individual; it also shows itself in complementary role playing. Stephanie's male partners increased their Mastery/*dominance,* Subterfuge/*deceit,* and Success/*exploitation* as they discovered her own penchant for Meekness/*weakness,* Innocence/*artlessness,* and Purgation/*frustration.* Each partner "feeds the other's sickness" as Delancey would say, or exacerbates the other's extremism. We saw this with Bill Toliver in Paris: the great giver pursued by takers (until *he* began to take), the Gnostic beset by spies and *voyeurs* (until *he,* too, became *hypervigilant*), the man of Mystery sucked dry by *primitive* freeloaders (until *he,* too, became *primitive*).

For both Bernado and Foster in Chapter 5 the crucial relationship was with their mothers. The further each son pushed his Courage/*recklessness,* his Steadfastness/*rigidity,* and his Glory/*gratification,* the more his Mama showed Caution/*cowardice,* Sacrificed/*surrendered* herself, and Suffered Nobly/*failed.* Why show emotion and be less than a macho kid when Mama is willing to shed tears for you? Does not *your* toughness elicit *her* tenderness?

In social science parlance a name has been given to this chronic form of overdifferentiation and acceleration of opposite tendencies. The term *schismogenesis* was first coined by the anthropologist Gregory Bateson as early as 1936, but only recently has it gained currency outside anthropological circles. Bateson distinguished two types of schismogenesis, symmetrical and complementary. In the symmetrical type the Strength/*brutality* and Dedication/*fanaticism* of Pepé and his gang of Barracudas vie with the identical values/disvalues of the King Cobras. In complementary schismogenesis members of each gang become Loyal/*con-*

forming to each other so that they can bring Revolution/*chaos* to their opponents. Arthur Koestler reminds us that Cosa Nostra means "our cause" and comments, "This is the infernal dialectics reflected in our history. The egotism of the group feeds on the altruism of its members; the savagery of the group feeds on the devotion of its members." *This* is the dilemma in trying to halt the tide of violence. If you show tenderness and concern for criminals as some liberals advocate, they will use these qualities to shore up their own toughness (complementary schismogenesis). If you show toughness toward criminals as some conservatives advocate, they will escalate their own toughness in response (symmetrical schismogenesis). *Whichever we do the crime rate worsens and the liberal-conservative shouting match becomes a part of the problem instead of a part of the solution.*

The Origins of the Pathology
   The pathology of schismogenetic patterning is everywhere. It is in America's Puritan heritage that pitted the Revolution of the Saints, their Vigilance, their knowledge of the Objective words of the scripture, their Selflessness, Mastery, and Self-disciplined Simplicity; against the Anglo-Catholic tradition of Obedience to the crown and bishops, Intuitions of the divine, and the embroidered Individuality of cavalier courtiers with their Grace and Passionate Mystery. The lines were drawn in not dissimilar ways in the Civil War between North and South, and today we live with this legacy of false dichotomies.
   Our scientific and technical heritage has taught us to analyze, to break into pieces, to search for discrete units of data, to think in linear terms, and to take the measure of all and anything. Every social science has a massive metaphysical bias in favor of the "independent variables" within its sovereignty, and these are believed to determine everyone else's variables. Hence, the social scientist alone gets to play Genius; his experimental subjects Obey/*conform to* the laws that the Genius discovers!
   Schismogenesis is imbedded in our whole tradition of liberal optimism. The more, the faster, the higher, the further, the bigger, and the purer a phenomenon is, the closer we come to perfection. We drool over stories of a sacred seagull who penetrates successive levels of paradise by improving his flight design. Onward and upward!
   Our institutions with their divisions of labor are schismogenetically designed to discharge "pure" objectives. The corporate sector projects Genius, Individualism, Mastery, and Courage. It is a systematized celebration of Success/*exploitation*. The welfare sector is (officially) Loyal to its clients' needs, Selfless on their behalf, Meek in their service, and Cautious with its aid. It is a systematized celebration of Suffering/*failure*. Schismogenetic systems try to avoid risk and thereby failure. If business fails to help the millions of marginal men and women, it is because *they* have failed to come up to corporate standards. If welfare fails to help

them, it is because *they* have failed to sink to levels of eligibility. The potential criminal writhes between these social shears—never quite man enough to make it but at the same time insufficiently slob-like for certification.

Schismogenesis seems inseparable from the commercial operation of the mass media. The mad Genius of Count Frankenstein, the Mastery of medical men, the Heroism of Superfly, the Innocence of Lucy, the pure Mystery of Kung Fu, the Martyrdom of some American Indian, the Suffering of rape victims, the Authority of marshals, and the Perfect Unity of lovey-dovey families—all vie for the greater glory of pancake syrup or the moving of assorted merchandise. "Violence is as American as apple pie," say the critics, who do not comprehend that apple pie morality is *in itself* violent.

When community begins to decay and mass communications try to fill the moral vacuum, then one-dimensional bombast replaces the subtlety of myriad opposite axioms and social cross-pressures. It is the lonely, the poor, the minorities subject to social discrimination who are most tempted to respond to a one-dimensional image. They swallow a poison undiluted by successful social experience, and much like schizophrenics they will seize upon the Strength of Julius Caesar, the Martyrdom of Joan of Arc, or the Noble Suffering of Jesus to find some virtue in their anguish.

I write this a few days after two attempts to shoot President Ford and the finding of Patty Hearst and her SLA captors. All the subjects concerned in these escapades seem manifestly demented and self-destructive. A girl called "Squeaky" appoints herself an avenger of redwood trees. A forty-five-year-old ex-Goldwater supporter and FBI informer asks to be taken into custody a day before she shoots at the President on her way to fetch her child from school. Two SLA "Revolutionaries" are captured *jogging* together near FBI headquarters and in the vicinity of their recent crimes. They have thoughtfully left behind for the police to find a diary that records their exploits.

In Delancey such palpable idiocy would win the Order of the Faucet for Half-assed Histrionics. Instead the media record every squeak with a breathless solemnity.

So what does the Delancey Street Foundation do for its members, and what can it teach us about the antidote to violent patterns? The first important lesson is as follows:

The use of negative evaluation and highly critical language is essential to trimming back inflated behaviors and pretentious exaggerations.

There is no permissive way of dealing with an obsessive need for Mastery that has become *dominant* and *brutal*. You have to call it by its negative names, just as you have to tell the Innocent Self-Sacrificer that she is a silly doormat, or she will go on and on. Both "on the street" and in prison collusions grow to confirm illusions. These have to be shattered.

People must learn to identify one-dimensional extensions of values for what they are—pathology. But shattering illusions can be dangerous. Therefore:

Highly negative judgments and denunciations can only take place within a community that cares for its members and assumes responsibility for them. We have almost reached a point where one cannot say anything unflattering about a person who is poor, black, or disadvantaged without being accused of discriminating against the entire class of persons. There is also the question of whether critics who have not shared his disadvantage have the knowledge to criticize him or the ability to distinguish his social burdens from his personal failures. Delancey shares with other self-help groups *a legitimate position from which to censure personal failure.* John tells his residents, "We gotta drop these ghetto habits of ours, like shouting up the stairs, 'Hey, Billie! You got the Brylcream? I wanna fuck the dog!'" Now a white upper-middle-class psychiatrist could *never* say this to poor or minority clients. Whole ranges of aspersions are out of bounds in exchanges between social classes.

Only if your commitment to help the disadvantaged is beyond question, evidenced by your entire mode of life, only then can furious censure be recognized for what it is, *anger in the context of a community's concern.* This introduces the next proposition.

All effective moral judgments are at least two-dimensional in the full range of their import, not one-dimensional. The second dimension is required to prevent the subject of censure swinging to the other polar position.

The moral messages at Delancey point in opposite ways. "We will take care of you (economically, physically), but as of today you start taking responsibility for your own behavior." "The system made you what you are, but if you want to change the system, you have to accept the responsibility for what you let the system do to you."

As we saw in Chapter 3, John Maher sets a brilliant example in the optimization of opposed values such as tribalism versus universalism, radicalism versus traditionalism, creativity versus productivity, etc. In his political rhetoric John has created *an ecology of mind.* Individuality is not placed *above* Living-for-Others but qualifies it through SYNERGY, as social concern becomes the measure of the individual. Strength is not placed above Refinement; they are fused, as in John's advice to Bill Toliver: "Have it quietly within yourself to know who you are."

More important still, Delancey is that very rare phenomenon, a nonschismogenetic institution. It is not just a business to make profit, and it is not just a church to bind up the wounds of pursuing profit. It is not just a political organization drunk with power, and it is not just a social club where the power-hungry relax. *It is all four in synthesis and more besides.* The objectives are in SYNERGY. The toughness is for the tenderness, and the tenderness sustains the toughness. Profit is for education, and the educated generate profit. Nothing is an end in itself or merely a means toward an end. All elements are a means-end continuum; they exist for their own sakes *and* for elements beyond. If that sounds like mysticism, the fault lies in our Aristotelian definitions of the rational.

What seems to have happened in the kinds of organizations we have called "Program" (Chapter 9) judging from the ex-"Program" people at Delancey, is that residents have been flipped from one polarity to the other, from *chaos* to Obedience, from *myopia* to Vigilance, from *egotism* to Selflessness, from *passivity* to Dedication. But a *fanaticism* peeps from beneath the Dedication, an *anonymity* from beneath the Selflessness. And if one of "Program's" members, like Dexter, plunges periodically from great heights, it is because these high and low estimates of himself charge out on a single limb together. Yet "Program" has at least half the answer, as my next proposition explains.

Persons cannot combine and synthesize moral axioms until they have the full range of these axioms at their command. They must first learn to exercise and to accept the polarities they have repressed.

The main purpose of the Dissipation is to get the "tough guy" who has never cried or the "nice girl" who has never blazed with fury to exercise those unused portions of their socioemotional anatomies. It is for the same reason that Delancey provides polarized roles. The Individualism of salesmanship counterpoints the Selflessness of pooling all your earnings and caring for patients in the House. Lou Ferronato returns from an exhausting day of Self-control with the moving company to realize, in a burst of Passion, that his work is keeping his friends alive. The experience both "stretches" him and shows him that the Eternal Verities grow in combination and fester in isolation. They are rational when synthesized and mutually qualifying, irrational when severed and apart.

Delancey's contribution to social progress is that it returns us to radical synthesis and turns us away from radical polarity.

Somewhere between 1966 and 1968 the Movement lost its virtue as a developmental force, turned ugly, and self-destructed into lethal shards. Martin Luther King was the inspiration of the earlier phase. He marched as in war and knelt as in prayer. He showed, paradoxically, that you develop courage by *sitting down* in the face of authority to delegitimize it. His Passion was wedded to the Self-Discipline of nonviolence. With his death the schismogenetic patterns reemerged and ran wild. Everything escalated. If you shouted at the Dean in September, you had to shit on his desk by December or some other lemming would be out in front, leading the televised rush to disaster. Demonstrations turned to "trashing," to spontaneous riot, and thence to organized terrorism. Members of the "love generation" proved their devotion to Charles Manson by butchering Sharon Tate, as social evil revealed its Janus faces, the juxtaposition of unreconciled opposites.

Delancey is *not* a golden mean or a *via media,* and those who read this appendix as a plea for compromise between moral absolutes have missed the whole point. Values can be increased if they are increased together. It is meaningful and rational to refer to Courage and to Caution, if they grow together. Growth is a human system in SYNERGY. It is meaningful and rational to refer to *recklessness* and to *cowardice*, if they increase at each other's expense. Disaster comes not with The Four Horsemen of the Apocalypse riding through the sky, but with the Eternal Verities mounted on a centrifuge.

Most residents at Delancey, even the senior ones, are not yet well. The system is designed to draw their fangs and maintain a remarkable degree of harmony. Most of them have yet to learn how to synthesize opposite values *for themselves.* It is here that Mimi Silbert's innovation of the Explorers, who must grope their different ways between Scylla and Charybdis, is of immense significance. The failure of so many marriages and intimate relationships at Delancey is a warning sign that the arts of reconciliation are yet to be learned by most residents. In those areas where social structure cannot guide them, they are still children, for there are two major steps on the road to moral awareness. You must first learn the moral axioms and social rules which, in your ignorance, are "outside" yourself (the conservative position). Only *then* can you make fine moral syntheses from within (the liberal position) in ways that enhance others. The next two years at Delancey should show whether this "gear change" can be transmitted. They should also show whether John can learn to share power with those newly trained in decision. This brings us to Delancey's final lesson.

Value synthesis is not a science but the art and act of creation itself.

No science can tell you, or ever will tell you, what you should do in a human encounter a few moments from now. You can be given the axioms and the principles involved, but the exact proportions of their combination is your existential decision. If a potential suicide arrives on your doorstep, the degree that you permit him to depend on you, and the degree that you urge him to the independence he needs to survive, are two elements in the art of judgment. You see it being practiced all around you in Delancey, in the humor, the drama, the style, the fury, and the compassion. Among a group of ex-cons and ex-junkies I found a greater range of human expression, activity, and endowment than I have encountered anywhere else in my eleven years in America.

I would like to end it all with a magnificent peroration. But that is not John's style—or Delancey's. As we have seen, John soars to a verbal "high" only to pause and mock himself with a wry smile. I once heard him being congratulated on pioneering a New Way of rehabilitation. He looked quizzically at the excited reporter and then shrugged.

"Yeah, you could say we have a 'new' way of fighting crime and drugs. We say, 'Look, punk! Go on oppressing your brothers and sisters, and we're gonna get very angry with you!' It's a way that hasn't been tried lately. We tell 'em to stop."

Additional Reading

A good description of schismogenesis is in Gregory Bateson's *Steps to an Ecology of Mind* (New York: Ballantine Books, 1972). A number of writers have intuitively recognized the pathology of polar extensions. See, for example, Aldous Huxley's classic *Point Counter Point* (New York: Harper, 1928) and the large number of books by Arthur Koestler with titles symbolizing a coincidence of opposites (*Darkness at Noon, The Yogi and the Commissar, The Lotus and the Robot, Insight and Outlook,* etc.). The idea that particular obsessions will convert to their opposites was argued by Denise de Rougement in *Love in the Western World* (New York: Pantheon Books, 1956) with specific reference to runaway romanticism.

Contemporary critiques of one-dimensionalism include Herbert Marcuse's *One Dimensional Man* (Boston: Beacon Press, 1964), *The Duality of Human Existence* by David Bakan (Boston: Beacon Press, 1966), and *Power and Innocence* by Rollo May (New York: Norton, 1972). Richard Sennett has been especially insightful on the "purification of identity" (see *The Uses of Disorder,* New York: Alfred A. Knopf, 1970), and Marcus Raskin has detailed the splitting and separating tendencies in American society (see especially "The Myth of No Connections" in *Being and Doing,* New York: Random House, 1971). For the psychic toll caused by a schizoid culture and the resulting split into "the true self" and "the false self" who sabotage each other, see *The Divided Self* by Ronald Laing (Baltimore, Penguin Books, 1965). An impassioned critique of American education by Jonathan Kozol in *The Night Is Dark and I Am Far from Home* (Boston: Houghton Mifflin, 1975) takes up similar themes (see especially the chapters on No Connections, Nonstop Forward Motion, and Extremes and Oppositions). *Home from the War*

293

by Robert J. Lifton (New York: Simon & Schuster, 1973) is excellent on the meeting ground of national and personal pathology, and much of his work is consistent with the position taken here.

For descriptions of alternative systems, see Abraham Maslow's work on synergy, especially his article "Synergy in Society and the Individual" in *The Journal of Individual Psychology,* Vol. 20, 1964, and Gregory Bateson's *Steps to an Ecology of the Mind.* This author has made a plea for Community Development Corporations similar in design to Delancey Street in *From Poverty to Dignity* (New York: Doubleday/Anchor, 1974). For his earlier theoretical work, see *Radical Man: The Process of Psycho-Social Development* (New York: Doubleday/Anchor, 1970).

The prison system from which many Delancey Streeters come is vividly described in *Kind and Usual Punishment* by Jessica Mitford (New York: Simon & Schuster, 1974). A good early description of Synanon, showing how similar to Delancey it once was, is *The Tunnel Back: Synanon* by Lewis Yablonsky (New York: Macmillan, 1964).

Acknowledgments

There are few of the three hundred or more who reside at Delancey to whom I am not in some way indebted. Everyone whose correct name or photograph appears in this book has contributed the often harrowing details of his or her life to make my work possible. I am immensely grateful.

But there are many who gave me valuable information and showed personal kindness, whose full names I was unable to include lest I drown readers in a huge cast of characters. There are others whose names and personal circumstances were changed to protect their privacy and the reputations of those associated with them.

In these last two categories I would like to thank specifically George Allen, Jose and Mary Amador, Meg Bancroft, Tom Bailey, Larry Burke, Dick Clapp, Milton Combs, Dawn Devaliti, Connie Ferronato, Verna Ford, Larry Herring, Laurie Hodges, Larry Jackson, Sue Jones, Edy Keeler, Fran MacKensie, Ed Marcellus, Dean Martin, Jim McDermott, Sue McFadden, Jerry Mirault, Vivian Neal, Andy and Debbie Nickolatos, Mary Nutter, Nate Paris, Nicolette Parker, Brad Pirie, Marty and Sunny Regan, Billie Ritchie, Miguel and Patty Rodriguez, Jesse Senore, Martha Skinner, Bernie Spevock, Barbara and Chester Stern, Lauretta Taylor, Rhonda Toliver, Barry Torgove, Jimmy Trujillo, Debbie Turner, Jeana Volk, John Wagner, Alice Watson, Chris Wall, Jay Webber, Larry Winer, Les Wisler, Richie Wosser, and Bill Zant. To Booker Morley, who was with me the night my son was born, I owe a personal appreciation of the idea of the Delancey Street family.

A number of Delancey's graduates and squares also showed me kindness. Pat and Sue Donnelly, Kerry Herchel, Kevin Hughes, Rubin Glickman, and Stefan and Gaby Ponek. Without the able photography of

295

Ed Turnbull, Ann Dowie, and Shelley Hampden-Turner this book would have been much impoverished. Shelley especially spent hours collecting prints and supervising the photography.

Kristin Shannon came to my house in Cambridge, Massachusetts, two years ago to tell me that the ideas I had visualized and written about were actually flourishing in San Francisco. She obtained funds to fly me out. I was met, housed, and greatly assisted by Sandra Hickey and a bountiful Ms. Y., whose family foundation underwrote my entire year of research and writing. Happy is the man for whom the Three Graces turn into organizers. Within the foundation Mimi Silbert has fought unrelentingly for the integrity of what I have written about Delancey.

Finally, my publisher Ernest Scott and Anita Scott and Patricia Holt of San Francisco Book Company have done wonders to sustain my morale amid a morass of release forms, revisions of revisions, and a flood of interested parties. If galley proofs have become my grave bands, page proofs my shroud, and legal advice my dirge, at least I shall have perished in the best of company.

C.H.-T.

Berkeley, California
November 1975

DATE DUE